What's Next
For Canada?

What's Next For Canada?

SECURITIES REGULATION
AFTER THE REFERENCE

Edited by Anita Anand

Published in 2012 by

Irwin Law Inc.
14 Duncan Street
Suite 206
Toronto, ON
M5H 3G8

www.irwinlaw.com

ISBN: 978-1-55221-312-4

Cataloguing in Publication data available from Library and
Archives Canada

The publisher acknowledges the financial support of the
Government of Canada through the Canada Book Fund for its
publishing activities.

We acknowledge the assistance of the OMDC Book Fund, an
initiative of Ontario Media Development Corporation.

Printed and bound in Canada.

1 2 3 4 5 16 15 14 13 12

Contents

∼

PART 3
REGULATORY STRUCTURE
109

∼

PART 4
MOVING FORWARD
195

Foreword

Peter W Hogg, QC

Professor Anita Anand, the editor of this collection of papers, had a constructive idea after the decision in the *Securities Reference* (2011) came down. She commissioned a group of outstanding scholars and practitioners to prepare papers on the future of securities regulation, she organized a conference, and she is now publishing the papers. The collection is very interesting and useful, as I will explain.

My own reaction to the decision was not in the least constructive. I was upset. I had been convinced for years of the policy reasons for a national securities regulator, and until the decision of the Supreme Court I was convinced that Parliament had the power to create a national securities regulator. And I was one of the counsel who represented the Government of Canada in the Supreme Court of Canada, arguing the case for a national securities regulator. The decision leaves Canada as the only country in the 107-member International Organization of Securities Commissions without a national regulator. (Canada is represented by Quebec and Ontario, neither of which has any power or mandate to speak for Canada as a whole.) I cannot pretend to be an unbiased observer, but it seemed to me that the Court in the Reference was wrong to treat the securities market as still predominantly of local concern, and wrong to apply a kind of squatters' rights doctrine to maintain exclusive provincial jurisdiction in a field that (like trademarks and competition) should have been treated as concurrent. ("First-mover advantage" has not been a doctrine of constitutional law until now.) These and many other critiques of the decision are to be found in the chapters by David Schneiderman, Poonam Puri, Michael Trebilcock, and Edward Iacobucci. However, the critical view is not universal, and arguments in support of the Court's decision are to be found in the chapters by Stéphane Rousseau and Jeffrey MacIntosh.

Federalism litigation is a win-lose game, and Canada lost this one and with it the policy to replace the existing thirteen provincial and territorial regulators with a single, federal, national regulator. In an effort to make the destruction of the federal initiative more balanced, the Court scattered vague suggestions of federal power in its reasons, and added some final paragraphs on the merits of federal-provincial cooperation. Of course, the proposed federal *Securities Act* already envisaged provincial cooperation: the proposed Act was only to come into force in provinces that willingly opted into the federal regime; provinces that did not opt in would retain their existing legislation and their provincial regulator. And the Reference decision itself increased the cost of achieving provincial cooperation because the federal Act was wholly struck down (despite the opt-in feature), and the provinces were left with their jurisdiction entirely intact and no obvious incentive to change the thirteen-regulator system that Quebec, Alberta, and four other provinces had successfully defended in the courtroom. (Only Ontario had supported the single national regulator in the Reference.) Lorne Sossin and Christopher Nicholls are sceptical of the prospects for a cooperative scheme, while Larry Ritchie and Mahmud Jamal accept that this has to be the way forward. As I write, federal efforts to achieve some measure of cooperation with the provinces on a "common securities regulator" are under way, and I very much hope that they bear fruit.

Many of the Court's suggestions of federal power were so vague that they could not easily serve as a firm basis for a federal role in the regulation of the securities market. Only Ian Lee's chapter holds out hope for a strong federal role after the Reference. However, one of the Court's suggestions was "systemic risk," the avoidance of which had in fact been one of the express purposes of the proposed federal Act. Systemic risk became a matter of great concern during the international financial crisis of 2007–08 — a crisis that was not averted by conventional disclosure-based securities regulation. Probably, as Stéphane Rousseau argues, systemic risk is not enough of a hook to support a full-fledged federal system of securities regulation, but the precise nature and regulatory implications of systemic risk are not yet clearly understood, and the chapters by Anita Anand, Janis Sarra, Cristie Ford and Hardeep Gill, and Andrew Green attempt to shed some light on the idea and how it might support a future federal role in the regulation of the securities market.

As I hope the foregoing suggests, this collection of essays will be of great interest to securities lawyers and others concerned with the regulation or functioning of the securities market. But it will be just as interesting for constitutional lawyers and others concerned with the functioning of our federal system. And the entire collection is a case study on the choice of regulatory tools for economic regulation. Many observers will agree with me that the Court made a strange choice for securities regulation, and this collection has the constructive goal of trying to help us make the best of it.

Introduction

A. Background

For years, scholars in Canada have debated the merits of, and the necessity for, a national securities regulator in this country. Now that the Supreme Court of Canada has opted not to endorse the *Securities Act* proposed by the federal government, this long-standing debate can take one of two turns: We can continue to work with the current, fragmented system, or we can take up the Supreme Court's call to work together to achieve a national model based on cooperation. The papers in this volume underscore the potential for cooperation consistent with the latter alternative. While diverse in viewpoint, they emphasize — explicitly or implicitly — that the status quo is unacceptable as a model of securities regulation in Canada.

Prior to the decision in *Reference Re Securities Act*, when I taught securities regulation and discussed the structure of the regulatory regime with my students, I explained that the one issue that has not been resolved is whether a federal or national securities regulator is constitutional. Now, even after the Court's decision, we still have no answer to this question. The federal government posed a very narrow question: Did the proposed Canadian *Securities Act* fall within the legislative authority of the Parliament of Canada?[1] Everything turned on the proposed

---

1   *Reference Re Securities Act*, 2011 SCC 66 at para 1 [*Securities Reference*].

Act, and the Court responded to the narrow question and to that question alone.

Thus, the Supreme Court's judgment leaves unanswered the larger question of which model of securities regulation would be best for Canada. The weaknesses inherent in the current structure persist despite the Court's decision, and they are weaknesses that even those who favour the structure might agree exist: weak and/or uncoordinated enforcement against financial market crimes; lack of unified representation on the international stage (the "one voice" problem); and the inability to respond coherently to macroprudential concerns as they arise. The question now is whether these problems will continue to persist or whether cooperation among the federal government and the provinces will allow the relevant stakeholders to achieve coordination and reach a new equilibrium.[2]

It goes without saying that capital markets have changed considerably over the decades since the implementation of the first *Securities Act* in the 1960s: secondary market trading far outpaces primary market trading; derivatives trading is explicitly within the realm of securities regulation; merger transactions are complex and span a variety of statutes; self-regulatory organizations are an integral complement to regulatory oversight; and securities markets are international and interconnected. It makes sense that the structure of securities regulation, the means by which regulation is dispensed, has changed also. But as the market has evolved, it has become disconnected from the regulatory structure that purports to regulate it.

Legally speaking, securities regulation has evolved as a matter of provincial jurisdiction. Provincial and territorial securities regulators have undertaken the responsibility, under provincial and territorial legislation, to ensure that the capital markets in their respective jurisdictions are well regulated. They have cooperated to some extent on an *ad hoc* basis under an umbrella organization called the Canadian Securities Administrators (CSA). Thus, the provinces have historically taken the lead in determining the type of cooperation that would occur. But they cannot control and together have not kept pace with the rapid development of capital market activity and the systemic issues that arise out of an interconnected global economy.

---

2 Anita I Anand & Andrew J Green, "Why Is This Taking so Long? The Move towards a National Securities Regulator" (2010) 60 UTLJ 663.

B. The Path to the Reference

Well before the federal government launched the *Securities Reference* case, it had established the Canadian Securities Transition Office (CSTO), whose mandate is to assist in the establishment of a Canadian securities regulatory authority. One of the CSTO's first accomplishments was to lead the development of the proposed *Canadian Securities Act*,[3] which the federal government tabled in Parliament in spring 2010. The federal government referred the Act to the Supreme Court of Canada to ask whether it was within the legislative authority of the Parliament of Canada. Similar questions were subsequently posed by Alberta[4] and Quebec[5] to their respective provincial Courts of Appeal.

The proposed Act was largely modelled on existing provincial securities legislation. As well as standard provisions relating to materiality, prospectus disclosure, liability for misrepresentations, and so on, it also contained a number of new provisions and, in particular, contemplated a new governance structure. The Canadian Securities Regulatory Authority, as it would be called, would have a regulatory division run by a Chief Regulator,[6] as well as a division independent of the Authority called the Canadian Securities Tribunal.[7] This Tribunal would have a Chief Adjudicator who would supervise and direct matters related to the performance of the Tribunal's adjudicative functions.[8] Thus, the proposed Act would have created a bifurcated structure, responding to previous calls for separation among the many functions (e.g., adjudicatory and policy making) of securities regulators.

As it happened, the decisions in Alberta and Quebec came down first, rejecting the proposed securities regulator and the model Act. The Alberta Court of Appeal, in a unanimous decision, held that the proposed Act exceeds the constitutional authority of the Parliament of Canada.[9] The Quebec Court of Appeal, in

---

3   Proposed *Canadian Securities Act* (25 May 2010), online: Department of Finance Canada www.fin.gc.ca/drleg-apl/csa-lvm.pdf [proposed Act].

4   *Reference Re Securities Act (Canada)*, 2011 ABCA 77 at para 1 [*Alberta Reference*].

5   *Québec (Procureure générale) c Canada (Procureure générale)*, 2011 QCCA 591 at para 1 [*Quebec Reference*].

6   Proposed Act, above note 3, s 24.

7   *Ibid*, s 28.

8   *Ibid*, s 36.

9   Alberta Reference, above note 4 at paras 47–49.

a split decision (Dalphond JA dissenting), held that the federal government does not have the constitutional jurisdiction to enact the proposed legislation.[10] In his dissenting reasons, Dalphond JA explains that a very large majority of securities transactions in Canada could be supported under the interprovincial and international branch of the trade and commerce power.[11] However, he goes on to uphold the proposed Act for all securities transactions under the general branch of the trade and commerce power.[12] Many believed that this dissent would be a toehold for an affirmative response from the Supreme Court in the *Securities Reference*.

But it was not to be. In a unanimous decision, the Supreme Court answered the Reference question in the negative, holding that the proposed Act is not within the jurisdiction of the Parliament of Canada. Many who read the decision found it surprising. The decision is difficult to explain on many levels, as several contributors to this volume argue: it did not take into account the context of capital markets regulation, but focused on doctrinal constitutional law alone; it did not fully consider experts' reports (particularly the evidence of Professors Milne and Trebilcock); and it did not fully address each of the branches of the trade and commerce power.

It is clear that the Court was aware of what seemed a powerful argument under the first branch of the trade and commerce power, relating to interprovincial trade and commerce. "No doubt," the Court stressed, "much of Canada's capital market is interprovincial and indeed international. Trade in securities is not confined to 13 provincial and territorial enclaves. Equally, however, capital markets also exist within provinces that meet the needs of local businesses and investors."[13] But the federal government did not argue the first branch of the trade and commerce power and instead argued that the proposed Act fell within the second branch. As a result, the Court did not consider in its reasons a constitutional argument based on the first branch.[14]

Some view the decision to rely exclusively on the second branch of the trade and commerce power as a shortcoming in the federal government's argument. Others believe that the proposed

10 Quebec Reference, above note 5 at paras 2–3.
11 *Ibid* at paras 489–90.
12 *Ibid* at paras 494–527.
13 *Securities Reference*, above note 1 at para 115.
14 *Ibid* at paras 47 and 129.

statute was drafted to be comprehensive in order to cover local as well as extraprovincial matters, underscoring why the federal government argued general trade and commerce alone. These arguments are made in hindsight, of course, and do not further current attempts being made in all quarters to move the policy discussion forward.

C. Looking Forward

Of course, the question to which we now turn is, where do we go from here? In its 2012 budget, the federal government set forth its plans to proceed on a cooperative basis toward the creation of a common securities regulator.[15] Some believe that the arrangement will be a "delegated" one, which would replace thirteen separate regulators.[16] In order to reach an agreement on the particular arrangement to be implemented, the CSTO[17] is now consulting with provinces and territories, some of which have affirmed — or reaffirmed, as the case may be — their interest in working cooperatively toward a common securities regulator.[18]

It is not definitively clear which provinces are in fact negotiating with the federal government. A review of Finance Minister Jim Flaherty's recent remarks suggests "there is a critical mass of support" from the provinces and territories, with the exception of Quebec, to work toward a regulatory model to oversee the country's capital markets.[19] According to Minister Flaherty, British Columbia, most of the Atlantic provinces, and the territories have joined Ontario in support of devising a solution.[20] Minister Flaherty also suggested that the new Conservative government

---

15 Department of Finance, *Jobs Growth and Long-term Prosperity: Economic Action Plan 2012* (Ottawa: Public Works and Government Services Canada, 2012), online: Government of Canada www.budget.gc.ca/2012/plan/pdf/Plan2012-eng.pdf at 128.

16 Theresa Tedesco, "Ottawa Pushes for National Securities Regulator within Year" *Financial Post* (27 April 2012), online: Financial Post business.financialpost.com/2012/04/27/ottawa-pushes-for-national-securities-regulator-within-year.

17 The government extended the term of the Canadian Securities Transition Office (CSTO) by only one year to 12 July 2013 in *Order Setting July 12, 2013 as the Date of Dissolution of the Canadian Securities Regulation Regime Transition Office*, PC 2012-341 (2012), C Gaz I, 875.

18 Department of Finance, above note 15 at 128.

19 Tedesco, above note 16.

20 *Ibid.*

in Alberta may be willing to cooperate, which the previous government had refused to do.[21] Indeed, in its 2011–12 annual report Alberta's Ministry of Finance stated that, "Alberta is committed to working co-operatively with all jurisdictions to improve the existing Canadian securities regulatory system."[22]

We are well aware that Alberta, along with Quebec, has been one of the major holdouts from a historical standpoint. While Quebec is unlikely to alter its oppositional stance, Alberta may well do so — and if it does, three of the four largest securities regulators in the country (Ontario, British Columbia, Alberta, and Quebec) would be onside. One of the most positive aspects of these negotiations, if they are ultimately successful, is that the new securities regulator would develop as a result of cooperation and coordination among all participating jurisdictions, rather than being imposed from the top down.

D. In this Volume

The *Securities Reference* is of interest to many, but particularly to a group of academics who have thought about these issues for years. Indeed, the broad issue of the structure of securities regulation has been central to many of the articles we write and the classes we teach. In compiling and editing this volume, I aimed to gather Canada's leading academics and other members of the profession on this issue to provide their analyses following the *Securities Reference*. The papers emanate from a conference that I organized following the release of the Supreme Court's decision. During the conference, and now in this volume, I grouped the papers loosely according to subject area, recognizing, of course, that these categories are not watertight.

The first set of papers in the volume analyzes the *Securities Reference* decision and provides context for the papers that follow. Poonam Puri examines Supreme Court reference decisions over twenty years, noting that this decision may appear to be inconsistent with other reference decisions. Adopting a similar

---

21 *Ibid.*

22 Alberta Treasury Board and Finance, *Finance: Annual Report 2011–2012* (Edmonton: Alberta Treasury Board and Finance, Communications, 2012), online: Alberta Treasury Board and Finance www.finance.alberta.ca/publications/annual_repts/finance/annrep12/Finance-Annual-Report-Financial-Statements-2011-12.pdf at 25.

stance, Michael Trebilcock sees little or no basis for optimism that cooperative efforts among the provinces and the federal government will prove more productive in the future. In his response piece, Edward Iacobucci suggests that there was much confusion in the Court's attempt to set aside considerations of efficacy in determining jurisdiction, using an analogy from competition law to help demonstrate this point.

The next set of papers examines the constitutional law implications of the *Securities Reference*. Ian Lee argues that a national regulator remains constitutionally available to Parliament under section 91(2). David Schneiderman concludes that the Court embraced a provincial rights discourse espoused by Stephen Harper's Conservative government in the realm of federal–provincial relations. In a lucid comment, Mahmud Jamal agrees with these points, arguing that the federal government did not necessarily lose, as the Court did recognize a federal role in financial market regulation (especially in certain areas such as systemic risk). Lorne Sossin's comment suggests that there is a need to focus on the public interest and a new commitment to "purposive federalism."

The third set of papers examines the administrative law implications of the Supreme Court's decision. Janis Sarra argues for the immediate creation of a national regulatory authority with legislative responsibility for regulating systemic risk and markets that cross national borders. Cristie Ford and Hardeep Gill argue that the combination of systemic risk and data-collection responsibilities could generate a "clearinghouse" regulatory body, which sets broad goals and regulatory requirements while leaving detailed implementation of regulation to more local units. In a thoughtful response piece, Andrew Green argues that the clearinghouse proposal raises concerns about how well systemic risk will actually be regulated and whether this regulatory model can overcome the difficulties of the current system.

The final set of papers addresses the question of moving forward: What's next in securities regulation? Stéphane Rousseau emphasizes the clarity of the Court's decision with respect to the provinces' jurisdiction over the securities sector and argues that systemic risk cannot form the basis of a full-fledged federal regulatory regime pertaining to securities. I take an opposing view and propose the creation of a Financial Market Regulatory Authority tasked with monitoring systemic risk issues, among other things. Jeffrey MacIntosh argues that the prospect of creating a single national regulator is and was a dream, and that some version of the passport system lies in Canada's securities regulatory future. In a thoughtful response piece, Christopher Nicholls comments on the Court's assessment of the political realities within which the federal government will operate following the *Securities Reference*. He argues that there will be challenges ahead in identifying compelling incentives for the provinces and territories to achieve a workable accord with the federal government.

The book begins and ends with short pieces from two key players in the *Securities Reference*. Peter Hogg, who was one of the counsel representing the federal government, opens the book with a thoughtful foreword that questions the Court's judgment. Lawrence Ritchie, a key leader within the CSTO, closes the book with fitting commentary about the road travelled and the road to be travelled from here.

E. Appreciation

When I asked the authors in this volume to contribute to the January conference, all of them answered immediately, positively, and enthusiastically. I sought to have a mix of academic viewpoints and comments from members of the practising bar. I thank each of the authors for being such a pleasure to work with and for preparing their respective papers and comments relatively quickly following the conference. A book such as this is only as strong as the contributions it comprises; in my view, we have here a set of top-notch papers from top-notch members of Canada's academy and practising Bar.

As the draft papers and comments rolled in from the authors, I edited each one and provided comments to the authors, as an editor does. However, my editing is only half the story, as Sylvia Hunter, an incredible copy editor, also reviewed each paper and comment. I was thrilled when Sylvia agreed to come on board, and I thank her for her tireless and excellent editing. She has helped to make the papers in this book consistent and accessible to a broad-based readership.

I also thank Hal Jackman, with whom I have debated these and other securities-related issues over the past few years. Hal's experience in this field is extensive, and his insights are profound.

We were all extremely fortunate that he attended the conference and offered his viewpoints on that day.

Law professors rely on their students in various ways (just as law students may, in other ways, rely on their professors). I was fortunate to have assistance from Grant Bishop, now a 3L, who did a wonderful job on all fronts — corresponding with conference attendees and authors, working the front desk, dealing with the program . . . the list goes on! I also thank Chava Schwebel, who has now graduated, for her invaluable assistance with the conference and for being a superb research assistant throughout the year. Finally, Adam Curran, now a 2L, has been an incredible support in terms of editing the papers in this volume (especially the footnotes), as well as compiling the index and table of contents.

Because the conference took place in the middle of term, finding space at the University of Toronto was difficult, as classes were in session. I contacted Les Viner from Torys, the law firm where I articled and practised after being called to the Bar, and Les invited us to hold the conference there; he and Dana Vitelli were so very gracious in extending the firm's physical space on the day of the conference. Deep thanks also to Dean Mayo Moran, who opened the conference for us.

Finally, I thank Jeff Miller at Irwin Law for his timeliness in getting this book into print. When choosing a publisher, timeliness was a key concern, given that I hope to see this volume contribute to the ensuing public policy debate. From our first telephone conversation, Jeff seemed to share my objectives, which is ideal in the publishing process.

Before signing off, I should mention that as a scholar, I have had the *Securities Reference* and the various issues to which it gives rise present in my thoughts, teaching, and writing for years. I am so pleased that this book has come to fruition, and I thank my children for their patience as I sat typing at the dining-room table when they would likely have preferred that I do other things.

Anita Anand
University of Toronto
July 31, 2012

～ PART 1 ～
The Securities Reference

CHAPTER 1

Twenty Years of Supreme Court Reference Decisions: Putting the *Securities Reference* Decision in Context

Poonam Puri

A. Introduction

In recent years capital markets have expanded dramatically throughout Canada and around the world. At present two-thirds of reporting issuers in Canada report in more than one jurisdiction, a phenomenon made possible, in part, by the development of electronic trading platforms and other technologies that allow investors to instantaneously purchase and sell securities of companies based outside their jurisdiction.[1] As a result of the increased integration of capital markets in Canada, the need for national oversight of the securities industry has become more pronounced.

The Supreme Court of Canada's decision in the *Reference Re Securities Act*[2] surprised many observers in the academic and legal communities who expected the Court to hold that the federal government has jurisdiction to create a national securities regulator.[3]

---

1   Poonam Puri, "Local and Regional Interests in the Debate on Optimal Securities Regulatory Structure" Research Study for the Wise Persons' Committee (7 October 2003), online: www.wise-averties.ca/reports/WPC_6.pdf [Puri, "Local and Regional Interests"].

2   *Reference Re Securities Act*, 2011 SCC 66 [*Securities Reference*].

3   See, generally, Poonam Puri, "The Capital Markets Perspective on a National Securities Regulator" (2010) 51 Sup Ct L Rev (2d) 603 [Puri, "Capital Markets"]; Peter W Hogg, *Constitutional Law of Canada*, 5th ed (Toronto: Carswell, 2010) at 16.4; Ian B Lee, "Balancing and its Alter-

Instead the Supreme Court adopted a highly de-contextualized and formulaic approach. This approach failed to engage the question of whether the securities industry had evolved to acquire a national dimension in the eighty years following the Privy Council's decision, in *Lymburn v Mayland* that the securities industry was a local matter falling under the provinces' property and civil rights powers and that offences within the Alberta Act at the time did not encroach on federal criminal law powers.[4]

At first blush the Supreme Court's reasoning in the *Securities Reference* appears inconsistent with other reference decisions rendered over the past twenty years. Unlike prior decisions, in which the Court thoroughly considered the legal dimensions of the policy issues before it as well as the evolution of the subject matter being considered and the submissions to the Court, by contrast, the *Securities Reference* adopted a very narrow, abstract approach and paid little regard to the submissions and substantial evidence from experts who demonstrated that the securities industry had become national in scope. However, the decision may be partly understood by examining the McLachlin Court's approach to history as well as other trends within the Court. While the *Securities Reference* was certainly the most pronounced example, an examination of the decisions of the McLachlin Court suggests that the *Securities Reference* was not completely unprecedented. Although the Lamer Court appeared willing to consider the evolving nature of an issue, references under the McLachlin Court seem to have adopted a more originalist jurisprudence. Thus, the Court's unwillingness to consider the evolution of Canadian capital markets is partially explicable by putting the *Securities Reference* decision into context.

---

natives: Jurisprudential Choice, Federal Securities Legislation and the Trade and Commerce Power" (2011) 50 Can Bus LJ 72; Expert Panel on Securities Regulation, *Creating an Advantage in Global Capital Markets: Final Report* (Ottawa: Department of Finance Canada, 2009); Wise Persons' Committee to Review the Structure of Securities Regulation in Canada, *It's Time* (Ottawa: Department of Finance, 2003), online: Wise Persons' Committee www.wise averties.ca/reports/WPC%20Final.pdf [WPC]; Crawford Panel on A Single Canadian Securities Regulator, *A Blueprint for a Canadian Securities Commission* (Ottawa: Crawford Panel on A Single Canadian Securities Regulator, 2006) [Crawford Report].

4   [1932] AC 318 [*Lymburn*]; *Securities Reference*, above note 2 (Record of the AG of Canada, Vol 1, Expert Report, Michael J Trebilcock, "National Securities Regulator Report" at paras 38–41) [Trebilcock Affidavit].

This chapter is divided into three sections. In Section B I critique the Supreme Court of Canada's decision by examining the contemporary nature of capital markets in Canada and the gaps in the Court's reasoning process. In Section C I compare the decision to other reference decisions from 1990 to 2012 to examine the structure and analytical approaches adopted by the Court during this period. In Section D I discuss the future of securities regulation in Canada and evaluate the Supreme Court's suggested options, including the cooperative federalism model, and the creation of a national regulator to address systemic risk.

B. Critique of the Supreme Court's Decision

In an effort to avoid discussing which regulatory approach is superior, the Supreme Court rendered a decision that lacked due consideration of the evolution or the present state of capital markets in Canada. Rather than focusing on the preliminary question of whether Parliament has the jurisdiction to enact securities legislation and then moving to a discussion of the application of the "paramountcy" doctrine, the Court immediately engaged in what appears to be a novel discussion of the appropriate balance between federal and provincial power and attempted to ensure that provincial regulatory capacity is not prejudiced by federal action. As a result the analysis ignored the pertinent issue of how capital markets have changed in recent years and allowed the Court to base its decision on minimal empirical evidence.

The Supreme Court held that the federal government "has not shown that the securities market has so changed that the regulation of all aspects of securities now falls within the general branch of Parliament's trade and commerce under s.91(2)."[5] This conclusion is questionable on three grounds. First, the decision assumes that the Court's role is to create balance between the provinces and the federal government, while dismissing the concept that such balance is achieved by the proper application of a division of powers analysis. Second, it artificially dissects the regulation of capital markets to focus on discrete elements rather than on the constitutionality of the Act as a whole. Finally, the Court ignored evidence provided by experts such as Frank Milne and Michael Trebilcock, who suggested that regulation of capital

---

5   *Securities Reference*, above note 2 at para 6.

markets requires national oversight. Instead, the Court focused on the fact that whether or not Canada should have a national securities regulator was not a new debate.[6]

In the *Securities Reference*, the Supreme Court appears to have introduced the balance between federal and provincial legislative capacity as a preliminary consideration that is addressed before considering whether or not the federal government has jurisdiction in the first place. Constitutional law has developed a series of doctrines, including paramountcy, inter-jurisdictional immunity, and the necessarily incidental doctrine to promote balance between federal and provincial jurisdiction. Rather than using one of these pre-established doctrines to determine whether Parliament has jurisdiction to create a national securities regulator, the Court appears to have been very concerned with the potential for section 91(2) to "permit federal duplication (and, in cases of conflict, evisceration) of the provincial powers"[7] and instead read down the federal trade and commerce power to prevent the loss of provincial legislative authority over securities.[8] By making balance a free-standing consideration, the Court effectively predetermined the outcome of the *General Motors* test[9] and allowed itself to make a conclusion on what is the proper allocation of legislative authority before working through the applicable test. Although a balancing approach may be consistent with the broader concept of cooperative federalism, where the matter is not pure *vires*, the Court should have allowed the Constitution and associated legal doctrines to determine the appropriate balance.

Also, the Supreme Court focused on discrete elements of securities regulation and failed to turn its attention to the market as a whole. In defining the securities industry, the Court juxtaposed its concession that Parliament may have jurisdiction to enact legislation dealing with systemic risk against the idea that regulation of "individuals engaged in the securities business" is a purely local concern.[10] Notwithstanding the federal government's

---

6   *Securities Reference*, above note 2 (Record of the AG of Canada, Vol 1, Expert Report, Frank Milne, "Impact of Innovation and Evolution on the Regulation of Capital Markets" at 8–13; Trebilcock Affidavit, above note 4 at 38–41.

7   *Ibid* at para 70.

8   *Ibid* at paras 7 and 128.

9   *General Motors of Canada Ltd v City National Leasing*, [1989] 1 SCR 641.

10 *Securities Reference*, above note 2 at para 117.

decision not to argue that provisions of the Act fall under federal legislative authority because they are necessarily incidental to the exercise of other federal powers, the Court's focus on these day-to-day, incidental elements of capital markets regulation detracts from the proper question of the federal government's capacity to regulate capital markets as a whole. The Court's failure to find "a necessary link" between the national interest in fair, efficient, and competitive capital markets and "a securities dealer in Saskatchewan or Quebec"[11] demonstrates a lack of understanding of the inter-jurisdictional character of securities regulation in Canada.

In addition the Court focused on the development of the securities regulation debate as a substitute for examining changes in Canadian capital markets in recent years. In considering the history of securities regulation in Canada, the Court noted that the debate over a national regulator is not new and surveyed numerous proposals dating back to 1935 to suggest that the federal government's position is neither novel nor a recent development precipitated by changes in Canadian capital markets but, rather, reflects the tension in the federalist system that has existed since Confederation.[12] By focusing narrowly on the lack of novelty of the debate, the Court implied that the determination of the appropriate jurisdiction is based on the novelty of the abstract legal issue rather than on the factual mischief the law seeks to address. Such an approach freezes the division of powers at the time when the issue first manifests, and is contrary to a "living tree" interpretation of the Constitution.[13]

This frozen, originalist interpretation of the regulation of securities was evident when the Court claimed a lack of evidentiary support for the federal government's assertion that the character of securities regulation had changed dramatically since the Privy Council's decision in *Lymburn* in 1932.[14] Throughout the decision,

---

11 *Ibid* at para 117.

12 *Ibid* at paras 11–27; A Douglas Harris, "A Symposium of Canadian Securities Regulation: Harmonization or Nationalization?" University of Toronto Capital Markets Institute, online: InvestorVoice.ca www.investorvoice.ca/Research/UofT_FMI_Symposium_Securities_Regulation_2002.pdf.

13 *Reference Re Same Sex Marriage*, [2004] 3 SCR 698 at para 22 [*Same Sex Marriage Reference*]; *Edwards v Canada (Attorney General)*, [1930] AC 124 (PC).

14 *Lymburn*, above note 4.

the Supreme Court emphasized that to evaluate expert evidence and select the superior regulatory option would go beyond its role. However, in doing so, the Court dismissed the content of the expert submissions provided as "irrelevant to the constitutional validity of the legislation."[15] The Court also turned a blind eye to evidence that the nature of the securities industry has, in fact, changed in response to the globalization of capital markets.[16]

In holding that the securities industry continued to be a local concern under the provinces' property and civil rights jurisdiction, the Court cited Professors JM Suret and C Carpentier's article on the location of the headquarters for reporting issuers, which establishes that corporate headquarters tend to be geographically clustered by industry.[17] Although the Court's assertion that issuers tend to be localized is objectively true and supported by a number of authors, including myself,[18] the location of issuers reveals little about trading in those companies' securities. In reality, many issuers distribute securities to investors throughout Canada and internationally, so that any connection to the reporting jurisdiction becomes even more remote when securities are traded in the secondary market.[19] The headquarters of an issuer is not a sufficient basis on which to conclude the relevant market and scope of the securities industry.

More pertinent evidence of the nature of capital markets was also ignored. For example, the Court did not consider the fact that two-thirds of reporting issuers in Canada report and raise capital in more than one jurisdiction.[20] Nor did it consider large cap issuers, which occupy 98 percent of market capitalization in Canadian markets and typically report in all jurisdictions.[21] This suggests that the majority of Canadian issuers do not structure their affairs around a particular province but, rather, appear to treat Canada as a single unified market.

When addressing the fourth and fifth elements of the *General Motors* test, the Supreme Court approvingly cited the provincial passport regime. The Court pointed to the passport system, which harmonizes regulations to allow market intermediaries

---

15 *Securities Reference*, above note 2 at para 127.
16 Trebilcock Affidavit, above note 4.
17 *Securities Reference*, above note 2 at para 127.
18 Puri, "Local and Regional Interests," above note 1.
19 *Ibid* at 240–42. See also Crawford Report, above note 3.
20 WPC, above note 3 at 5.
21 *Ibid.*

to operate in multiple jurisdictions while dealing directly only with a single principal regulator, as an example of the provinces' ability to effectively accommodate the high number of cross-listed issuers.[22] However, the fact that provinces now have to resort to interprovincial harmonization agreements to effectively regulate capital markets suggests that it is no longer commonplace to classify capital markets as a strictly provincial concern; the industry has in fact acquired a general trade dimension. Therefore, the Court's holding that Canadian capital markets remain an exclusively provincial concern appears arbitrary and no longer consistent with the present-day reality of capital markets.

C. Comparison with Other Supreme Court References

Since 1990, the Supreme Court has released twenty-two reference decisions. As is demonstrated in this Section, a review of these decisions suggests that the *Securities Reference* deviated from the approach taken in many previous references. Reference decision making tends to differ fundamentally from conventional cases, in which there is an adversarial *lis*.[23] Through references, the Court is directly engaged in policy development, and thus they must undergo an abstract analysis of potential legal issues that could emerge from the legislation under review. Since references emphasize a distinct set of considerations, the Court's reasoning in the *Securities Reference* is most appropriately evaluated in relation to other reference decisions.

Section C therefore compares the *Securities Reference* decision with the twenty-two Supreme Court references released since 1990 and, more specifically, with the ten[24] that address federalist issues. The Court's approach in considering history and the evolution of the division of powers is followed by an analysis of the degree to which the Court directly engages the parties' submissions and expert evidence in its decision, and the influence of prior decisions by a Court of Appeal on the Supreme Court's

---

22 *Securities Reference*, above note 2 at paras 118–28 (whether the provinces, acting in concert, are capable of creating a similar scheme and whether the absence of a province from the scheme would prevent the effective operation of the federal scheme).

23 Gerald Rubin, "The Nature, Use and Effect of Reference Cases in Canadian Constitutional Law" (1960) 6 McGill LJ 168 at 168–69.

24 See Appendix A for a list of the ten Supreme Court References.

decision making. Finally, I consider the Court's approach to determining the appropriate balance between federal and provincial legislative power. Review of recent reference decisions clearly indicates that the Court adopted a narrower perspective in the *Securities Reference*, which differed substantially from previous reference decisions. This analysis affirms the concerns of many observers that the Supreme Court failed to give full consideration to the modern realities of capital markets in Canada and to the submissions provided.

1) Consideration of the History of the Regulated Subject

The central question before the Court in the *Securities Reference* was whether the trade of securities had evolved to acquire a national dimension under section 91(2) of the *Constitution Act, 1867*.[25] In considering the history of securities regulation in Canada, the Court focused narrowly on the evolution of the debate over a national regulator without considering the evolution of capital markets as an observable event.[26] Instead, the Court considered, at great length, the development of jurisprudence on the division of powers and the general regulation of trade provision.[27] This analysis is highly abstract and makes only negligible reference to securities regulation in Canada.[28] Fifty-five of the 134 paragraphs in the Court's decision are devoted to surveying the legal landscape — a discussion that fails to provide germane insight into the regulation of capital markets in Canada or how this prior jurisprudence relates to the securities context.

By contrast, prior reference decisions consider in detail both the legal issue at bar and the historical evolution of the constitutional provision as it relates specifically to the reference question. For example, in the *Quebec Sales Tax Reference*,[29] Gonthier J, writing for the Court, engages in a detailed discussion of the evolution of what constitutes a "direct" tax under section 92(2) of the *Constitution Act, 1867*[30] directly considering the proposed amendments in relation to past jurisprudence and distinguishing the

25 (UK), 30 & 31 Vict, c 3, reprinted in RSC 1985, App II, No 5.
26 *Securities Reference*, above note 2 at paras 11–31.
27 *Ibid* at paras 55–90.
28 *Ibid* at paras 67–68 (states Canada's submission).
29 *Reference Re Quebec Sales Tax*, [1994] 2 SCR 715 [*Quebec Sales Tax Reference*].
30 *Ibid* at 20–23.

instant case from the previous decision in the *GST Reference*.[31] This approach of interweaving the facts of the case with the historical evolution of the provision under review also appears in subsequent reference decisions and helps to provide a robust connection between the Court's rationale for their decision and prior case law.[32]

In the *Nova Scotia Residential Tenancies Reference*, two divergent approaches to the role of history emerge in the Court's jurisprudence. In his dissenting opinion, Chief Justice Lamer adopted a living tree approach to the scope of the provision and attempted to place the legislation on an evolving spectrum, such that the jurisdiction of a particular issue is not fixed in time but can shift as a result of changing circumstances. For Lamer CJ, relying on prior classifications as the sole basis for determining the applicable constitutional provision would be "tantamount to evading a review of the scope of the constitutional amendment."[33] The same principle is seen in the *Same Sex Marriage Reference*, where the Court allowed the scope of the definition of marriage to evolve to reflect changing social realities.[34] This decision clearly indicates the Court has not traditionally felt bound by the way a provision was originally defined and by the way the jurisdiction was originally allocated.

The second approach to applying history is seen in the majority opinion of Justice McLachlin in the *Nova Scotia Residential Tenancies Reference*, in which the Court refused to adopt Lamer CJ's living tree approach. From McLachlin J's perspective, since provincial courts "have been performing this function since before Confederation," the proposed legislation cannot be novel and thus does not violate section 96 of the *Constitution Act*.[35] McLachlin J's approach considers the jurisdiction of the issue at the time when the legislation was first enacted and does not allow the jurisdiction to shift over time. This approach examined the nature of section 96 of the *Constitution Act* when it was first defined

---

31 *Ibid* at 21; *Reference Re Goods and Services Tax,* [1992] 2 SCR 445 [*GST Reference*].

32 See e.g. *Same Sex Marriage Reference*, above note 13 at paras 23–30; *Reference Re Employment Insurance Act (Can.), ss 22 & 23*, 2005 SCC 56 at paras 37–49 [*Employment Insurance Reference*].

33 *Reference Re Amendments to the Residential Tenancies Act (N.S.)*, [1996] 1 SCR 186 at para 38 [*Nova Scotia Residential Tenancies Act Reference*].

34 *Same Sex Marriage Reference*, above note 13 at paras 21–30.

35 *Nova Scotia Residential Tenancies Act Reference*, above note 33 at para 69.

and then relies on subsequent jurisprudence to provide further clarification for the scope of the provision.[36] McLachlin J further distinguishes between questions that consider truly novel legislation and those that involve analogous situations or the development of a previously determined issue.[37]

Although the Lamer approach, which uses history and the evolution of the issue to determine whether there has been a shift in jurisdiction, appears to represent the Court's conventional approach to reference decisions, the McLachlin Court has not embraced this approach and appears less willing to accept that jurisdiction may shift over time. The shift from the Lamer to the McLachlin Court's jurisprudence is clearly seen in the *Employment Insurance Reference* where the Supreme Court overturned the Quebec Court of Appeal's decision and held that the federal government has jurisdiction to provide maternity benefits under the employment insurance scheme. In reaching this decision, Deschamps J, writing for the Supreme Court, rejected the Quebec Attorney General's submission that jurisdiction over unemployment should be limited by the parameters defined in early legislation. In doing so, Deschamps J stated that although the views of the Constitution's framers provide a starting point, Parliament should not be bound by the original scope or application of the provision.[38] Despite the aforementioned statements, Justice Deschamps goes on to hold that maternity benefits are constitutional *because* they fall within the original scope of employment.[39] The *Employment Insurance Reference* demonstrates the shift from the Lamer Court's willingness to accept the possibility of jurisdiction changing from federal to provincial, or vice versa, over time. Unlike previous decisions where the Court did not perceive itself as bound by the way a provision was previously defined, the Court in the *Employment Insurance Reference* strains its reasoning to read maternity benefits into the original definition of employment, rather than allowing the scope of the provision to change over time.

---

36 *Ibid* at paras 72–80.
37 Justice McLachlin distinguishes the *Reference Re Young Offenders Act (PEI)*, [1991] 1 SCR 252 and *Sobeys Stores Ltd v Yeomans*, [1989] 1 SCR 238.
38 *Employment Insurance Reference,* above note 32 at paras 39–40 and 45.
39 *Ibid* at paras 67–68.

Now that all the judges who originally endorsed Lamer CJ's approach have retired from the bench, there appears to be greater acceptance of McLachlin CJ's approach to allocating jurisdiction that seems more originalist in nature. The Court's approach to history in the *Securities Reference* appears to continue this shift toward using history to determine the original scope of the provision when jurisdiction was first conferred, rather than considering how the provision has changed over time and whether the original determination remains valid.

Constitutional references are important for supporting the development of the Constitution and furthering the dialogue between Parliament and the courts, but meaningful dialogue is best achieved when the Court is willing to directly consider whether the mischief being addressed has changed over time. In the *Same Sex Marriage Reference*, the Court emphasized that "a large and liberal, or progressive, interpretation ensured the continued relevance and, indeed, legitimacy of Canada's constituting document."[40] The need for a progressive interpretation is particularly pronounced in the context of reference decisions where the Court frequently lacks direct evidence on or insight into the effects of the statute.

Given the substantial policy role of reference decisions, the Lamer Court's practice of examining the evolution of the issue ensures that prior case law remains consistent with current realities. Had the Supreme Court engaged in a thorough analysis of the evolution of capital markets, it would have been clear that the industry has changed dramatically in recent years. For instance, in the time since the Privy Council initially decided that securities fall under provincial jurisdiction, the four pillars of Canadian capital markets have gradually collapsed, and federally regulated banks and trust companies have been permitted to acquire securities brokerage firms.[41] As capital markets have expanded, Canadian retail investors have become heavily invested in funds with nationwide and international positions.[42] Because of the overlapping jurisdictions, these issues cannot be regulated under the present provincial model, and I am of the opinion that,

---

40 *Same Sex Marriage Reference*, above note 13 at para 23.
41 Puri, "Capital Markets," above note 3 at 618.
42 *Ibid* at 613.

had the Court examined the nature of the securities industry more thoroughly, it may have come to this same conclusion.[43]

2) Responsiveness to Expert Submissions and Arguments of the Parties

In concluding that the trade of securities should remain exclusively under provincial jurisdiction, the Court expressed the view that an extensive review of the expert evidence submitted by both sides was unnecessary. The Court indicated that it was not "necessary or helpful to set out a detailed analysis" to consider these reports because their analysis was assumed to concern securities regulation from a policy perspective alone rather than from a jurisdictional perspective.[44] The Court did not engage the submissions of the parties or judgments from the Alberta and Quebec Courts of Appeal and in particular, did not respond to the arguments raised in the dissenting opinion of Dalphond J, beyond stating the parties' positions at the start of the decision.[45] Because the federal government requested a reference on the *Securities Act*, the Supreme Court was not technically required to review the provincial reference decisions. However, the unwillingness to respond directly to the parties, lower courts, or to the relevant opinions marks a departure from prior reference decisions, in which the Court devoted significant attention to responding to submissions and arguments regardless of whether they supported or opposed the Court's final decision.

In all the reference decisions considered since 1990, the Court responded to the arguments of the parties in the analysis section of the decision. Although the degree of attention to these submissions varied from case to case, a core feature of reference decisions appears to be the importance of dialogue between the bench and the parties. In the *Reference Re Assisted Human Reproduction Act*, McLachlin CJ directly and methodically engaged the submissions, generally beginning by stating each party's argument and then explaining why she had accepted or rejected this

---

43 *Ibid* at 615–17.
44 *Securities Reference*, above note 2 at para 127.
45 *Ibid* at paras 32–39; see also *Reference Re Securities Act (Canada)*, 2011 ABCA 77, *Québec (Procureure générale) c Canada (Procureure générale)*, 2011 QCCA 591 (Dalphond JA's dissenting opinion is only mentioned for one sentence in *Securities Reference*, above note 2 at para 39.).

approach.[46] The same approach is adopted in the reasons of LeBel and Deschamps JJ.[47] Given that the Court devoted two full days to hearing submissions in the *Securities Reference*,[48] and considered submissions from sixteen parties and interveners offering arguments from a variety of perspectives, the Court's choice not to respond directly to these arguments is troubling and may suggest an overall lack of comfort with or appreciation for the arguments submitted.

In dismissing the numerous expert reports submitted on both sides of the issues as not "necessary or helpful" in determining the proper jurisdiction, the Court also asserted that its role does not include determining which policy scheme is preferable.[49] Although there is certainly a policy element involved in determining whether securities can be regulated effectively at the provincial level or whether federal regulation is necessary, this policy choice also includes a fundamental jurisdictional question that the Court cannot abdicate. In prior reference decisions, the Court embraced the legal, political, and policy elements of its decisions and exercised appropriate discretion to fully address the legal issues while circumscribing the non-justiciable content. In the *Reference Re Secession of Quebec*,[50] the Court clearly addressed the abstract policy issue of what would be required for Quebec to secede from Canada; by creating a duty to negotiate, the Court made a policy decision concerning a largely political matter. Similarly, in the *Same Sex Marriage Reference*,[51] the Court directly engaged the evidence submitted and rendered a decision that substantially limited the range of legislative options available to Parliament.

It is arguable that the *Securities Reference* is distinguishable from prior policy decisions made by the Court because in previous cases the policy issue was incidental to an established legal issue, whereas in the *Securities Reference* the policy question of whether

---

46 [2010] SCR 457 [*Assisted Human Reproduction Reference*]. See also *Reference Re Broadcasting Act*, 2012 SCC 4.

47 *Assisted Human Reproduction Reference, ibid.*

48 Supreme Court of Canada, "SCC Case Information: Docket 33718: In the Matter of a Reference by the Governor in Council concerning the proposed *Canadian Securities Act*, as set out in Order in Council PC 2010-667, dated May 26, 2010" online: Supreme Court of Canada www.scc-csc.gc.ca/case-dossier/cms-sgd/dock-regi-eng.aspx?cas=33718.

49 *Securities Reference,* above note 2 at para 127.

50 [1998] 2 SCR 217 [*Secession Reference*].

51 *Same Sex Marriage Reference*, above note 13.

a national regulator is more capable than provincial regulators is both abstract and, in some respects, severable from the jurisdictional question. However, this approach to considering the policy question before the Court presumes that expert evidence is not relevant to the jurisdictional question. By refusing to explore the boundaries of the policy issues surrounding its legal determination, the Court summarily disregarded valuable evidence as relevant only to a non-legal policy debate. As a result of the Court's desire to avoid non-legal policy matters, the discussion of legal issues addressed in the *Securities Reference* was far less comprehensive and informative than in previous reference decisions.

3) Review of Reference Decisions with Prior Consideration by the Court of Appeal

A review of reference decisions originating in a provincial Court of Appeal reveals no discernible pattern in the Supreme Court's decisions, nor does the Court appear to show any deference to decisions of the Courts of Appeal. Notably, however, in four of the five Court of Appeal references to which the Attorney General of Canada was a party, the Supreme Court ruled in favour of the federal government, and in the fifth — the *Reference Re Assisted Human Reproduction Act* — the Attorney General of Canada's appeal was allowed in part.[52] This analysis also highlights the significant degree of dialogue between the Courts of Appeal and the Supreme Court on reference decisions, even where the Supreme Court is affirming a decision by the Court of Appeal. In the *Firearms Reference*, the Court had to consider whether the *Firearms Act*, enacted by the Federal Government, concerning the registration and licensing for gun owners, was *ultra vires* federal jurisdiction. While upholding the majority decision of the Alberta Court of Appeal, the Supreme Court refuted the main

---

52 *Reference Re Canada Assistance Plan (BC)*, [1991] 2 SCR 525 (Appeal by the Attorney General of Canada allowed); *GST Reference*, above note 31 (Appeal by the Attorney General of Canada allowed in full. Cross-appeal by the Attorney General of Alberta rejected); *Reference Re Firearms Act (Can)*, 2000 SCC 31 [*Firearms Reference*] (Appeal by the Attorney General of Alberta rejected); *Employment Insurance Reference*, above note 32 (Appeal by the Attorney General of Canada allowed); *Assisted Human Reproduction Reference*, above note 46 (Appeal by the Attorney General of Canada allowed in part).

arguments from Conrad JA's dissenting opinion.[53] Interestingly, in the *Assisted Human Reproduction Reference*, McLachlin CJ's written opinion does not engage the Quebec Court of Appeal's reasons, despite fully rejecting the latter's holding that the impugned sections of the *Assisted Human Reproduction Act* were not valid criminal law.[54] By contrast, the reasons of LeBel and Deschamps JJ respond directly to the Court of Appeal's decision by discussing the submissions before the Court of Appeal,[55] gaps in the latter's reasoning,[56] and how their decision fits with the submissions made by the parties before the Supreme Court.[57] Although it is difficult to read deeply into a single set of opinions, the division and approach of the Supreme Court in the *Assisted Human Reproduction Reference* is significant because this decision involved the same bench that heard the *Securities Reference*.

The three securities reference decisions provided by the Supreme Court of Canada, the Alberta Court of Appeal, and the Quebec Court of Appeal, were unique in that the proposed Act was referred directly to the Supreme Court by the Governor in Council, and concurrently by Quebec and Alberta to their Courts of Appeal, rather than being appealed as of right to the Supreme Court; thus, the Supreme Court was providing a *de novo* assessment of the proposed Act's constitutionality, rather than acting in an appellate capacity.[58] However, since the provincial decisions were rendered prior to the Supreme Court's hearing the Reference and were directly cited in the background of the decision,[59] it would appear reasonable for the Court to continue to consider and engage this jurisprudence.

The Supreme Court's unwillingness to respond directly to the submissions of the parties, the concerns of stakeholders, or to Dalphond J's dissent leaves many lingering questions for those who read the Court's decision. In justifying its rather vague reasoning,

---

53 *Firearms Reference, ibid* at paras 28–29 and 46–47.

54 *Assisted Human Reproduction Reference*, above note 46 at para 10.

55 *Ibid* at para 177.

56 *Ibid* at paras 181 and 267.

57 *Ibid* at para 200.

58 Following the Court of Appeal's Reference decision *Québec (Procureur général) c Conseil scolaire de l'île de Montréal*, [1990] RJQ 2498 (CA), Quebec's National Assembly amended the impugned legislation. Thus, in *Reference Re Education Act (Que)*, [1993] 2 SCR 511, the Supreme Court was asked to decide on the constitutionality of the legislation as amended.

59 *Securities Reference*, above note 2 at paras 36–39.

the Court suggested that it did not want to render a highly circumscribed decision that might prejudice future negotiations
regarding a cooperative federalist national regulator.[60] Unfortunately, the resulting lack of clear guidance creates uncertainty
for any attempt by the federal government to draft securities
legislation and dramatically shifts the balance of power to those
provinces that continue to oppose a national regulator.

4) Federal–Provincial Balance

In the *Securities Reference*, the Supreme Court approached the
question of securities regulation from the perspective of ensuring proper balance, stating that "federalism demands that a balance be struck, a balance that allows both the federal Parliament
and provincial legislatures to act effectively in their respective
spheres."[61] In emphasizing the importance of balance between
federal and provincial jurisdictions, the Supreme Court relied
heavily on the federalist principle from the *Secession Reference*[62]
and on the concept of cooperative federalism articulated in the
Employment Insurance Reference.[63] But whereas in these previous decisions, balance was the outcome of the proper application
of federalist doctrines, the *Securities Reference* appears to elevate
balance to a freestanding and intrinsically valuable feature of
Canadian constitutional law.

In previous reference decisions, balance between federal and
provincial jurisdiction was achieved through the proper application of the Constitution and the tests developed by the courts.
In the 1992 *GST Reference*, the Supreme Court considered the
decision of the Alberta Court of Appeal on the constitutionality
of the federal Goods and Services Tax, and in particular how the
agency and trust provisions of the Act encroached on provincial
property and civil rights jurisdiction. In upholding the constitutionality of the tax, the Court unanimously held that the extent
to which a federal power affects a province is irrelevant to the
constitutionality of the legislation. La Forest J succinctly stated
the Court's perspective on balance between the federal and provincial powers: "that the collection provisions may have an impact

---

60 *Securities Reference, ibid* at paras 10 and 132–33.
61 *Ibid* at para 7.
62 Above note 49 at para 50.
63 *Employment Insurance Reference,* above note 32 at para 10.

on property and civil rights is of no moment."[64] Despite lengthy commentary on the interaction between federal and provincial jurisdiction, the *GST Reference* is not cited in the *Securities Reference*. Moreover, the approach adopted in the *GST Reference* is consistent with subsequent federalist references in which the Court underscores the notion that federal and provincial powers should be treated equally.

The Supreme Court's approach to balancing federal and provincial powers was elaborated on in the *Firearms Reference*, in which the Court determined the appropriate balance using an effects-based approach. Although the Court discussed the abstract notion of legislation's upsetting the balance of federalism, this notion is understood using conventional tests for the division of powers.[65] Thus, as in the *GST Reference*, constitutional balance appears to be the desired result rather than a freestanding consideration. This test-based approach to balance ensures that the Court is not required to make a policy decision on what the appropriate federal–provincial balance is. In the *Securities Reference*, the Court departed from this principle and, in expressing concern about the reduction of provincial regulatory capacity, asserted its own perspective on balance.[66]

Because reference decisions commonly address issues that have both legal and political implications, the Court has traditionally endeavoured not to prejudice negotiations between stakeholders. In this respect, the *Securities Reference* does not depart from the Court's preference for espousing cooperative federalism. However, whereas prior courts have emphasized that "maintaining the balance between federal and provincial powers falls primarily to governments,"[67] the Court in the *Securities Reference* has blurred the line between the dynamic balancing that occurs through federal–provincial negotiations and the more static balance of powers under the Constitution. As a result, the Court has effectively shifted power toward the provincial governments by not providing an adequate legal framework for federal–provincial negotiations on a cooperative, national securities regulator.

Review of prior reference decisions strongly supports the conclusion that the Supreme Court in the *Securities Reference* deviated

---

64 *GST Reference*, above note 31.
65 *Firearms Reference*, above note 52 at paras 48–50.
66 *Securities Reference*, above note 2 at paras 98–102.
67 *Employment Insurance Reference*, above note 32 at para 10.

from its traditional approach in previous references. From a structural perspective, the Court was far less willing to consider how the subject matter of securities regulation might have evolved since 1932, when jurisdiction over securities was first allocated to the provinces. Another common feature of reference decisions that was absent from the *Securities Reference* was a robust dialogue with the submissions of the parties, expert evidence, and prior Court of Appeal decisions. Instead, the Court moved directly from a discussion of the general regulation of trade and commerce power jurisprudence to its decision. Finally, the Court changed its approach to considering balance between federal and provincial jurisdictions, emphasizing the need to protect provincial powers rather than regarding balance as the proper outcome of the division of powers tests.

D. Options for Moving Forward with the National Regulation of Capital Markets

In holding that the federal government lacked jurisdiction to unilaterally create a national securities regulator, the Supreme Court encouraged the federal government to move forward in pursuing constitutionally valid options for regulating capital markets. Unilaterally, the federal government could expand its criminal law powers by enhancing the capacity of the Integrated Market Enforcement Teams (IMETs), or it could create a national regulator narrowly focused on systemic risk. Acting jointly with the "willing" provinces, it could create a national regulator through a system of cooperative federalism. Alternatively, the federal government could choose to maintain the *status quo*.

The problem with maintaining the *status quo* is that the current passport system does not provide a uniform approach to securities regulation and there is no one ultimate decision maker capable of ensuring the efficacy of the system. Although the harmonization of securities legislation among the provinces is certainly desirable, similar legislation remains inefficient because enforcement priorities differ among provinces[68] and there

---

68 Poonam Puri, *Enforcement Effectiveness in the Canadian Capital Markets* (Toronto: Capital Markets Institute, 2005) at 22.

is a lack of centralized accountability.[69] Thus, there are internal limits on the provinces' ability to cooperatively regulate capital markets while retaining independent jurisdiction. Given the recent evolution of capital markets in Canada, it is my belief that provincial securities regulation in Canada is rapidly nearing this limit. By contrast, a national regulator would have the ability to pool resources, harmonize enforcement efforts throughout the provinces, and provide Canada with unified representation at the International Organization of Securities Commissions. A national regulator would be capable of effectively integrating securities regulation into broader macroeconomic planning and financial system regulation, which is predominately under federal jurisdiction. Given the inadequacy of the *status quo*, it is my opinion that the federal government should explore the remaining options for creating a national securities regulator.

The Supreme Court strongly endorsed the concept of the federal government's creating a national systemic risk regulator[70] empowered to regulate a narrow portion of the securities industry in order to protect against catastrophic failures such as the 2007 asset-backed commercial paper crisis.[71] In doing so, however, the Court did not define the scope of "systemic risk" and failed to indicate how a systemic risk regulator would fit within the provincially regulated framework. This ambiguity may result in regulators' becoming preoccupied with defining what constitutes "systemic risk" rather than focusing on how best to regulate it.[72]

My principal concern with a systemic risk regulator is that it would add another regulatory layer to Canada's patchwork system of capital markets regulation. Because regulating systemic risk would require in-depth consideration of risk factors from multiple perspectives, an independent systemic risk regulator would likely be inefficient for both the government and private

---

69 The Honourable Peter de C Cory & Marilyn L Pilkington, *Critical Issues in Enforcement* (Toronto: Task Force to Modernize Securities Legislation in Canada, 2006) at 247–48.

70 *Securities Reference*, above note 2 at para 117.

71 Poonam Puri, "Securities Litigation and Enforcement: The Canadian Perspective" Brook J Int'l L at 35 [forthcoming in 2012] [Puri, "Securities Litigation and Enforcement"].

72 See Poonam Puri, "The Supreme Court's *Securities Act* Reference Fails to Demonstrate an Understanding of the Canadian Capital Markets" (2012) 52 Can Bus LJ at 190.

actors, unless integrated into a pre-existing comprehensive regulatory framework.

A systemic risk regulator might be effective if the regulator works directly with the provincial securities regulators and does not make issuers subject to an additional regulatory agency. Systemic market incidents are rare and generally occur when the accumulation of risk factors reaches a tipping point. Thus, regulating systemic risk would be highly information intensive and would require the federal government to assume an oversight role as opposed to implementing an enforcement-based model. This could be accomplished through a cooperative federalist model whereby the provinces supply pertinent information to the national regulator, which in turn provides a national regulatory framework and enforcement directly to the issuers. The challenge for a systemic risk regulator would be to ensure that it has sufficient information while not adding an additional regulator to whom issuers make filings.

Another major challenge in establishing a systemic risk regulator would be to obtain sufficient cooperation from the provinces to meet the regulator's information needs. As exemplified in previous federal–provincial negotiations to create a national securities regulator, some provinces may be reluctant to facilitate the federal government's entry into securities regulation, regardless of the form or purpose of such regulation. Fortunately, because systemic risk regulation would presumably focus on the largest issuers who already report in multiple jurisdictions, the federal government's information needs could be met by obtaining information only from the cooperating provinces.

Though this topic is not discussed in any detail by the Supreme Court, the federal government has jurisdiction to enact criminal laws dealing with capital market offences. In 2003, the federal government established IMETs to investigate criminal capital market offences;[73] over the past nine years, however, the government has had difficulty in effectively developing the IMETs and integrating them into provincial enforcement activities.[74] These types of challenges will likely continue following the *Secur-*

---

73 Royal Canadian Mounted Police, Backgrounder, "Integrated Market Enforcement Team Program" (21 October 2011), online: Royal Canadian Mounted Police www.rcmp-grc.gc.ca/imet-eipmf/backgrounder-information-eng.htm.
74 Cory & Pilkington, above note 69 at 208.

ities Reference decision. However, if the federal government were to abandon the idea of pursuing a national regulator, it might instead consider expanding its capacity to target criminal law activities. Though the capacity of the federal government is limited by the scope of the criminal law power, a criminal law body for capital markets would certainly be beneficial.[75]

A final option is for the federal government to work cooperatively with the willing provinces to create a national regulator with broad jurisdiction. The Supreme Court strongly advocated for the federal government to negotiate with the provinces to develop a cooperative model that respects and recognizes the pre-existing jurisdiction of the provinces to regulate securities.[76] This approach is consistent with the federal government's opt-in model under the rejected *Securities Act*, but requires the federal government to be less absolute in its jurisdiction. A cooperatively negotiated federal regulator, involving even some of the provinces, would significantly reduce redundancy and inefficiency in Canada's securities regulation landscape, regardless of how many provinces choose to participate.

Following the *Securities Reference*, federal Finance Minister Flaherty set a May 2013 deadline for negotiations to create a federal securities regulator, noting that the national securities regulator debate has persisted for more than thirty years with limited meaningful progress.[77] This aggressive stance appears, in part, to be an effort by the Minister to reclaim the negotiating power lost to the provinces following the Supreme Court's decision, and it provides a clear indication of the federal government's continued desire to create a comprehensive regulator. Ultimately, I believe that a national regulator operated by the federal government would be the most effective option because it would not be limited by the capacity of thirteen provinces and territories to reach a consensus on priorities and other administrative matters. However, because the federal and provincial governments have not engaged in public negotiations since the *Securities*

---

75 Poonam Puri, "Of Regulatory Reform and Enforcement Effectiveness: Models for a Common Enforcement Agency for Canada" (2008), online: Rotman School of Management www.rotman.utoronto.ca.

76 *Securities Reference*, above note 2 at para 132.

77 Tim Kiladze, "Flaherty Sets One-Year Goal for National Regulator Plan" *The Globe and Mail* (27 April 2012), online: The Globe and Mail www. theglobeandmail.com/globe-investor/flaherty-sets-one-year-goal-for-national-regulator-plan/article2416477.

Reference was released, it is unclear whether the provinces who were originally supportive of a national regulator will maintain their original position and cede jurisdiction to a federally managed securities regulator or advocate in favour of a provincially managed model.

Alternatively, the provinces could jointly, and without the federal government's involvement, establish a national securities regulator — similar to what was done with the passport system in 2004.[78] This option would likely receive greater support from Quebec and Alberta, which have strongly opposed increased federal control over their financial markets on the basis that a federally operated securities regulator would undermine the strength of these economic centres.[79] Though this approach may be helpful in gaining the support of the holdout provinces, I believe that a securities regulator managed jointly by the provinces would be less effective than a regulator managed by the federal government. In negotiating the structure of the securities regulator, there is the possibility that the provinces will want to retain jurisdiction in certain areas to pursue certain policies of interest, such as developing local priorities for civil enforcement.[80] With thirteen provincial/territorial actors competing to promote their individual interests, a provincially managed regulator could lack the unified voice necessary to effectively regulate securities domestically and represent Canada internationally. More importantly, a provincially managed regulator would maintain the jurisdictional separation between the four pillars of the Canadian financial system, and thus it would remain difficult for the Canadian government to develop a unified approach to financial regulation. Therefore, a federally managed securities regulator, supported by the willing provinces, appears to be the most effective solution for capital markets regulation in Canada.

---

78 "A Provincial/ Territorial memorandum of Understanding Regarding Securities Regulation" (2004) online: www.securitiescanada. org/2004_0930_mou_english.pdf.

79 Bertrand Marotte, "Alberta, Quebec Ramp up Fight over Securities Regulator" *The Globe and Mail* (15 June 2010), online: The Globe and Mail www.theglobeandmail.com/globe-investor/alberta-quebec-ramp-up-fight-over-securities-regulator/article1604858.

80 See Puri, "Securities Litigation and Enforcement," above note 71 at 16.

E. Conclusion

The Supreme Court's decision in the *Securities Reference* represented a major setback for the federal government's efforts to create a national securities regulator. The decision came as a surprise to many observers, both in terms of the outcome and in terms of the Court's reasons justifying its decision. The Supreme Court's reasons failed to fully explore the evidence on the key issue of whether capital markets have changed sufficiently so as to no longer be a matter of property and civil rights, and thus making their regulation subject to the federal government's general regulation of trade and commerce power. Instead, the Court adopted a narrow perspective that focused on particular elements of the securities trade rather than on the industry as a whole. As a result, the Court does not appear to have developed a full understanding of the modern realities of capital markets in Canada.

Above I have reviewed Supreme Court Reference decisions since 1990 in an attempt to determine whether the Court's reasoning process in the *Securities Reference* was consistent with prior reference decisions. My analysis revealed that the Supreme Court's decision departed from prior reference decisions in several respects.

First, the Court's consideration of the history of securities regulation in Canada did not follow the pattern established in prior reference decisions, in which the Court developed a detailed narrative addressing how the reference topic has evolved over time. In the *Securities Reference*, the Court focused instead on whether the issue itself was novel or whether the question was subsumed by the Privy Council's 1932 decision that securities fall under provincial jurisdiction. This approach may reflect changes in the composition of the Court: the McLachlin Court has taken a more originalist approach in its decisions than the Lamer Court, which was amenable to arguments that the character of the issue had changed over time.

Second, the *Securities Reference* failed to fully engage the submissions, Court of Appeal decisions, and expert evidence. A central feature of previous reference decisions was the Court's willingness to engage in a policy dialogue with other stakeholders and to provide a comprehensive discussion of the constitutional limits affecting a particular legislative action. Such discussion was absent in the *Securities Reference* decision, and this lacuna has left many lingering questions about the range of options available to the federal government.

Finally, the Court shifted its approach to establishing balance between federal and provincial jurisdictions. In previous reference decisions, the Court allowed the division of powers tests to establish the appropriate balance between jurisdictions; in the *Securities Reference*, however, the Court articulated the appropriate balance between the federal and provincial governments as a freestanding consideration and sought to protect the legislative capacity of the provinces as a concern distinct from the outcome in the *General Motors* test.

The federal government has drawn a line in the sand with the provincial governments by establishing May 2013 as the deadline for negotiations on a comprehensive national securities regulator. This strong position demonstrates the federal government's commitment to developing a national regulator. Although both federal and provincial governments have a variety of options moving forward, such as a provincially organized national regulator, a federal systemic risk regulator, or a renewed focus on expanding the capacity of criminal law enforcement, it is my opinion that a national regulator managed by the federal government remains the best option for Canadian capital markets.

CHAPTER 2

More Questions than Answers: The Supreme Court of Canada's Decision in the National *Securities Reference*

Michael J. Trebilcock

A. Introduction

My perspective on the issues before the Supreme Court of Canada in this case is not that of a constitutional expert, nor that of an expert in securities markets and their regulation, but rather that of an international trade lawyer-economist steeped in the academic literature and international policy environment bearing on tariff and non-tariff barriers to trade and on the relevance of this framework of analysis to internal barriers to trade within a federation such as Canada's (to which I have devoted considerable attention in the past).[1] I also acknowledge at the outset that as one of the experts whose opinions were filed with the Court by the federal government in support of its proposed legislation, I may be considered less objective on that account.

In much of this literature, a fundamental distinction is drawn between negative and positive integration. The term "negative integration" refers to prohibitions on measures that states (or, in federations or economic unions, sub-national levels of government) are prohibited from taking because they discriminate against out-of-jurisdiction interests. "Positive integration" refers

---

1   See e.g. Michael J Trebilcock *et al*, *Federalism and the Canadian Economic Union* (Toronto: University of Toronto Press, 1983); Michael J Trebilcock & Daniel Schwanen, eds, *Getting There: An Assessment of the Agreement on Internal Trade* (Toronto: CD Howe Institute, 1995).

to affirmative obligations of states (or sub-national levels of government) to remove impediments to the mobility of goods, services, capital, and, in some cases, labour across jurisdictional boundaries. The issues before the Supreme Court in the *Reference Re Securities Act*[2] principally involve the latter: historically, concerns about the decentralized and uncoordinated nature of the regulation of securities markets in Canada, in their essence, reflect apprehensions that such a regime carries serious risks of creating impediments to the movement of capital within Canada to its most productive uses (as reflected in a long line of expert reports over the past seventy-five years, as the Court noted in its decision). Many of these concerns have been exacerbated in recent years by the evolution of capital markets from local to national to international in nature. In Section B below I briefly review key features of the Supreme Court's response to these concerns that seem to me to yield more questions than answers.

B. Problematic Features of the Court's Decision

1) The Irrelevance of Policy Considerations

The Court stressed several times that the policy question of whether a national securities scheme is preferable to multiple provincial schemes — the subject of a long line of expert reports and academic commentary — is not one for the courts to decide.[3] Rather, the question before the Court was to be resolved solely by the text of the Constitution, fundamental constitutional principles, and the relevant case law.[4] The Court, therefore, barely referred to any of the voluminous expert reports filed on behalf of various parties and intervenors. While acknowledging that the Constitution must be viewed as a "living tree capable of growth and expansion within its natural limits"[5] and "that Confederation can be adapted to new social realities,"[6] the Court simply refused to engage with the central policy issues at stake in this case, in striking contrast to its own constitutional jurisprudence

---

2   *Reference Re Securities Act*, 2011 SCC 66 [*Securities Reference*].
3   See e.g. *ibid* at para 10.
4   *Ibid.*
5   *Ibid* at para 56.
6   *Ibid.*

in other contexts, such as abortion, same-sex marriage, and the *Reference Re Secession of Quebec.*[7] Rather, the Court emphasized on several occasions that the provinces have long been active in the field of securities regulation, and the *status quo* should not be easily disturbed.[8] This *status quo* bias is reinforced by the Court's refusal to engage with relevant policy considerations or to engage seriously with the evolving factual matrix in Canadian and global capital markets. Moreover, it stands in striking contrast to the "living tree" approach adopted by the Court in other constitutional contexts, such as abortion and same-sex marriage.

2) The Irrelevance of the Factual Matrix

The Court stated that the federal government must establish that the Proposed *Canadian Securities Act,*[9] read as a whole, addresses concerns that transcend local provincial interests.[10] The federal government's argument was that this area of economic activity has been so transformed that it now should be regulated under a different head of power. According to the Court, this argument requires not mere conjecture but evidentiary support; the legislative facts adduced by the federal government in the *Securities Reference* do not establish the asserted transformation.[11] The Court goes on to say that a review of the expert evidence does not lead to a different conclusion. The Court did not find it necessary or helpful to set out a detailed analysis of the many reports filed on both sides of the issue. A reasonable reading of the reports suggests that routine securities regulation is concerned mainly with regulating securities as an industry; it also confirms the local nature of much of Canada's securities industry. The Court then cited a study by Suret and Carpentier that points to different focuses and specializations from province to province.[12] According to this study, mining listings make up approximately two-thirds of the securities market in British Columbia; about half

---

7   [1998] 2 SCR 217.
8   See e.g. *ibid* at paras 114 and 126.
9   Proposed *Canadian Securities Act*, as set out in Order in Council PC 2010-667 (26 May 2010) [Proposed Act].
10 *Securities Reference*, above note 2 at para 116.
11 *Ibid.*
12 Cécile Carpentier & Jean-Marc Suret, "Securities Regulation in Canada" (23 July 2003), online: Social Science Research Network papers.ssrn.com/sol3/papers.cfm?abstract_id=1505002.

of Ontario's securities market is attributable to large financial services companies; Alberta is the dominant national market for oil and gas; and roughly one-quarter of technology listings emanate from Quebec. This discussion of the nature of Canadian securities markets represents the sum total of the Court's discussion of the factual matrix and occupies a total of about six lines in its judgment, despite the voluminous evidence submitted to the Court on this issue.

While citing Suret and Carpentier as supporting the degree of regional specialization in securities markets, the Court failed also to note that investors in these issues are often from out-of-province, or that almost all public offerings of securities in Canada are issued in two or more provinces and trade in secondary markets in even more. As I noted in my rebuttal opinion filed in the *Securities Reference*, Professors Carpentier and Suret, in their report filed with the Court,[13] attempt to disprove the jurisdictional externalities inherent in securities regulation in Canada by focusing on the extent of what they term "intra-provincial activity" and seeking to characterize the Canadian capital market as "local with international elements."

First, Carpentier and Suret analyze exchange listing transactions between 2004 and 2008 to argue that the extent to which issuers deal with multiple regulators is exaggerated, contending that the majority (60 percent) of exchange-listing transactions involve no more than three securities commissions. Carpentier and Suret's own data, however, prove the extent of jurisdictional externalities: Table 13 of their report demonstrates that the vast majority of offerings are interprovincial, 94.9 percent of exchange listings involve more than one securities regulator and 70.6 percent involve three or more.[14]

Second, Carpentier and Suret argue that capital markets in Canada are "local" by focusing on a narrow segment of the capital market: exempt offerings of private equity (including venture capital). Their sample, however, represents only a small percentage of the capital markets activity that is the subject of securities regulation. Table 2 of Professor Milne's report filed with the Court indicates that the total value of portfolio investments in Canada

---

13 *Securities Reference*, above note 2 (Report, Cécile Carpentier & Jean-Marc Suret, "Réglementation des valeurs mobilières au Canada").

14 *Ibid* at 141.

in 2009 was over $100 billion;[15] according to data published by McKinsey & Company, venture capital investments in Canada represented just over $1 billion in 2009, and other forms of private equity totalled another $3.1 billion,[16] for a total of roughly 4 percent of total portfolio investments in Canada in 2009.

Carpentier and Suret's limited sample of private equity offerings is also problematic for at least two other reasons. First, many private placements are offered primarily to sophisticated investors or "family and friends"; as such, they are typically exempt from provincial securities regulation.[17] Thus, it is difficult to accept that these activities form the basis of an argument in support of *local* regulation (from which they are exempt). Second, and more importantly, the private placement market includes a built-in slant toward intra-provincial offerings, due to the well-established "home bias" effect in private equity and, in particular, venture capital investing — that is, the tendency for such investors to fund firms that operate within their own region. The very nature of the investment (early-stage, with limited public information about the issuer and the potential for the investor to provide value to the issuer through hands-on involvement in management) means that such investors are generally more confident investing locally, being more familiar with local ventures, especially during the earlier stages of development.

Finally, Carpentier and Suret's finding that roughly 60 percent of exchange listing transactions involve three or fewer provincial regulators means that many such transactions, including IPOs, are not available in every jurisdiction in Canada and that a great many Canadian investors are shut out of a portion of Canada's capital markets. I have difficulty accepting that this could be considered a *positive* feature of Canada's capital market. In this respect, one ought to be cautious in interpreting data concerning the "local character" of securities markets, to be sure to identify what is cause and what is effect. It may be that even where one can point to a local feature of capital markets, that feature is the *result* of the existing regulatory structure.

---

15 *Securities Reference*, above note 2 (Record of the AG of Canada, Vol 1, Expert Report, Frank Milne, "The Impact of Innovation and Evolution on the Regulation of Capital Markets" at para 3.8).

16 McKinsey & Company, "Private Equity Canada 2009" (2010) Exhibits 6 & 7, online: McKinsey & Company www.mckinsey.com.

17 See *Prospectus and Registration Exemptions*, NI 45-106 (containing the "accredited investor" exemption).

Curiously, of the three courts that have issued judgments on the constitutional validity of the proposed *Canadian Securities Act* (the Quebec Court of Appeal, the Alberta Court of Appeal, and the Supreme Court of Canada), only Dalphond JA, dissenting in the Quebec Court of Appeal, bothered to review in any detail evidence of the increasingly national and international nature of Canadian securities markets.[18] He cited data on the extent of Canadian investors' investments in foreign countries; foreign investors' investments in Canadian securities; the "miniscule" portion (5 percent) of even small IPOs involving only one securities commission, suggesting that "even small public securities issues constitute essentially extra-provincial activities" (citing Carpentier and Suret's own data); the integration of Canadian stock exchanges into three commonly owned exchanges specializing in separate classes of securities that are traded nationally; and the national regulation of investment dealers and mutual fund dealers.[19] For the other judges involved in the three decisions, the facts — along with their policy relevance — appeared not to matter.

3) The Boundaries between Federal and Provincial Jurisdiction over Securities Regulation

a) The General Trade and Commerce Power

According to the Court, a law will not fall under the general trade and commerce power unless the matter regulated is genuinely national in importance and scope.[20] For a matter to be genuinely national in importance and scope, it is not enough that it be replicated in all jurisdictions throughout the country; it has to be something that the provinces, acting either individually or in concert, could not effectively achieve.[21] To put it another way, the situation must be such that if the federal government were not able to legislate, there would be a constitutional gap. Such a gap is constitutional anathema in a federation.

The Court concluded that the proposed Act includes provisions that go beyond provincial powers, especially as they pertain

---

18 *Québec (Procureure générale) c Canada (Procureure générale)*, 2011 QCCA 591, Dalphond JA, dissenting.

19 *Ibid.*

20 *Securities Reference*, above note 2 at para 70.

21 *Ibid* at para 80.

to the control of systemic risk and provide for data collection on
a nationwide basis.[22] Systemic risks have been defined as risks
that occasion a domino effect, whereby the risk of default by one
market participant will affect the ability of others to fulfil their
legal obligations, setting off a chain of negative economic consequences that pervade an entire financial system. By definition,
such risks can evade provincial boundaries and usual methods
of control. Without attempting an exhaustive enumeration, the
following provisions of the proposed Act would appear, in the
Court's view, to address or authorize the adoption of regulations
directed at systemic risk: sections 89 and 90 relating to derivatives; section 126(1) on short-selling; section 73 on credit rating;
section 228(4)(c) relating to urgent regulations; and sections 109
and 224 on data collection and sharing.[23] Prevention of systemic
risk may require a national regulator empowered to issue orders
that are valid throughout Canada and to impose common standards, under which provincial governments can work to ensure
that their markets will not transmit any disturbance across Canada or elsewhere. Preserving capital markets to fuel Canada's
economy and maintain its financial stability is a matter that goes
beyond a particular industry and engages trade as a whole within the general trade and commerce power. Legislation aimed at
imposing minimum standards applicable throughout the country
and preserving the stability and integrity of Canada's financial
market might well relate to trade as a whole. However, the proposed Act reaches beyond such matters and descends into the
detailed "day-to-day" regulation of all aspects of trading and
securities, long viewed as within provincial jurisdiction.

The Court noted that the provinces opposing the Proposed
Act argued that if there is a national interest in fair, efficient,
and competitive capital markets and the need for an effective national response to systemic risk, they can meet it by legislating
in concert. No doubt the provinces possess constitutional capacity
to enact uniform legislation on most of the administrative matters covered by the proposed Act, such as registration requirements and the regulation of participants' conduct. By way of
administrative delegation, they could delegate provincial regulatory powers to a single pan-Canadian regulator. The difficulty
with the provinces' argument, however, according to the Court,

---

22 *Ibid* at para 102.
23 Proposed Act, above note 9.

is that as a matter of constitutional principle, neither Parliament nor the legislatures can, by ordinary legislation, fetter themselves against future legislative action.[24] The provinces' inherent prerogative to resign from an interprovincial scheme aimed, for example, at managing systemic risk limits their constitutional capacity to achieve the truly national goals of the proposed federal Act as there is no assurance that they can effectively address issues of national systemic risk in competitive national capital markets on a sustained basis. A federal scheme aimed at such matters, then, might well be qualitatively different from what the provinces, acting alone or in concert, could achieve.

However, the Court failed to note that minimizing systemic risk, as a major objective of securities market regulation, has only begun to attract sharp policy and academic focus in recent years (especially since the advent of the global financial crisis in 2008), and systemic risk is not yet well understood in terms of where it may arise in a country's financial system, or in interconnected national financial systems; what factors are likely to trigger the phenomenon; what factors are likely to lead to its transmission throughout a financial system or interconnected financial systems; and what macro-prudential measures might most effectively pre-empt its occurrence or mitigate its consequences after it has occurred.[25] Thus, the Supreme Court's decision provides very little guidance as to the scope and form that federal regulation may take with respect to regulating systemic risk. Indeed, most disclosure requirements — the heart of securities regulation — can be conceived of as addressing systemic risk (*inter alia*), especially when securitization and trading of financial claims have become commonplace (as they have). Moreover, concerns about systemic risk have not been the central motivation for proposals to rationalize and integrate securities market regulation in Canada over the past seventy-five years. These motivations have been much more prosaic: Does it make sense for a corporation wishing to make a public offering of securities across Canada to be

---

24 *Securities Reference*, above note 2 at para 119.
25 See Anita Anand, "Is Systemic Risk Relevant to Securities Regulation?" (2010) 60 UTLJ 941; Nick Le Pan, "Look Before You Leap: A Skeptical View of Proposals to Meld Macro- and Micro-Prudential Regulation" (2009) CD Howe Institute Commentary No 296; Chapter 9; Paul Jenkins & Gordon Thiessen, "Reducing the Potential for Future Financial Crises: A Framework for Macro-Prudential Policy in Canada" (2012) CD Howe Institute Commentary No. 351.

obliged to obtain approvals from, and to be subject to continuing oversight by, thirteen different provincial and territorial securities regulators? In any event, in pursuing a unilateral regulatory initiative under the general trade and commerce power with respect to systemic risk, the federal government will be entering largely uncharted territory in terms of both the powers and functions appropriate to such a mandate and the choice and design of an appropriate regulatory forum.[26]

b) The Interprovincial and International Trade and Commerce Power

The Court noted on several occasions that the federal government had not chosen to rely on the interprovincial and international trade and commerce power, as opposed to the general trade and commerce power.[27] While seeming to accept, following earlier case law, that the provincial power over securities extends to impacts on market intermediaries or investors outside a particular province, the Court did not consider it appropriate to venture any views on the scope of Parliament's powers over interprovincial and international trade and commerce, given that the federal government had not sought to rely on this head of jurisdiction (although this seems unlikely to have affected the outcome of the case). This is particularly unfortunate, in retrospect, given the Court's reference to comparative experience in other federations, especially the US experience, where federal pre-emption under the inter-state commerce power has essentially provided the basis for a predominant federal presence in securities regulation in the United States, and given my concerns, as a trade lawyer-economist, with interjurisdictional barriers to trade. Thus, this Reference has passed up an opportunity to clarify exactly what set of activities falls within the scope of interprovincial trade and commerce in the securities field. As my earlier comments on Carpentier and Suret indicate, and as other evidence submitted to the Court by Professor Milne, myself, and others further corroborates, almost no public offerings, even by small and medium-sized enterprises, are entirely intraprovincial in that issuers, initial subscribers, and subsequent traders in secondary markets are all located within the same province. Only offerings

---

26 See Le Pan, above note 25; Jenkins and Thiessen, above note 25.
27 See e.g. *Securities Reference*, above note 2 at para 32.

in exempt markets — and not all of these — are likely to lack a substantial interprovincial element, and in any event, by virtue of being exempt, such offerings are not effectively subject to provincial regulation. Thus, on this view of interprovincial trade, very few aspects of securities regulation would be left within exclusive provincial jurisdiction. With respect to the international trade power, the federal government could equally make a case for assuming the role of representing Canada in international financial fora, in particular the International Organization of Securities Commissions (IOSCO), leaving provinces to seek observer status in such bodies if they wish (presumably with the consent of other members).

c) The Competition Law Analogy

In the course of its judgment, the Court sought to distinguish federal competition law, the constitutional validity of which had previously been upheld in *General Motors of Canada Ltd v City National Leasing*,[28] from securities regulation, arguing that competition law is not confined to a set group of participants in an organized trade, nor is it limited to a specific location in Canada.[29] Rather, according to the Court, it is a diffuse matter that permeates the economy as a whole, as the deleterious effects of anti-competitive practices transcend provincial boundaries.[30] Anti-competitive behaviour that is subject to weak standards or sanctions in one province could distort the fairness of the entire Canadian market.[31] The Court's claimed disanalogy between competition law and securities regulation is unconvincing, however. Capital is an input or factor of production in all industries across Canada, and the effective functioning of capital markets is as important to the Canadian economy as the regulation of anti-competitive practices; indeed, the impact of capital markets on the efficient functioning of the Canadian economy may be more pervasive than the impact of competition laws. If we were to assume instead that the two fields are indeed analogous in many respects, we might ask, counterfactually, how one might view decentralized administration of competition laws. Suppose, for

---

28 *General Motors of Canada Ltd v City National Leasing*, [1989] 1 SCR 641 [*General Motors*].
29 *Securities Reference*, above note 2 at para 87.
30 *Ibid*.
31 *Ibid*.

example, that a large merger in Canada could potentially affect the competitiveness of local geographic markets across the country (e.g., a merger between two large retail chains). At present, such a merger would require pre-merger notification to the federal Competition Bureau and, in effect, clearance of the merger by either the Bureau or the Competition Tribunal. Under a decentralized system of competition law administration, on the other hand, such a merger would require notification to and approval by thirteen provincial and territorial competition authorities. No competition law regime in the world (to the best of my knowledge) operates in this fashion; and no securities regulation regime in the world (to the best of my knowledge) operates in this fashion, except in one country — Canada.

C. Conclusion

My reading of the Supreme Court's decision is that it leaves significant scope for unilateral federal action in the field of securities regulation, relying on the general trade and commerce power and perhaps the interprovincial and international trade and commerce power. However, the limits on the scope of these two heads of federal jurisdiction in the securities context are far from clear, and this may presage further constitutional litigation in the event of a reconceived focused federal initiative in this field. Whether such an initiative is desirable from a policy perspective is entirely another matter. Such a regime would add one more regulator to the thirteen regulators we already have, potentially complicating respective spheres of regulatory responsibility, as well as failing to address diffuse and uncoordinated enforcement responsibilities and continuing to confront participants in Canadian securities markets with multiple (and probably additional) compliance costs associated with multiple regulators. In this respect, we are left only with the Court's encomium to the virtues of cooperative federalism and the importance of seeking cooperative solutions that meet the needs of the country as a whole, as well as its constituent parts: "Cooperation is the animating force."[32] However, this view reflects a blissful disregard of all the tortuous and unedifying efforts at intergovernmental cooperation in this field over the past several decades, and suggests little or no basis

---

32 *Ibid* at para 133.

for optimism that such efforts are likely to prove more productive in the future. In this respect, efforts at achieving intergovernmental cooperation in harmonizing laws and rationalizing their administration and enforcement can be likened to the problems confronting participants in economic markets who see private advantages to cartelizing the market: experience shows that cartels, amongst very different kinds of actors, are hard to form and are even harder to sustain where frequent renegotiation of the terms of the cartel is required in the light of changing external circumstances. While critics of the federal legislation in this case offer as an alternative some form of multijurisdictional commission (although sometimes mischaracterizing this as a model of regulatory competition),[33] an inter-governmental cartel of regulators is likely to be much less effective in regulating Canadian securities markets than a "benign" monopolist in the form of a single federal regulator. I say "benign" because the realities are that Canada is competing for capital in global capital markets and that national regulators are constrained by this imperative and will increasingly need to cooperate with other national regulators in establishing some basic ground rules for this competitive process and, in particular, in containing the transmission of systemic risks across national capital markets — a role that Canada's system of decentralized securities regulation largely disqualifies us from playing.

---

33 See Chapter 12.

CHAPTER 3

Competition Policy, Efficacy, and the National *Securities Reference*

Edward M. Iacobucci

A. Introduction

In this brief comment on the Supreme Court of Canada's decision in the *Reference Re Securities Act*,[1] I will expand and elaborate on a point raised by Michael Trebilcock in his excellent critique of the Court's approach in Chapter 2.[2] Trebilcock concludes that the Court inappropriately distinguished competition policy from securities regulation. The Court contended that competition policy is an intrinsically national matter, while securities regulation is not. It engaged in this exercise in order to determine the applicability to the reference of the *General Motors of Canada v City National Leasing* case, which upheld a civil remedy in a federal competition policy statute as within the federal government's general trade and commerce authority.[3]

I agree with Trebilcock that the Supreme Court failed to distinguish competition policy from securities regulation in a meaningful way, but would go further. In my view, as I explain below, securities regulation is of *greater* national significance than competition policy, and thus is even more suitably covered by the general trade and commerce power. Trebilcock also describes what

---

1   *Reference Re Securities Act*, 2011 SCC 66 [*Securities Reference*].
2   See Chapter 2.
3   *General Motors of Canada Ltd v City National Leasing*, [1989] 1 SCR 641 [*General Motors*].

the competition policy regime would look like if jurisdiction were provincial. His point is to demonstrate the absurdity of provincial jurisdiction over securities regulation; in addition I suggest that the example helps illustrate the confusion that the Court suffered in attempting to set aside considerations of efficacy in determining jurisdiction. I consider each point in turn.

B. Competition Policy and Local Jurisdiction

Trebilcock takes the Court to task for its approach to competition policy — rightly, in my view — for two important reasons. First, he points out that "[c]apital is an input or factor of production in all industries across Canada, and the effective functioning of capital markets is as important to the Canadian economy as the regulation of anti-competitive practices; indeed, the impact of capital markets on the efficient functioning of the Canadian economy may be more pervasive than the impact of competition laws."[4]

I agree with Trebilcock's observation, but would add to the latter point. Given capital's mobility, securities markets are not inherently local in today's world, though legal regulation might encourage certain transactions to take place within certain geographic bounds. Buyers and sellers of securities may be located anywhere in the world, and in fact, for diversification reasons, it makes sense for buyers in one region to look to acquire securities from businesses located in another region.[5] And, of course, there are no transportation costs to undermine far-flung sales of securities.

In contrast, competition policy often concerns markets that are inherently very localized. A leading mergers case, for example, involved print advertising in community newspapers in the north shore area of Vancouver.[6] It turns out that, for demand-side reasons, community newspapers sell in local markets: people in one small area do not want to read about local news from another small area. The outcome in this case would have had only

---

4   See Chapter 2, Section B(3)(c) .
5   To elaborate, if performance in two geographic areas is not perfectly correlated, someone owning shares that derive value from economic activities in both areas will face lower risk in her portfolio than someone who owns shares in only one region, all other things equal.
6   *Canada (Director of Investigation and Research) v Southam Inc*, [1997] 1 SCR 748.

a focused impact in one neighbourhood of Vancouver and was hardly a matter of national significance. This is not an isolated example. Many cases in competition policy involve price-fixing in local markets, such as cement (which tends to be a local market because of supply-side considerations, specifically high shipping costs) or gasoline. A conviction of two neighbouring gasoline retailers does not come anywhere close to affecting national markets. Trebilcock is correct to point out that securities markets are at least national in scope, if not international, and there is no reason for *General Motors* not to apply. But it would be fair to go further and conclude that as between the two forms of economic regulation, competition policy is in fact much more likely than securities regulation to involve intrinsically local matters. The Court's analysis of the national significance of competition policy is naïve.

C. Efficacy and Jurisdiction

Trebilcock's second point on competition policy concerns the institutional implications of provincial jurisdiction. He asks what mergers policy would look like if it took the same approach as the *status quo* in securities regulation. Rather than pre-notifying a merger to one competition authority, merging parties would have to prepare thirteen different notifications to send to thirteen different regulators, and then contend with the decisions of thirteen different agencies. Trebilcock relies on this example to provide perspective on the absurdity of the *status quo* in securities regulation.

While I wholeheartedly agree that thirteen pre-notifications would be absurd, I would also rely on Trebilcock's example for a different reason. In my view, the Supreme Court is terribly muddled in its treatment of the distinction between the optimality of institutional arrangements as a matter of policy, and the question of legislative competence and jurisdiction. As I find it difficult to know precisely what the Court meant to say on this matter, rather than paraphrase, I reproduce paragraph 90 of the decision in its entirety:

> We would add that, in applying the *General Motors* test, one should not confuse what is optimum as a matter of policy and what is constitutionally permissible. The fifth *General Motors* criterion, it is true, asks whether failure of one or more provinces

to participate in the regulatory scheme would "jeopardize the successful operation of the scheme in other parts of the country". However, the reference to "successful operation" should not be read as introducing an inquiry into what would be the best resolution in terms of policy. Efficaciousness is not a relevant consideration in a division of powers analysis (see *Reference re Firearms Act (Can.)*, at par. 18). Similarly, references in past cases to promoting fair and effective commerce should be understood as referring to constitutional powers that, because they are essential in the national interest, transcend provincial interests and are truly national in importance and scope. Canada must identify a federal aspect distinct from that on which the provincial legislation is grounded. The courts do not have the power to declare legislation constitutional simply because they conclude that it may be the best option from the point of view of policy. The test is not which jurisdiction — federal or provincial — is thought to be best placed to legislate regarding the matter in question. The inquiry into constitutional powers under ss. 91 and 92 of the *Constitution Act, 1867* focuses on legislative competence, not policy.[7]

Thus, according to the Court, optimal policy is irrelevant in determining what is constitutionally permissible. The reference to "successful operation" in *General Motors* is not about efficacy. Promoting "fair and effective commerce" should be understood to be about powers that are national in importance and scope. Canada must identify a distinct federal aspect. There is a question of legislative competence, not policy.

These observations by the Court do not make sense. For example, how can "successful operation" not have anything to do with efficacy? The Court appears to treat jurisdiction under *General Motors* as a kind of light switch: only if the light does not come on at all when the provincial jurisdiction switch is thrown would the federal government assume jurisdiction over a given matter; the fact that the light may be very dim with provincial jurisdiction, while it would be bright with federal authority, is irrelevant.

The obvious difficulty with such an approach to *General Motors* is that it would be a rare case in which the provinces could not assume jurisdiction over a matter and establish some kind of workable regime. To use the above metaphor, provinces will

---

7   *Securities Reference*, above note 1 at para 90.

almost always generate some kind of dim light when assuming jurisdiction over a matter.

To illustrate, consider a matter that the Court identified in the *Securities Reference* as within federal jurisdiction: securities regulation aimed at systemic risk. It is difficult to know exactly what regulating systemic risk with securities regulation would entail, but let us accept for the sake of argument the Court's approach to the question. The Court observed at paragraph 103:

> Systemic risks have been defined as "risks that occasion a 'domino effect' whereby the risk of default by one market participant will impact the ability of others to fulfill their legal obligations, setting off a chain of negative economic consequences that pervade an entire financial system" (M. J. Trebilcock, National Securities Regulator Report (2010), at para. 26). By definition, such risks can be evasive of provincial boundaries and usual methods of control. The proposed legislation is aimed in part at responding to systemic risks threatening the Canadian market viewed as a whole. Without attempting an exhaustive enumeration, the following provisions of the proposed Act would appear to address or authorize the adoption of regulations directed at systemic risk: ss. 89 and 90 relating to derivatives, s. 126(1) on short-selling, s. 73 on credit rating, s. 228(4)(c) relating to urgent regulations and ss. 109 and 224 on data collection and sharing.[8]

A key sentence in this passage is that systemic risks, "[b]y definition, . . . can be evasive of provincial boundaries and usual methods of control." Federal jurisdiction follows. But the Court's analysis of systemic risk is not consistent with its rejection of efficacy as a criterion for determining jurisdiction. The key differences between federal and provincial jurisdiction over matters concerning systemic risk turn on efficacy. There is no reason, for example, that provinces could not regulate short-selling. Indeed, as MacIntosh points out in his comment on the case, provinces do regulate short-selling.[9] What MacIntosh does not acknowledge, however, is that there is a difference in the predictable efficacy of provincial and federal regulatory schemes aimed at systemic risk. For example, a provincial government whose objective is to maximize well-being in the province will have a bias against close regulation (including enforcement) of a practice that may create

8   *Ibid* at para 103.
9   See Chapter 12.

systemic risks across the country but is nevertheless good for the province. Even absent such a bias, a failure to regulate in one province for whatever reason could affect systemic risk elsewhere. This is the Court's implicit point in observing that systemic risks are "evasive of provincial boundaries."

But this analysis of the efficacy of provincial regulation says nothing about whether the provinces could put in place some kind of regime that addresses systemic risk. Of course they could: nothing prevents provinces from regulating securities with an eye to systemic risk. To be sure, given the localized nature of provincial jurisdiction and the associated spillovers, provinces may regulate suboptimally. But suboptimality, the factor that invites federal jurisdiction over systemic risk, is elsewhere in the *Securities Reference* decision characterized as irrelevant. Thus, the Court's acceptance of federal jurisdiction in the systemic risk context, based as it must be on efficacy, is not consistent with the Court's rejection of optimality as a criterion for deciding jurisdiction.

The other example of legitimate federal jurisdiction invoked by the Court is national data collection. There are two ways of thinking about what drives federal jurisdiction with respect to this kind of regulation. First, federal jurisdiction could follow because provinces can mandate the production of data only within their own borders, while the federal government may mandate data production across the country. Federal jurisdiction is thus superior to provincial jurisdiction if the objective is to gather comprehensive data. But, again, the functional superiority of a regime is not supposed to be a criterion in determining jurisdiction according to the Court elsewhere in its decision. Provinces obviously have the power to create a data collection regime within their borders; the fact that such regimes will be operationally inferior to a federal scheme should, the Court tells us, be irrelevant to the question of jurisdiction.

The other possible way of looking at the authority to establish a national data collection regime is that it is the "national" aspect that creates federal jurisdiction. It is tautological that a province (at least on its own) cannot create a national data collection regime. If, however, the label "national" is what drives jurisdiction here, then why does it not drive jurisdiction generally? That is, the federal government wants to establish a "national" securities regulator, something that no province has the power to do. Why not take the label "national" seriously in this context if one takes it so seriously in the data collection context? The difference in contexts turns on efficacy: a national data collection regime is obviously superior to a provincial regime in achieving the goal of gathering data, while a national securities regulator, according to some (though not me), is not obviously superior. But efficacy, according to the Court, is an irrelevant criterion, and the Court's willingness to confer jurisdiction on the federal government to establish a national data collection regime is therefore puzzling.

Given the availability of some kind of provincial regulatory regime in almost any context, the test for jurisdiction that the Supreme Court set out in the *Securities Reference* under the general trade and commerce clause is unsatisfactory. The Court's distinction between whether the switch turns on a light and whether the light is bright is not helpful: provinces generally can establish some sort of regulatory regime over a matter, and thus the federal government will generally fail to meet the fifth *General Motors* criterion. This could not be what *General Motors* intended. Rather, *General Motors* meant what it said: whether the failure of a province to regulate a matter jeopardizes the successful operation of a scheme is relevant both to the efficacy of a provincial regime and to jurisdiction.

Let me return to Trebilcock's analysis of competition policy to illustrate this point still further. *General Motors* concluded that competition policy was vital to the national interest, and given the wide range of activities that would be affected by it, could be implemented effectively only by the federal government. The idea that federal jurisdiction is *necessary* for competition policy is simply wrong, however: competition policy could be implemented at the provincial level. Trebilcock's analysis of pre-notification of mergers in a provincial scheme is useful in responding to the Court's unsuccessful attempt in the *Securities Reference* to draw a distinction between good policy and constitutional authority. If competition policy were provincial and territorial rather than federal, two merging parties would have to notify thirteen authorities and satisfy all thirteen that the merger does not pose a competitive threat. This is an unwieldy and undesirable institutional arrangement, but it is entirely conceivable. And this would be true of all areas of competition policy, not just mergers: there is no reason that there could not exist thirteen authorities charged with investigating price-fixing or other market abuses in their territories. Indeed, there was, and remains, a common law of restraint of trade that, by its common law nature, is under provincial authority, and thus some aspects of competition policy are in fact provincial.[10]

The fact that provincial jurisdiction over competition policy would produce a patchwork of inefficient overseers of potentially anticompetitive activities such as mergers does not undermine the proposition that provinces can establish competition policy regulation. Trebilcock's example of merger pre-notification is intended to illustrate the peculiar nature of the *status quo* in securities regulation, but it also points out the inconsistency of the *Securities Reference* with the *General Motors* approach to jurisdiction. When the Court in *General Motors* speaks of the necessity of federal jurisdiction, it is implicitly taking efficacy seriously. The Court in the *Securities Reference*, on the other hand, rejects efficacy as a relevant consideration, but is internally inconsistent on the question. When considering systemic risk and national data collection, the Court implicitly must have relied on efficacy as a significant factor in deciding jurisdiction. It is a pity that the Court did not go further and consider the efficacy of a national securities regulator in a more robust way.

D. Conclusion

Michael Trebilcock was correct, in my view, to claim that the Court's invocation of competition policy in the Reference as a comparison to securities regulation is flawed. I would add two further points. First, competition policy is in fact more local than securities regulation. Second, the acceptance of federal jurisdiction over competition policy in *General Motors* (and the acceptance of federal jurisdiction over systemic risk and information collection in the *Securities Reference*) must turn on efficacy. Efficacy is a key criterion in determining jurisdiction under the *General Motors* test: the Court in the *Securities Reference* was incorrect to reject it.

---

10 See Michael J Trebilcock, *The Common Law of Restraint of Trade: A Legal and Economic Analysis* (Toronto: Carswell, 1986).

PART 2
Constitutional Considerations

CHAPTER 4

The General Trade and Commerce Power after the *Securities Reference*

Ian B. Lee

A. Introduction

In this comment, I argue that the Supreme Court of Canada's decision[1] that the proposed *Canadian Securities Act*[2] exceeded Parliament's powers does not entail the more general conclusion that Parliament lacks the power to enact national securities legislation. The Court's rejection of the proposed Act was driven by two characteristics of that legislation that are not essential to a federal securities regime: namely, that it was intended to be "comprehensive" and that its stated objectives mirrored, for the most part, the microeconomic objectives of existing provincial legislation. A federal securities law not possessing these two characteristics remains constitutionally available to Parliament, under the same head of legislative power that could not, in the Court's opinion, sustain the proposed Act.

I acknowledge that such a law may not be politically feasible, and I also make no claim that a parallel (i.e., non-comprehensive) federal securities regime would be desirable as a matter of policy. At least in the short term, such a regime would not achieve the federal government's avowed aim of reducing the fragmentation which, in its view, characterizes the Canadian securities regulatory system.

---

1   *Reference Re Securities Act*, 2011 SCC 66 [*Securities Reference*].
2   Order in Council PC 2010-667 (26 May 2010).

However, the stakes of the *Securities Reference* were not limited to the shape of the Canadian securities regulatory system. The Reference was also a test of the limits of the federal trade and commerce power and therefore, more generally, of federal power to regulate the economy. For this reason, it is important to distinguish between what the Supreme Court held that Parliament may not do, and what federal politicians and officials may subsequently decide is not worth doing.

In Section B below, I begin by summarizing the doctrinal requirements for the exercise of the "general trade and commerce" power. This is the power on which the federal government relied as the basis for its proposed Act. In Section C, I explain the characteristics of the legislation that were central to the Supreme Court's decision to reject it, before describing a hypothetical federal securities law that avoids these weaknesses and therefore, on the best interpretation of the general trade and commerce power, should be considered valid. In Section D, I consider alternative sources of federal authority to enact a general securities regulatory law. Section E concludes.

B. The General Trade and Commerce Power

The *Constitution Act, 1867*[3] confers authority on Parliament to enact laws in relation to "the regulation of trade and commerce" (section 91(2)) while conferring authority upon the provinces to legislate with respect to "property and civil rights in the province" (section 92(13)). During its tenure as the court of final appeal for Canada, the Judicial Committee of the Privy Council upheld scarcely any federal laws under the trade and commerce power[4] and rejected many.[5] The main ground on which federal laws were held to exceed the power conferred by section 91(2) was

---

3   (UK), 30 & 31 Vict, c 3.

4   The conventionally cited exceptions are *John Deere Plow Co v Wharton*, [1915] AC 330; *AG Canada v AG Ontario*, [1937] AC 405 ("Canada Standard Trademark Case"). Also, in *Reference Re Validity of Section 5(a) Dairy Industry Act*, [1949] SCR 1, aff'd [1950] AC 31, an import restriction was upheld under s 91(2) even though the remainder of the Act was ruled invalid.

5   See e.g. *Local Prohibition Reference*, [1896] AC 348; *Insurance Reference*, [1916] 1 AC 588; *Board of Commerce*, [1922] 1 AC 191; *Toronto Electric Commissioners v Snider*, [1925] AC 396; *Attorney-General for British Columbia v Attorney-General for Canada*, [1937] AC 377.

that they purported to regulate "particular trades." According to the Judicial Committee, the regulation of particular trades, or industries, within a province did not come within the concept of the regulation of trade and commerce, but instead came within the exclusive purview of the provinces by virtue of section 92(13).[6]

Since 1949, when it replaced the Judicial Committee as the court of last resort, the Supreme Court of Canada has upheld several federal laws under section 91(2). Some of these laws dealt primarily with the regulation of cross-border transactions.[7] Thus, Parliament has a well-established power, under section 91(2), to regulate international and interprovincial trade. In its 1989 decision in *General Motors of Canada Ltd v City National Leasing*, the Court held that, in addition, Parliament can regulate transactions (even those taking place within a province) if the legislation can be described as regulating "general trade and commerce."[8] The Court articulated five indicia of legislation qualifying under this second branch of the trade and commerce power,[9] which may be summarized in terms of two requirements: the legislation must not amount to the regulation of a single industry, and the legislation must be a regulatory scheme directed at a national economic concern rather than a collection of local concerns.

---

6   See e.g. *Citizens Insurance Co v Parsons* (1880), 7 AC 96 (PC); *Board of Commerce*, above note 5.

7   *Murphy v CPR*, [1958] SCR 626; *Caloil Inc v Attorney General of Canada,* [1971] SCR 543.

8   *General Motors of Canada Ltd v City National Leasing*, [1989] 1 SCR 641 [*General Motors*]. The expression originates with the Judicial Committee's opinion in *Citizens Insurance Company of Canada v Parsons* (1881), 7 AC 96 [*Citizens Insurance*], observing, in *obiter dicta*, that power conferred by s 91(2) "may . . . include general regulation of trade affecting the whole dominion."

9   *General Motors, ibid* (The criteria are as follows: "First, the impugned legislation must be part of a general regulatory scheme. Second, the scheme must be monitored by the continuing oversight of a regulatory agency. Third, the legislation must be concerned with trade as a whole rather than with a particular industry . . . . [fourth,] the legislation should be of a nature that the provinces jointly or severally would be constitutionally incapable of enacting; and [fifth,] the failure to include one or more provinces or localities in a legislative scheme would jeopardize the successful operation of the scheme in other parts of the country" at 661–62). The Court noted in General Motors, *ibid* at 663 that the criteria are not "determinative"; rather, they aid in determining whether "what is being addressed in a federal enactment is genuinely a national economic concern and not just a collection of local ones."

In the *Securities Reference*, the Attorney General of Canada did not suggest that the proposed Act dealt primarily with the regulation of cross-border transactions. Instead, the federal government argued that the proposed Act met the criteria for the exercise of the "general trade and commerce power."

C. Analysis of the Opinion

1) Vulnerabilities of the Proposed Act

In order to ascertain the scope that remains available for enacting federal securities regulatory legislation, we must first understand the Supreme Court's objections to the proposed Act.[10] From the Supreme Court's perspective, the legislation contained three main vulnerabilities.

a) Pith and Substance

The first vulnerability concerned the "pith and substance" of the proposed Act. In Canadian constitutional analysis, the first step in determining whether a law comes within federal or provincial jurisdiction is to describe what the law does and what its purpose is — that is, to describe its "pith and substance." The next step is to determine whether any of the powers conferred upon Parliament and the legislatures encompasses the power to enact a law having such a pith and substance.

According to the Attorney General of Canada, the pith and substance of the proposed Act was "comprehensive national securities regulation."[11] The government's argument at the next

---

10   In a previous article, while the Reference opinion was pending, I argued that the proposed Act should be upheld under the general trade and commerce power. See Ian Lee, "Balancing and its Alternatives: Jurisprudential Choice, Federal Securities Regulation and the Trade and Commerce Power" (2011) 50 Can Bus LJ 72. Although the Court reached the opposite conclusion, the purpose of this comment is not to criticize the Court's opinion but, instead, to offer a sympathetic interpretation of that opinion, with a view to ascertaining its implications for the scope of federal authority.

11   *Securities Reference*, above note 1 (Factum of the AG of Canada) ("[t]he Pith and Substance of the Law is Comprehensive National Securities Regulation; The Government's Goal is to Create a Single National Securities Regulator" at para 47).

stage would be that the provinces could not enact a comprehensive securities regime;[12] their incapacity to do so was an indication that the legislation was directed at a national rather than a local economic concern, and that its enactment therefore came within the "general trade and commerce power."[13]

Unfortunately for the federal government, the Supreme Court read "comprehensive" as a code word for "exclusively federal." The federal lawyers protested, with good reason, that the legislation had a provincial opt-in mechanism: the regulatory provisions would not enter into force in any province without the provincial government's consent.[14] Nor, of course, did the federal lawyers contend that the provinces lacked the legislative jurisdiction to regulate securities transactions: in this sense, the federal government was not claiming "exclusive" jurisdiction. But the fact remained that the objective of the legislation, according to the federal government itself, was to establish a "single regulator, and not a fourteenth."[15] The Supreme Court concluded that the "main thrust [or pith and substance] of the Act [was] to regulate, on an exclusive basis, all aspects of securities trading in Canada."[16]

The result was that the decisive question in the *Securities Reference* would not be whether the provinces could enact a comprehensive regime but, rather, whether Parliament was entitled to enact a law the point of which was to regulate, on an exclusive basis, all aspects of securities trading in Canada. Or, to put it another way, could Parliament effect a "complete takeover of provincial regulation"?[17] The federal government was much less likely to receive an affirmative answer to this question than to the question that it had hoped the Court would ask, namely whether the provinces lacked the capacity to enact comprehensive legislation.

Some commentators have pointed out that the Supreme Court's judgment is reminiscent of the early-twentieth-century

---

12 *Ibid* ("[t]he legislation is of a nature that the provinces . . . would be incapable of enacting, because the limitations on their powers preclude them from establishing a comprehensive regime of securities regulation" at para 137).

13 See above note 9 for more.

14 Proposed *Canadian Securities Act*, above note 2, s 250.

15 *Securities Reference*, above note 1 (Factum of the AG of Canada at para 71).

16 *Securities Reference*, above note 1 at para 106.

17 *Ibid* at para 117. See also *ibid* ("wholesale takeover" at para 128); ("attempt to take over regulation of the entirety of the securities trade" at para 126); ("wholesale displacement of provincial regulation" at para 117).

judgments of the Privy Council.[18] This is a valid observation, and there is a good reason for the resemblance. The Privy Council was preoccupied by the mutually exclusive nature of the federal and provincial powers conferred by the *Constitution Act, 1867*, and often felt obliged to interpret a given federal power narrowly because, in a system of mutually exclusive powers, every inch of federal power is an inch subtracted from provincial power.[19] The modern view is that there is considerable overlap, in practice, between the legislative spheres,[20] and that the recognition of federal power to enact a given law does not, in itself, reduce provincial legislative authority. With this awareness, the Supreme Court has been less reluctant than the Judicial Committee to uphold federal legislation. In the *Securities Reference*, however, the Court perceived that what was being asserted was a federal power to regulate — on an exclusive basis — all aspects of a hitherto provincially regulated activity. The Court viewed the case, therefore, as presenting a zero-sum game to which, it is true, the Court reacted in much the same way as the Judicial Committee in analogous circumstances: It said no to Parliament in order to prevent provincial legislative autonomy from being "swe[pt] . . . out to sea."[21]

b) Regulatory Aims

The second difficulty encountered by the legislation concerned the substantive aims of the scheme as set forth in section 9 of the proposed Act:

---

18 E.g., Barry Cooper, "A Return to Classical Federalism? The Significance of the *Securities Reference* Decision" Frontier Centre for Public Policy, Policy Series No. 129 (February 2012) ("Classical federalism initially affirmed by the JCPC in Parsons [was] reaffirmed in the *Securities Act* Reference").

19 An example is the so-called doctrine of mutual modification developed in *Citizens Insurance,* above note 8.

20 *Canadian Western Bank v Alberta*, [2007] 2 SCR 3 (the "dominant tide" in Canadian jurisprudence favours the simultaneous operation of federal and provincial statutes at paras 36–37).

21 *Securities Reference*, above note 1 at para 62.

The purposes of this Act are:

(a) to provide protection to investors from unfair, improper or fraudulent practices;

(b) to foster fair, efficient and competitive capital markets in which the public has confidence; and

(c) to contribute, as part of the Canadian financial regulatory framework, to the integrity and stability of the financial system.

The first two aims listed — in particular, investor protection and transactional fairness — appeared to the Court to be paradigmatic provincial concerns,[22] and, indeed, the provinces confirmed that these were the aims of their own legislation, the validity of which was unchallenged. The third stated aim of the legislation, the management of systemic risk, was more distinctively national in character, but this did not appear to be what the legislation was mainly about.[23]

c) Regulation of the Securities Professions

The opponents of the proposed Act had also argued that, insofar as the regulation of brokers and other intermediaries was a substantial element of the scheme, the legislation was regulating a particular industry, something which Parliament is not entitled to do under the general trade and commerce power.[24] The Supreme Court appears to have been receptive to this objection,[25] although I suspect that it would not, on its own, have been fatal to the validity of the legislation. If the other features of the Act had been valid, a more than reasonable argument could have

---

22 *Ibid* ("the proposed Act is chiefly directed at protecting investors and ensuring the fairness of capital markets through the day-to-day regulation of issuers and other participants in the securities market. These matters have long been considered local concerns subject to provincial legislative competence over property and civil rights within the province" at para 6).

23 *Ibid* at paras 121–22.

24 *Citizens Insurance*, above note 8.

25 *Securities Reference*, above note 1 ("on their face, the provisions of the proposed Act aimed at government registration and the day-to-day conduct of brokers or investment advisers are not obviously related to trade as a whole" at para 112); ("[i]ndividuals engaged in the securities business are still, for the most part, exercising a trade or occupation within the province" at para 117).

been made that the industry-specific features were valid under the "ancillary powers doctrine."[26]

2) Hypothetical Federal Securities Regulatory Legislation

It appears to me that it is possible to draft a federal securities law that avoids the above-mentioned difficulties. I am referring here not to a law directed primarily or only at systemic risk but to what most people would recognize as a garden-variety securities regulatory law.[27]

Obviously, such a law would need to be designed so as to oper-ate in parallel to provincial securities legislation, rather than to be comprehensive. It may be that, over time, one or more prov-inces might choose to align their regulatory framework on the federal regime, for reasons of efficiency, as has happened, to some extent, in the case of business corporations legislation.[28] However, it must not be the aim of the federal legislation to supplant the existing provincial schemes.

In addition, the primary objective of the law should *not* be investor protection or the fairness of transactions. The provinces have argued that these are the intrinsic objectives of securities regulation,[29] but that is not true. From a federal perspective, and

---

26 Under the ancillary powers doctrine, if minor provisions of an otherwise valid legislative scheme encroach on the jurisdiction of the other level of government, the encroaching provisions are valid provided that they are sufficiently functionally related to the achievement of the objectives of the scheme. *General Motors*, above note 8.

27 As David Schneiderman and Mahmud Jamal observe in their respective contributions to this volume, the Court extolls the virtues of a coopera-tive, intergovernmental approach to securities regulation (e.g. *Securities Reference*, above note 1 at para 9). The Court alludes, in particular, to "the management of systemic risk or Canada-wide data collection" as the federal component of a possible cooperative scheme (para 121). In this section, I suggest that a valid federal securities regulatory law need not be limited to these specific concerns, provided that it avoids the pitfalls of the proposed Act.

28 Ronald J Daniels, "Should Provinces Compete? The Case for a Competi-tive Corporate Law Market" (1990–1991) 36 McGill LJ 130.

29 *Securities Reference*, above note 1 (Factum of the AG of Alberta) ("[t]he primary purpose of regulating trading in securities is to protect inves-tors . . . ." at para 59); *Securities Reference, ibid* (Record of the AG of Alberta, Expert Report, Eric Spink [Spink Expert Report]) ("investor protection has always been the fundamental objective of securities regu-lation and the other objectives [such as market efficiency] merely extend investor protection concepts into the operational details of markets" at 5).

more generally from an economic perspective, these goals are not ends in themselves. The ultimate end of securities regulation, from a federal perspective, is macroeconomic, not microeconomic: it is the efficient allocation of financial resources to productive ventures across the economy, regardless of industry sector.[30] Allocative efficiency is a valid national concern; in light of the Supreme Court's opinion, investor protection can be, at most, a means to this end.

A federal securities law can validly impose standard securities regulatory requirements relating to prospectus and continuous disclosure, the purpose of which is to promote allocative efficiency by facilitating the incorporation of information into stock prices.[31] A federal law could similarly regulate takeover bids and insider trading.[32] All of these requirements apply to market participants regardless of what industry they are in.

Imposing requirements specifically on broker-dealers and other securities professionals would be a more delicate matter because this would be regarded as the regulation of a particular

---

30 Zohar Goshen & Gideon Parchomovsky, "The Essential Role of Securities Regulation" (2006) 55 Duke LJ 711 (describing as "widespread, yet misguided" the belief that securities regulation is primarily concerned with investor protection. "Securities regulation is not a consumer protection law . . . . [T]he ultimate goal of securities regulation is to . . . improve the allocation of resources in the economy." at 713); George J Stigler, "The Public Regulation of the Securities Markets" (1964) 37:2 J Bus 117 ("[s]o far as the efficiency and growth of the American economy are concerned, efficient capital markets are even more important than the protection of investors" at 124).

31 Iris H-Y Chiu, *Regulatory Convergence in EU Securities Regulation* (Alphen aan den Rijn: Kluwer Law International, 2008) (the purpose of mandatory disclosure on the secondary market is "to achieve stock price accuracy in order to maintain allocative efficiency and investor confidence" at 16); John C Coffee, "Market Failure and the Economic Case for a Mandatory Disclosure System" (1984) 70 Va L Rev 717 (describing the rationale for mandatory disclosure in terms of "the allocative efficiency of the capital market" at 722).

32 This point seems to have been recognized, albeit obliquely, in the Reference. The Court noted the federal government's argument, in the Reference, that the securities market serves a general allocative function (*Securities Reference*, above note 1 at para 113), then acknowledged that "legislation aimed at imposing minimum standards applicable throughout the country and preserving the stability and integrity of Canada's financial markets might well relate to trade as a whole" (*ibid* at para 114). The measures I describe in the accompanying text are, of course, "minimum standards" adopted with a view to economy-wide allocative efficiency.

trade, something the trade and commerce power does not allow Parliament to do except as an ancillary part of an otherwise valid scheme. In essence, broker-dealer regulation would have to be a minor part of what the legislation does.

In short, my claim is that it is possible to draft a federal securities regulatory act that does not have the weaknesses of the Act rejected by the Court. Whether such an act is desirable as policy or politically feasible are, of course, separate questions.

3) Double Aspect Doctrine

Because provincial securities laws are undoubtedly valid, the validity of any federal securities law will depend on the operation of the so-called "double aspect doctrine," which allows valid federal and provincial laws to coexist even though their legal consequences overlap.[33]

The legislation rejected by the Court did not present an unassailable case for the application of the double aspect doctrine. For one thing, the legislation was not intended to coexist with overlapping provincial legislation but ultimately to supplant it. For another, the first two aims set forth in section 9 of the proposed Act were identical to those set forth in provincial securities legislation. This is not a promising foundation for a double aspect argument: usually, the coexisting provincial and federal laws have *different* primary purposes. This is what generates their distinct constitutional aspects.

By contrast, the parallel federal regime I have outlined above is a more promising candidate. A federal macroeconomic objective — specifically, the optimal allocation of resources throughout the economy — presents the required distinct federal aspect.

4) The Trade and Commerce Power and Subsidiarity

There is a school of thought according to which federal legislative capacity under the "general trade and commerce power" should depend upon demonstrating the provinces' inability to regulate

---

33 This doctrine was confirmed by the Court in its opinion in the Reference: "federal legislation adopted from [a] distinct perspective will be constitutional even if the matter, considered from a different perspective, also falls within a provincial head of power" (*Securities Reference*, above note 1 at para 85).

that activity successfully. This idea, which finds support in one of the indicia developed by the Court in *General Motors*,[34] is sometimes said to flow from the principle of subsidiarity,[35] that is, the principle that political decisions should be taken by the level of government that is closest to the citizen.[36]

From the perspective of subsidiarity, some have sought to explain the outcome in the Reference by the fact that the federal government did not succeed in showing that the provinces are incapable of successfully regulating securities markets.[37] In the absence of such a showing, securities regulation must come within the exclusive jurisdiction of the provinces.

I do not subscribe to this interpretation of the *Securities Reference*. I have already explained that, in my view, the Supreme Court's objection to the proposed Act was that its pith and substance was to establish an exclusively federal regulatory scheme having as primary aims such quintessentially provincial concerns as investor protection and transactional fairness.

I have misgivings, moreover, with the normative argument that federal jurisdiction under the general trade and commerce power should depend upon a showing of provincial regulatory ineffectiveness.[38] These reservations do not rest upon any disagreement with subsidiarity as a political principle: any government,

---

34 See specifically, the fourth indicium developed by the Supreme Court in *General Motors*, above note 8.

35 See also Jean Leclair, "'Please, Draw Me a Field of Jurisdiction': Regulating Securities, Securing Federalism" (2010) 51 Sup Ct L Rev (2d) 555 at 597–99; Noura Karazivan & Jean-François Gaudreault-Desbiens, "On Polyphony and Paradoxes in the Regulation of Securities within the Canadian Federation" (2010) 49 Can Bus LJ 1. Article 5 of the Treaty Establishing the European Community is said to exemplify the principle ("[i]n areas which do not fall within its exclusive competence, the Community shall take action, in accordance with the principle of subsidiarity, only if and in so far as the objectives of the proposed action cannot be sufficiently achieved by the Member States and can therefore, by reason of the scale or effects of the proposed action, be better achieved by the Community. Any action by the Community shall not go beyond what is necessary to achieve the objectives of this Treaty").

36 See also the preamble to the Treaty on European Union ("[r]esolved to continue the process of creating an ever closer union among the peoples of Europe, in which decisions are taken as closely as possible to the citizen in accordance with the principle of subsidiarity").

37 See e.g. Sébastien Grammond, "Flaherty's Supreme Court Loss Is Federalism's Gain" *National Post* (22 December 2011).

38 These reservations were also discussed in Lee, above note 10.

before acting, should indeed consider whether its aims could be attained just as well by a lower level of government, or even by private ordering.

However, I am not convinced that subsidiarity should be a constitutional constraint upon legislative action. The application of the principle involves assessing legislative efficacy; this is not a task for which the judiciary is unquestionably well suited.[39] The idea of entrusting such determinations to judges may be criticized from the perspective of subsidiarity itself, for one cannot say that the Supreme Court is "closer to the citizen" than are the members of the elected branches of government.

I am also concerned that subsidiarity, as a legal constraint, may prove a false friend to provincial autonomy. Sometimes, the judicialization of a political principle diminishes the degree of compliance with that principle. On the one hand, the courts, conscious that they lack a democratic mandate, may apply the principle less than vigorously;[40] on the other hand, political actors may find that the existence of a judicial review mechanism gives them an excuse to be less careful in policing their own compliance.

D. Other Heads of Power

The Supreme Court's opinion has caused some supporters of comprehensive federal securities legislation to consider whether some other head of federal power might be able to accomplish what the "general regulation of trade" power cannot. The two most obvious candidates are the power to regulate international and interprovincial trade[41] and the federal power to legislate with respect to interprovincial works and undertakings.[42] A promising third strategy, not often discussed, is that followed in Australia

---

39 Indeed, in the Reference, the Supreme Court disavows any inquiry into the relative "efficaciousness" of federal and provincial securities regulation (*Securities Reference*, above note 1 at para 90).

40 The experience with subsidiarity in European Union law is instructive: although the principle has been justiciable since 1992, the European Court of Justice has yet to annul an act of the EU legislature on the basis of subsidiarity.

41 *Constitution Act, 1867*, above note 3, s 91(2). See text accompanying note 5.

42 *Ibid*, s 92(10)(a) ("[l]ines of Steam or other Ships, Railways, Canals, Telegraphs, and other Works and Undertakings connecting the Province with any other or others of the Provinces, or extending beyond the Limits of the Province").

in 1989, whereby the provisions of a federal statute enacted for the federal territory were adopted wholesale by state legislation in each of the states.[43]

With respect to the international and interprovincial trade power, which the Supreme Court itself mentions as an unexplored source of potential federal authority in relation to securities regulation,[44] one challenge for the federal government is how to surmount the vigorously argued provincial position that what is colloquially referred to as a transaction between two investors living in two different jurisdictions is in fact two legally disconnected intrajurisdictional transactions, between each investor and her broker.[45]

As for "interprovincial works and undertakings," this expression is the Canadian equivalent of the US concept of "instrumentalities of interstate commerce," the use of which is the basis of US federal securities regulatory jurisdiction. It is lawful to offer securities to the public in the US without filing a registration statement with the SEC, but only if the offeror manages to do so without using the telephone, the Internet, or an interstate courier service.[46] Could a similar theory be a basis for federal securities jurisdiction here?

---

43 The Australian scheme was invalidated by the High Court of Australia on grounds relating to the jurisdiction of Australia's federal courts; these grounds are irrelevant in the Canadian context. See *Re Wakim; ex parte McNally* (1999), 198 CLR 511 (HC Aust).

44 *Securities Reference*, above note 1 at paras 47 and 129.

45 See e.g. Spink Expert Report, above note 29 ("a typical securities market transaction described colloquially as a single cross-border trade in securities is actually a series of separate contractual and property arrangements, none of which involve any movement of property, cross-border or otherwise" at 2).

46 See e.g. *Securities Act* of 1933, s 5. One implication of this basis for US federal jurisdiction is that even intrastate transactions are, in principle, subject to federal jurisdiction, so long as an instrumentality of interstate commerce is employed. Intrastate securities offerings are, in fact, statutorily exempted from registration requirements under s 3(a)(11) of the *Securities Act*. This fact does not mean, however, that intrastate transactions (even in securities exempt from registration) are not subject to other US federal securities law provisions, including the requirements of the *Securities Exchange Act* of 1934. See Daniel J McCauley Jr, "Intrastate securities transactions under the federal *Securities Act*" (1958–1959) 107 U Pa L Rev 937; Robert S Kant, "SEC Rule 147 – Further Narrowing of the Intrastate Offering Exemption" (1974–1975) 30 Bus Law 73.

In evaluating these possibilities, we should bear in mind a major lesson of the *Securities Reference*, which is that the Supreme Court may not be persuaded by a technically clever argument that, in the Court's perception, fails to do justice to the reality of what is at stake. It follows that an argument that Parliament should be able to regulate any activity that the provinces currently regulate, provided that the activity requires the use of the telephone or the Internet, stands a good chance of suffering the same fate as the argument that because of the opt-in clause in the proposed Act, Parliament was not technically effecting a takeover of provincial securities regulatory jurisdiction.

By the same token, however, the provincial argument that intermediation by market-makers transforms what is, in economic terms, a cross-border nexus of contracts into a collection of disconnected local transactions might suffer this fate, too, so I would not entirely discount the argument that a federal securities regulatory law could be drafted in such a manner as to bring it within Parliament's power to regulate international and interprovincial trade.

Finally, given that the federal government appears to be comfortable with an opt-in scheme, under which national rules would apply only in the willing jurisdictions, a third option, little discussed by Canadian academic commentators, is to employ the method used by Australia in 1989. There, the federal Parliament began by enacting a federal corporate and securities law for the Australian Capital Territory.[47] Each state legislature then enacted a law adopting, by reference, the federal regime as a law of the state.[48] Given the undisputed power of the Parliament of Canada to enact a securities law for the Canadian federal territories — Yukon, the Northwest Territories, and Nunavut[49] — a similar strategy would appear to hold promise here as a means

---

47 *Corporations Act 1989 (Cth)*. Section 82 of this Act set forth the provisions of a "corporations law"; section 5 of the Act adopted these provisions as the law of the Australian Capital Territory. A legislative provision enacted by each state parliament adopted section 82 of the federal Act as the law of that state.

48 For instance, the *Corporations (New South Wales) Act 1990* provides, at section 7, that the federal corporations legislation "applies as a law of New South Wales."

49 *Constitution Act 1871* (UK), 34 & 35 Vic, c 28, s 4.

of creating a valid federal regime into which willing provinces could opt by legislation.[50]

E. Conclusion

I have advanced the argument that the general trade and commerce power remains available as a basis for the enactment of a federal securities regulatory law. In the *Securities Reference*, the Court decided that this power does not permit the Parliament to effect a "wholesale takeover" of provincial jurisdiction. This proposition should not be confused with the proposition that a garden-variety federal securities law cannot be enacted using this power. Such a law is constitutionally possible, provided that its content and legislative history support its characterization as a parallel federal macroeconomic policy instrument rather than as substitute investor protection legislation.

---

50 Although the proposed Act rejected by the Court in the *Securities Reference* also involved an opt-in scheme, the scheme described here is more respectful of provincial legislative autonomy than was the proposed Act. Under the scheme described here, the legal force of the federal provisions in each province would rest upon a provincial legislative act. Moreover, under the usual rules, a province wishing at a later date to exit the federal securities regime would be free to amend or even repeal its reference to the federal rules. By contrast, under the proposal rejected by the Court, the consent of the provincial *executive* would be sufficient to authorize Ottawa to apply its Act in that province, and it was not clear that this consent could be effectively revoked.

CHAPTER 5

Making Waves:
The Supreme Court of Canada
Confronts Stephen Harper's
Brand of Federalism*

David Schneiderman

A. Introduction

The confidence with which English-speaking constitutionalists[1] (and even French-speaking ones[2]) predicted that the Supreme

---

* With apologies to Tom Flanagan for playing with the title of his book on Stephen Harper, *Waiting for the Wave: The Reform Party and the Conservative Movement*, 2d ed (Montreal and Kingston: McGill-Queen's University Press, 2009).

1 Both among practitioners: letter from Allan McEachern, Counsel, Fasken Martineau Dumoulin LLP to Michael Phelps, Chair, WPC-Committee to Review the Structure of Securities Regulation in Canada (10 November 2003), online: Wise Persons' Committee www.wise-averties.ca/reports/WPC_1C.pdf; letter from L Yves Fortier, Ogilvy Renault to Michael Phelps, Chair, WPC-Committee to Review the Structure of Securities regulation in Canada (10 November 2003), online: Wise Persons' Committee www.wise-averties.ca/reports/WPC_1A.pdf; letter from John B Laskin, Torys LLP to Michael Phelps, Chair, WPC-Committee to Review the Structure of Securities regulation in Canada (10 November 2003), online: Wise Persons' Committee www.wise-averties.ca/reports/WPC_1B.pdf; and among scholars: Philip Anisman & Peter W Hogg, "Constitutional Aspects of Federal Securities Legislation" in Philip Anisman *et al*, eds, *Proposals for a Securities Market Law for Canada*, vol 3 (Ottawa: Consumer and Corporate Affairs Canada, 1979); Patrick J Monahan, *Constitutional Law*, 3d ed (Toronto: Irwin Law, 2006) at 297; Ian B Lee, "Balancing and Its Alternatives: Jurisprudential Choice, Federal Securities Legislation and the Trade and Commerce Power" (2011) 50 Can Bus LJ 72.

2 See Noura Karazivan & Jean François Gaudreault-Desbiens, "On Polyphony and Paradoxes in the Regulation of Securities Within the Canadian Federation" (2010) 40 Can Bus LJ 1; Jean Leclair, "'Please Draw

Court of Canada would validate the proposed *Canadian Securities Act*[3] was breathtaking. It was uncontroversial to claim, first, that federal regulation of cross-border trade in securities was authorized by section 91 of the *Constitution Act, 1867*, under the "first branch" of *Citizens Insurance Co v Parsons*, as a matter falling under interprovincial and international trade.[4] Only a short leap of logic was required to maintain that federal authority extended to the establishment of a single national regulator under the "second branch" of the trade and commerce power — a matter concerning *general* trade and commerce — because the Supreme Court of Canada had condoned the use of the general trade and commerce authority in the *General Motors of Canada Ltd v City National Leasing* case.[5] Long denied the federal government by the courts, the second branch of trade and commerce authority extends to largely intraprovincial transactions so long as the federal government satisfies the five criteria laid down by Dickson C.J. in *General Motors*.[6] There seemed little basis for hesitation in concluding that all five of these factors could be met by the proposed *Securities Act*. As legal federalism was no longer obsessed with exclusive jurisdictional domains, the Court would now be expected to tolerate all kinds of overlap between the two levels of government. All that seemed to be required was federal boldness, and the Court would pretty much get out of the way. Opposition seemed futile.

Admittedly, there were good grounds for this confidence, which are canvassed in Section B below. Yet the Court turned against this dominant consensus. The burden taken up in Section C is to understand why the Court decided the *Securities Reference*[7] the other way. In addition to doctrinal and comparative constitutional observations, some of the explanations and influences I offer are non-legal. This is because much of the Court's constitutional doctrine cannot be explained with reference to legal resources alone

---

Me a Field of Jurisdiction': Regulating Securities, Securing Federalism" (2010) 51 Sup Ct L Rev (2d) 551.

3   Proposed *Canadian Securities Act*, Order in Council PC 2010-667.
4   *Citizens Insurance Co v Parsons* (1881), 7 AC 96 (PC) [*Parsons*].
5   *General Motors of Canada Ltd v City National Leasing*, [1989] 1 SCR 641 [*General Motors*].
6   *Ibid.*
7   *Reference Re Securities Act*, 2011 SCC 66 [*Securities Reference*].

(i.e., text, structure, history, precedent).[8] With respect to many of the deeply divisive constitutional questions that the Court faces, rarely does any single or even obvious resource exist to help explain judicial outcomes. "The constitution is as open as the minds of those called upon to interpret it,"[9] wrote Bora Laskin some time ago, in which case, there will be no "inevitability" in constitutional decision making.[10] For this reason, we should understand the Court's room to manoeuvre in these matters as quite capacious. We can better understand the Court's doctrine, then, by reference to a variety of influences, some of them non-legal. For this reason I canvass both legal arguments and non-legal factors to help explain the Court's turn away from a model of "flexible" federalism to one resembling the "classical legal" outcomes of times past. Paradoxically, it turns out that the Court better reflects a dominant strain in the Harper government's federalism rhetoric, one that gives due respect to "exclusive" provincial domains. This is an orientation at odds with the over-confident constitutional argumentation the federal government tendered, and which the Court turned against, in the *Securities Reference*.

B. With the Flow

1) The Dominant Tide

There has been a long-standing dispute within English-speaking constitutional theory about the utility of having the Supreme Court of Canada resolve federalism disputes. In the postscript to his book-length tirade, Paul Weiler famously proposed that federalism without a judicial umpire was both "probable and desirable."[11] The preferable technique for resolving federalism

---

8   See Richard A Posner, *How Judges Think* (Cambridge: Harvard University Press, 2008). Posner offers a "positive decision-theoretic account of judicial behavior in what I am calling the open area — the area in which a judge is legislator" (at 15). Though Posner's concern is with US appellate court decision making, I assume that his arguments have some traction in the Canadian context.

9   Bora Laskin, "Tests for the Validity of Legislation: What's the 'Matter'?" (1955) 11 UTLJ 114 at 127.

10 *Ibid* at 121 and 123.

11 Paul Weiler, *In the Last Resort: A Critical Study of the Supreme Court of Canada* (Toronto: Carswell/Methuen, 1974) at 174.

disputes, Weiler concluded, was "continual negotiation and political compromise"[12] — what is known in the United States as the "political safeguards of federalism" doctrine.[13] On the other side was Katherine Swinton, who offered a forceful reply to Weiler in her book *The Supreme Court and Canadian Federalism*.[14] Abdication of the judicial role in federalism cases makes little sense, she wrote, where consensus can be hard to achieve and where there is a danger of federal expansion at the expense of "regional and other interests."[15] For the most part, the Weiler side had won. As Bruce Ryder observes,[16] there is little question that until recently the Court had "almost entirely abandoned, for more than two decades, the use of the declaration of ultra vires to police the division of powers."[17] An unprecedented number of exercises of legislative authority, at both the federal and the provincial levels, have been granted judicial sanction by the Court. This posture of deference is reinforced by the numerous interpretive doctrines that the Court has embraced: an emphasis on pith and substance (characterizing laws for the purpose of classification that is not overly anxious about overlap), reliance on the "double aspect" doctrine (enabling the same subject to be regulated by both levels of government), and progressive interpretation (the "living tree" approach to constitutional growth and adaptation). These have trumped classical interpretive concerns such as trenching (exhibiting an anxiety associated with overlap), exclusivity (an emphasis on a single regulatory authority associated with "watertight compartments"), or interjurisdictional immunity (limiting legislative impacts on the regulatory authority of the other level of government).[18]

---

12 *Ibid* at 175.

13 Herbert Wechsler, "The Political Safeguards of Federalism: The Role of the States in the Composition and Selection of the National Government" (1954) 54 Colum L Rev 543.

14 Katherine E Swinton, *The Supreme Court and Canadian Federalism: The Laskin-Dickson Years* (Toronto: Carswell, 1990).

15 *Ibid* at 52.

16 Bruce Ryder, "Equal Autonomy in Canadian Federalism: The Continuing Search for Balance in the Interpretation of the Division of Powers" (2011) 54 Sup Ct L Rev (2d) 565.

17 Bruce Ryder, "The End of Umpire? Federalism and Judicial Restraint" (2006) 34 Sup Ct L Rev (2d) 345 at 347 [Ryder, "End of Umpire"].

18 Many of these doctrines are ably addressed in the first 120 pages of Albert S Abel & John I Laskin, ed, *Laskin's Canadian Constitutional Law*, revised 4th ed (Toronto: Carswell, 1975).

I will return to the political safeguards of federalism in Section C below. I wish only to underscore here what Dickson CJ said in the *OPSEU v Ontario* case:[19] that the doctrines associated with classical legal federalism do not well reflect the "dominant tide" in legal federalism. There were, indeed, ample judicial resources to decide the case in the federal government's favour.

2) The Doctrinal Laxity in General Trade and Commerce

It might be said that Exhibit A in these trend lines was the Court's articulation and then application of the five-part test outlined in *General Motors* for determining when the general trade and commerce authority — the so-called second branch of *Parsons*[20] — is available to the federal government. It is the last three criteria[21] that are most pertinent here. These are the indicia that ensure the legislation concerns trade as a whole, not any particular industry ("trade-as-a-whole"), for which the provinces jointly or severally are constitutionally incapable of enacting ("constitutional incapacity"), and where failure of one province to participate in the scheme would jeopardize its successful operation elsewhere in the country ("provincial inability"). Having articulated the criteria, we learn much more about them in their application. As concerned the *Combines Investigation Act* at issue in *General Motors*, which was previously authorized under the criminal law power,[22] Dickson CJ relocated authority to general trade and commerce. He found easily that all five criteria were met, including the most difficult last two. The fourth and fifth criteria appear to have collapsed into a single inquiry — seemingly dispensing with the fourth criterion entirely — about the desirability of federal uniformity in the area of anti-combines. Lengthy quotations from

---

19 *OPSEU v Ontario (Attorney General)*, [1987] 2 SCR 2 at 18, cited in *Securities Reference*, above note 7 at para 59.

20 *Parsons*, above note 4.

21 The first three were identified by Laskin CJ in *Macdonald v Vapor Canada Ltd*, [1977] 2 SCR 134 (general regulatory scheme, monitored by general regulatory agency, and concerning trade as a whole). Justice Dickson added two criteria to this list initially in *General Motors*, above note 5.

22 *Proprietary Articles Trade Association v AG Canada*, [1931] AC 310 (PC) [*PATA*].

the work of Hogg and Grover,[23] AE Safarian,[24] and the Canadian Economic Council[25] lent force to the Court's conclusion that competition could not be regulated properly unless regulated nationally.[26] Reiterating conclusions he had articulated in *Canadian National Transportation*,[27] Dickson CJ described Canada as, "for economic purposes, a single huge marketplace."[28] The tenor of the Court's ruling appeared entirely in sync with proposals that had been advanced for some time to enhance positive integration of Canada's economic union via federal harmonization.[29] All of this lent weight to the inference that the Court would welcome federal intervention in the area of securities regulation.

The lax nature of the criteria for invoking federal authority over general trade and commerce was underscored in *Kirkbi AG v Ritvik Holdings Inc*,[30] where the Court upheld the civil cause of action in the federal *Trade-marks Act* under general trade and commerce authority, applying the five criteria from *General Motors*. Whereas *General Motors* merely relocated authority from the criminal law power to the commerce clause, the case here appeared to be more difficult: the federal trademarks law had yet to be declared constitutionally valid by the Court. Justice LeBel nevertheless declared the law valid according to all five *General Motors* criteria, without any substantive discussion of the individual criteria. This decision appears to have been justified by the

---

23 Peter W Hogg & Warren Grover, "The Constitutionality of the Competition Bill" (1976) 1 Can Bus LJ 197.

24 Albert E Safarian, *Canadian Federalism and Economic Integration* (Ottawa: Privy Council Office, 1974).

25 Economic Council of Canada, *Interim Report on Competition Policy* (Ottawa: Queen's Printer, 1969).

26 Chief Justice Dickson quoting approvingly from Anisman & Hogg, above note 1, on the constitutional authority to enact national securities regulation (*General Motors*, above note 5 at 686), albeit for different purposes, namely, that of upholding under ancillary authority the civil cause of action in the *Combines Investigation Act*.

27 *AG Canada v Canadian National Transportation*, [1983] 2 SCR 206 [*Canadian National Transportation*].

28 *General Motors*, above note 5 at 683.

29 See Safarian, above note 24. For a critique of constitutional reform proposals to enhance Canada's economic union, see David Schneiderman, "Economic Citizenship and Deliberative Democracy: An Inquiry into Constitutional Limitations on Economic Regulation" (1995) Queen's LJ 125.

30 *Kirkbi AG v Ritvik Holdings Inc*, [2005] 3 SCR 302 [*Kirkbi*].

absence of disagreement amongst the parties about Parliament's constitutional capacity to enact the law.[31]

3) Legitimacy Concerns

It should be uncontroversial to claim that the Court is attuned to legitimacy concerns. This is something different than the observation of Mr. Dooley, the fictional Irish-American saloonkeeper, that "th' Supreme Coort follows th' illiction returns."[32] It has been said of the US Supreme Court, back even to the time of John Marshall CJ, that it serves the ruling regime's interests and promotes its policies. For this reason, Lucas A Powe Jr concludes that the US Court "is a majoritarian institution . . . [that] identifies with and serves ruling coalitions."[33] This is how the decision in *Brown v Board of Education*[34] is explained, for example: as a national ruling coalition having its way over the objections of a regional (Southern) ruling coalition.[35] Quebec constitutional scholars have made a similar point, though in negative terms: that the Supreme Court of Canada, since its inception, has served the interests of the federal government.[36] With the Judicial Committee of the Privy Council out of its way, the Court has had freer rein in facilitating a national agenda; its largely deferential stance in recent decades lends support to this view. We could say, then, that the Court is attuned (or sensitive) to the needs of the national ruling coalition, however that coalition may be config-

31 *Ibid* at para 28; Ryder, "End of Umpire," above note 17 at 362, n 56, observes that the Quebec Attorney General was the only provincial AG to intervene in the case and did so in support of federal authority.

32 Finley P Dunne, *Mr. Dooley at His Best* (New York: C. Scribner's Sons, 1938) at 77 quoted in Lucas A Powe Jr, *The Supreme Court and the American Elite, 1789–2008* (Cambridge: Harvard University Press, 2009) at 162.

33 Powe, *ibid* at ix. See also Barry Friedman, *The Will of the People: How Public Opinion Has Influenced the Supreme Court and Shaped the Meaning of the Constitution* (New York: Farrar, Straus and Giroux, 2009).

34 *Brown v Board of Education*, 349 US 294 (1955).

35 Mark V Tushnet, "The Warren Court as History: An Interpretation" in Mark V Tushnet, ed, *The Warren Court in Historical and Political Perspective* (Charlottesville: The University of Virginia Press, 1993) at 16.

36 See e.g. Andrée Lajoie, Pierrette Mulazzi, & Michelle Gamache, "Political Ideas and the Evolution of Canadian Constitutional Law, 1945 to 1985" in Ivan Bernier & Andrée Lajoie, eds, *The Supreme Court of Canada as an Instrument of Political Change* (Toronto: University of Toronto Press, 1986).

ured. In this instance, it was given expression by the governing Conservative Party of Canada, together with the passive support of the Liberal Party of Canada and the active support of peak business organizations. It is significant, of course, that the national ruling coalition's proposal was repudiated by elites (both courts and legislatures) in various provinces (and, less significantly, by the federal New Democratic Party of Canada).

In social science terms, we can say that the Court is concerned with maintaining the diffuse support, as opposed to the specific support, of the Canadian public.[37] With this deep well of diffuse support to draw upon, it has the requisite freedom to manoeuvre and, indeed, to lose specific support in particular cases.[38] In my own work, I have tried to map out instances in which the Court is attuned to these legitimacy concerns, and have analyzed cases such as the *Reference Re Secession of Quebec, R v Marshall* (No. 2), *R v Sharpe*,[39] and *Canada (Prime Minister) v Khadr* (No. 2)[40] in this light. The results in these cases, I argue, are best explained with reference to the Court's ongoing legitimacy concerns. In the *Securities Reference*, legitimacy concerns could have led the Court to tilt in the direction of the will of the national ruling coalition.

4) Exigencies of Economic Globalization

Connected to legitimacy concerns and the demands of national ruling coalitions are the exigencies of economic globalization, which the Court has occasionally acknowledged as a significant contextual factor in constitutional litigation. I have suggested

---

37 On specific and diffuse support see Valerie J Hoekstra, *Public Reaction to Supreme Court Decisions* (Cambridge: Cambridge University Press, 2003) at 12.

38 In the United States, the data suggest that this deep reservoir of support (what the authors call "positivity theory") will ensure that the Court's legitimacy is not impaired even by controversial judicial appointments. See James L Gibson & Gregory A Caldera, *Citizens, Courts and Confirmations: Positivity Theory and the Judgments of the American People* (Princeton: Princeton University Press, 2009).

39 See *Reference Re Secession of Quebec*, [1988] 2 SCR 217 [*Secession Reference*]; *R v Marshall*, [1999] 3 SCR 533; *R v Sharpe*, [2001] 1 SCR 245. The three cases are discussed in Florian Sauvageau, David Schneiderman, & David Taras, *The Last Word: Media Coverage of the Supreme Court of Canada* (Vancouver: UBC Press, 2006).

40 *Canada (Prime Minister) v Khadr*, [2010] 1 SCR 44 discussed in David Schneiderman, "Khadr and Prerogative Power" (2010) 3 Rights Review 1.

elsewhere that the Court was driven by such exigencies in a case where it read in a US-style "full faith and credit clause" into the *Constitution Act, 1867* so that a Quebec statute blocking the production of documents in Ontario would be declared constitutionally invalid.[41] Rules respecting diversity of jurisdiction were anachronistic, Justice La Forest observed, in an "era in which numerous transactions and interactions spill over the borders defining legal communities in our disorganized legal world."[42] The Quebec blocking statute would have had the effect of "discouraging international commerce" and constituting an infringement on "the unity and efficiency of the Canadian marketplace."[43] Justice LaForest was building on foundations he had articulated in *Morguard*,[44] where he declared that "modern states . . . cannot live in splendid isolation" and that rules of comity must be grounded in the modern need to facilitate "the flow of wealth, skills and people across state lines," which has now "become imperative."[45] The Court's discourse complements well the picture of a borderless world that necessitates coordination of economic subjects at national, if not supranational, levels. The exigencies of economic globalization, in particular the rise of "systemic risks" associated with global financial markets,[46] could have helped the Court move in a more centralizing direction.

In light of the judicial resources available to the Court, the conclusion seems unassailable that the ruling is a slap in the face to the Harper government. In Section C below, I turn to some mitigating factors that provide a supportive context for the Court's repudiation of the initiative. In addition to a number of more doctrinal observations, I argue that the case does not buck dominant trends so much as tap into thinking about federalism

---

41   *Hunt v T&N plc*, [1993] 4 SCR 289 [*Hunt*] discussed in David Schneiderman, "Exchanging Constitutions: Constitutional Bricolage in Canada" (2002) 40 Osgoode Hall LJ 401 at 412–14.

42   *Hunt, ibid* at 295.

43   *Ibid* at 327 and 330.

44   *Morguard Investments v De Savoye*, [1990] 3 SCR 1077.

45   *Ibid* at 1095 and 1098. These sentiments are reflected in *obiter* in the *Canadian Western Bank v Alberta*, [2007] 2 SCR 3 at para 23: "the interpretation of . . . powers and of how they interrelate must evolve and must be tailored to the changing political and cultural realities of Canadian society." This is referred to approvingly in Binnie J's minority decision in *Consolidated Fastfrate Inc v Western Canada Council of Teamsters*, [2009] 3 SCR 407 at para 89 [*Fastfrate*].

46   See Chapter 2.

that is congenial to the Harper government in most other policy domains. I turn first to a couple of doctrinal considerations.

C. Against the Tide

1) The Wrong Head of Power

General trade and commerce authority does not function as a plenary source of authority in the same way as the criminal law or banking powers. Only the so-called first branch of the trade and commerce power, encompassing both interprovincial and international trade, functions as a fully independent head of federal authority. The same cannot be said for its second branch, which played little[47] or no role in federalism jurisprudence until 1989, when it was resuscitated in *General Motors*. Even eighty-eight years after Confederation, the Supreme Court could describe the general authority as "yet undefined."[48] Having been denied access to this federal authority for so long a period of time, its availability in *General Motors* was predicated on some pretty extraordinary circumstances. Chief Justice Dickson added the last two indicia precisely to "ensure that federal legislation does not upset the balance of power between federal and provincial governments."[49] Moreover, the judicial branch has long confirmed that securities regulation falls within provincial jurisdiction,[50] despite its cross-border elements;[51] extant precedent simply does not support the invasion of provincial domains under the general trade and commerce authority. One could say that Dickson CJ's "belt and suspenders" approach to expanding the general trade and commerce authority was intended to prevent federal power grabs of just this sort. From this angle, in so far as federal securities legislation

---

47 See e.g. *AG Ontario v AG Canada* (sub nom Canada Standard Trade Mark) [1937] AC 405 (PC) [*AG Ontario*].

48 *Re Validity of the Industrial Relations and Disputes Investgation Act*, [1955] SCR 529 at 551, Rand J. In what is still the only book-length treatment of trade and commerce authority, Professor Smith declared "the content of this general power, however, had remained a mystery" in Alexander Smith, *The Commerce Power in Canada and the United States* (Toronto: Butterworths, 1963) at 77.

49 *General Motors*, above note 5 at 662.

50 *Smith v The Queen*, [1960] SCR 776.

51 For instance, *Gregory & Company Inc v Quebec Securities Commission*, [1961] SCR 584.

upset that balance, the general trade and commerce argument seemed doomed to fail from the start. This is why the Court, in the *Securities Reference*, repeatedly described the general trade and commerce authority as "circumscribed"[52] and would not apply the double aspect doctrine (authorizing the same matter to be the subject of legislation by either level of government) without identifying a federal aspect that was "distinct" from the provincial one.[53]

The federal initiative, furthermore, did not resemble earlier judicial validations of the general trade and commerce authority. Federal legislation regulating business combinations, a version of which was upheld in *General Motors*, had already been authorized under the federal criminal law power.[54] Federal trademark authority was implicitly authorized by the second branch of *Parsons* in *Canada Standard Trade Mark*,[55] as well as in later cases, and was not contested by any of the provinces in *Kirkbi*.[56] In sum, the general trade and commerce power simply seemed to be the wrong head of federal power with which to justify the initiative.[57]

2) The Narrative of a Federal Takeover

The Court rejected the narrative of the case offered by the federal government — that this was an instance of "cooperative federalism"[58] — and instead characterized the case as one of federal "overreach" amounting to a "wholesale takeover" of provincial jurisdiction.[59] Given the Act's "opt-ins" and "progressive implementation," however, the Court would not go so far as to characterize it as the "unilateral[] impos[ition] of securities

---

52 *Securities Reference*, above note 7 at paras 73–74.
53 *Ibid* at para 90.
54 *PATA*, above note 22; *Canadian National Transportation*, above note 27.
55 *AG Ontario*, above note 47.
56 *Kirkbi*, above note 30 at paras 18–19.
57 Perhaps what the federal government was hoping to pull out of the hat was the sort of jurisdictional grant it obtained under s 92(10)(a) in *Alberta Government Telephones v Canada (CRTC)*, [1989] 2 SCR 225, which declared provincially run telephone services to be a federal work or undertaking. As regards federal jurisdiction over intraprovincial carriage of goods, the Court preferred to keep such matters within provincial domains in *Fastfrate*, above note 45.
58 *Securities Reference*, above note 7 (Factum of the Attorney General of Canada at para 69).
59 *Securities Reference*, above note 7 at para 127.

regulation for the whole of Canada."[60] Yet it is hard to read the
Reference as anything but a repudiation of federal unilateralism
— a recurring theme in the law of Canadian federalism. This is
a worry traceable back to *Parsons* itself and, to my mind, a dominant strain in the jurisprudence;[61] it reached its apotheosis in
the *Secession Reference*,[62] where the Court would not condone
the unilateral secession of a constituent unit from the federation
without negotiations, leaving aside the requirements imposed by
the amending formula. Unilateralism of all sorts is condemned
in the Court's decision — not only a unilateral declaration of independence by Quebec, but also a unilateral refusal to negotiate by the federal government and the provinces in the face of a
clear majority in Quebec responding positively to a clear question.
Even during negotiations, the parties were expected to act in accordance with the underlying constitutional principles identified
by the Court, one of which was federalism: unilateralism was
inconsistent with the workings of a federal system, in which political power is shared. This antipathy to unilateralism — to the
"wholesale takeover" on an "exclusive basis" of "all aspects" of securities regulation — seems once again to have roiled the Court.

3) "Hello, We're Here," or, the Argument from Institutional Self-Preservation

Another possible explanation is that the Court decided the case as
it did in order to preserve its place in the legal hierarchy of Canadian federalism, that is, in order to maintain its own relevance
in federalism disputes. This sort of claim was not very successfully made about the work of the Judicial Committee of the Privy
Council. Murray Greenwood argued that the JCPC continually
overruled the Supreme Court of Canada in the late nineteenth
century in order to preserve its appellate jurisdiction in the face
of increasing worries that Canada would no longer tolerate this

---

60 *Ibid* at para 31.
61 This anxiety is captured, in part, by Lederman's interpretive claim that
    the "balance between federal and provincial subjects should remain
    stable — reasonably constant — subject only to a process of gradual
    changes when these are rendered truly necessary by the demands of new
    conditions in our society from time to time": William R Lederman, "Unity
    and Diversity in Canadian Federalism" (1975) 53 Can Bar Rev 597 at
    607–608.
62 *Secession Reference*, above note 39.

form of judicial subordination.[63] By continually ruling in favour
of the provinces, the Board could be confident that a powerful
constituency of support could be found there. Having nothing to
say about classical legal thinking of the period,[64] the argument
could hardly explain why the judges reasoned as they did.

My argument is more context specific, though it also reson-
ates in institutional terms. Recall the debate in English-speaking
constitutional circles about the utility of a judicial umpire in the
realms of legal federalism (discussed in Section B(1) above). Until
now, it looked as though the "Weiler side" had won, given decades
of judicial deference in these realms; that is, the Court appeared
to have accepted that political safeguards of federalism were
sufficient to police jurisdictional lines of authority. That argument runs as follows: we can reasonably rely on ordinary political processes operating within a federalist system to ensure that
the division of powers between two levels of government will be
respected.[65] By reviving concerns about exclusive jurisdictional
authority — the watertight compartments approach associated
with classical legal federalism — the Court appears to have made
itself relevant again.[66]

The *Securities Reference* looks similar, from this institutional
angle, to what the US Supreme Court did with the opportunity
presented to it by the *US v Lopez* case.[67] After deferring for some
fifty years to the use of federal commerce clause authority — not
since the New Deal crisis had the Court invalidated a federal

---

63 Murray Greenwood, "Lord Watson, Institutional Self-Interest, and the
   Decentralization of Canadian Federalism in the 1890s" (1974) 9 UBC L
   Rev 244.

64 On this, see Richard CB Risk, "Canadian Courts under the Influence"
   (1990) 40 UTLJ 687.

65 Ryder, "End of Umpire", above note 17 at 375, made precisely this point
   in 2006, though not with reference to US doctrine: "Just as the Court
   placed its faith in the politics of federalism to prevent abuse of the dis-
   allowance and declaratory powers, it may also be confident that expansion of the legal potential for federal dominance resulting from judicial
   interpretation of the division of powers carries little risk for the federal
   principle in practice. Federal governments in Canada pay a heavy political price for running roughshod over provincial interests, even though
   they have a growing legal capacity to do so."

66 The Court may have initiated this new phase in *Reference re Assisted Human Reproduction Act*, 2010 SCC 61.

67 *US v Lopez*, 514 US 549 (1995) [*Lopez*].

exercise of the clause[68] — the majority in *Lopez* invalidated the federal *Gun-Free School Zones Act*. Chief Justice Rehnquist declared that they had reached the "outer limits" of federal commerce clause authority, drawing a line in the sand beyond which the Court would decline to "proceed any further."[69] Justices Kennedy and O'Connor, in their concurrence, admit that the case "requires us to consider our place in the design of the Government."[70] Why is it, they ask, that in other areas where judicial review is exercised under the Constitution, the Court's "legitimacy is undoubted," whereas "[o]ur role in preserving the federal balance seems more tenuous"?[71] It would be wrong, they concluded, to cede jurisdiction entirely to the political safeguards of federalism.

The ruling in the *Securities Reference* serves similar functions. "Inherent in a federal system," the Court declares, "is the need for an impartial arbiter of jurisdictional disputes over the boundaries of federal and provincial powers."[72] The Court admits that the "'dominant tide' of flexible federalism" points in the other direction — one that upholds the validity of the federal law. Yet it will resist that tug: "however strong its pull may be, [the dominant tide] cannot sweep designated powers out to sea, nor erode the constitutional balance inherent in the federal state."[73] The Court here expresses in seafaring terms the line in the sand that the Supreme Court in *Lopez* was also intent on drawing.[74]

4) The New/Old Federalism

The Court's decision in the *Securities Reference*, it turns out, is not entirely dissonant with a version of federalism that Prime Minister Stephen Harper has been promoting for some time, a version that is faithful to the classical lines of the division of legislative powers and which censures federal incursions into traditionally provincial domains. Preston Manning, leader of the

---

68 The new paradigm, associated with Justice Stone's famous footnote 4, was explained in *US v Carolene Products*, 304 US 144 (1938).

69 *Lopez*, above note 66 at 557 and 567, Rehnquist CJ.

70 *Ibid* at 575, Kennedy J.

71 *Ibid.*

72 *Securities Reference*, above note 7 at para 55.

73 *Ibid* at para 62.

74 The extraordinary nature of the case, and its dissonance with the version of "enabling" federalism that the Court has practised over the last couple of decades, is underscored by the Court's repeated invocation of what the *Secession Reference* referred to as the "fundamental principle" of federalism.

Reform Party in 1993, proposed a "new federalism" that would go some distance in restoring this lost reading of Canadian federalism. Manning's strategy was intended specifically to lure Quebec back into the federalist fold by (1) retreating from the use of the federal spending power in provincial areas of jurisdiction and (2) strengthening the economic union by removing barriers to interprovincial trade.[75] We can safely assume that Harper supported this policy initiative, and may even have had a hand in designing it. A former research director for the Reform Party, Harper was serving as Member of Parliament for Calgary Southwest by 1993; shortly after taking the helm of the Conservative Party of Canada (successor to the Reform Party of Canada and the Canadian Alliance), he introduced, first in an important speech in Quebec City and then in a *National Post* op-ed, a modified version of Manning's proposal that he called "open federalism." This opaque idea, again meant principally to address Quebec grievances, was intended to "re-establish a strong central government that focuses on genuine national priorities like national defence and the economic union, while fully respecting the exclusive jurisdiction of the provinces."[76] What, specifically, did Harper mean by this? I trace here the development of the idea with a view to determining the degree to which it bears any relation to the Supreme Court's decision in the *Securities Reference*.

Open federalism had its own short chapter in the 2005 *Conservative Party of Canada Policy Declaration*,[77] which spoke of restoring "constitutional balance" (code for the federal government's withdrawal from provincial jurisdiction) and of a commitment "to the federal principle, to the notion of strong provinces within Canada," and to working "co-operatively with the provinces to improve the lives of Canadians while respecting the division of power and responsibilities outlined in the Constitution."[78] The document committed the party to limiting use of the federal spending power and to remedying the problem of "fiscal imbalance," referring to the revenue-generating capacity of the federal government and the diminished capacity of the provinces in the

---

75 Flanagan, *Waiting for the Wave*, above note 1 at 188–89.

76 Stephen Harper, "My Plan for 'Open Federalism'" *National Post* (27 October 2004).

77 *Conservative Party of Canada Policy Declaration* (19 March 2005), online: Conservative Party of Canada www.conservative.ca/media/20050319-POLICY%20DECLARATION.pdf.

78 *Ibid* at 6.

face of rising expenditures.[79] The only reference to policies associated with enhancing the economic union appears under the heading "Interprovincial Trade" and commits the party to "take the lead in working with its provincial partners to eliminate interprovincial trade barriers in commerce, labour, and capital mobility."[80]

In the Conservative Party's election platform of 2006, "open federalism" is associated with strengthening "national unity,"[81] which will be achieved by devising "practical intergovernmental mechanisms to facilitate provincial involvement in areas of federal jurisdiction where provincial jurisdiction is affected, and enshrine those practices in a Charter of Open Federalism."[82] There is mention of expanding the "economic and social union in Canada" but very few specifics.

In the 2006 budget document *Restoring Fiscal Balance in Canada: Focusing on Priorities*,[83] the Department of Finance declares that the government will ensure "respect for local autonomy and diversity" of the provinces, "whether by virtue of their exclusive constitutional jurisdiction or because they have a comparative advantage in the delivery of programs and policies in particular areas."[84] The government commits to improving the competitiveness and efficiency of the economic union by "collaborating" with provinces to reduce barriers to internal trade and to work "[t]oward a common securities regulator that administers a single code, is responsive to regional needs, and has a governance structure that ensures broad provincial-territorial participation."[85] There otherwise is no specific mention of open federalism.

The party's 2008 election platform refers to entering into a "Charter of Open Federalism" that will "respect the jurisdiction of the provinces and territories in the *Constitution Act, 1867*, and

---

79 *Ibid* at 7.
80 *Ibid* at 14.
81 "Stand Up for Canada, Conservative Party of Canada Federal Election Platform 2006", online: CBC www.cbc.ca/canadavotes2006/leadersparties/pdf/conservative_platform20060113.pdf at 42.
82 *Ibid.*
83 Canada, Department of Finance, *Restoring Fiscal Balance in Canada: Focusing on Priorities, Canada's New Government Turning a New Leaf*, Budget 2006, online: Department of Finance Canada www.fin.gc.ca/budget06/pdf/fp2006e.pdf.
84 *Ibid* at 56.
85 *Ibid* at 69 and 50.

will enshrine our principles of federalism in a new Charter of Open Federalism."[86] There are commitments to enhancing the economic union, but these are confined to removing barriers to interprovincial trade.[87]

Subsequent to the Conservative's 2008 election victory, on 22 June 2009 Finance Minister Jim Flaherty announced the establishment of the Canadian Securities Regulator Transition Office,[88] and on 16 October Justice Minister Rob Nicholson announced that the question of the constitutionality of a proposed federal securities act would be put to the Supreme Court. Nicholson expressed satisfaction that the government would be "supported by Canada's foremost constitutional experts."[89]

In the Conservative Party's 2011 platform, "open federalism" is referred to just once: in the context of "renewing the Health Accord" with the provinces, the document states that a Conservative government "will respect the fact that health care is an area of provincial jurisdiction."[90] It is acknowledged that the government will take steps to establish a national securities regulator, a federal role that is made more self-evident by the "global financial crisis."[91]

What this brief review of Stephen Harper's idea of "open federalism" suggests is that, both historically and in present-day terms, it is meant to signal a respect for the division of legislative

86 "The True North Strong and Free: Stephen Harper's Plan for Canadians [2008]", online: Conservative Party of Canada www.conservative.ca/media/2008-Platform-e.pdf at 26.

87 "A re-elected Conservative Government led by Stephen Harper will work to eliminate barriers that restrict or impair trade, investment or labour mobility between provinces and territories by 2010. In 2007, the government announced that it was prepared to use the federal trade and commerce power to strengthen the Canadian economic union. Since that time, we have seen progress among the provinces and territories in strengthening the existing Agreement on Internal Trade. We hope to see further progress, but are prepared to intervene by exercising federal authority if barriers to trade, investment and mobility remain by 2010": *ibid* at 16.

88 Department of Finance Canada, Press Release, "Minister of Finance Announces Launch of Canadian Securities Regulator Transition Office" (22 June 2009), online: Department of Finance Canada www.fin.gc.ca/n08/09-064-eng.asp (accessed 15 May 2012).

89 Les Whittington, "Ottawa Seeks Guidance on Regulator Proposal" *Toronto Star* (17 October 2009) B7.

90 "Here for Canada" online: Conservative Party of Canada www.conservative.ca/media/ConservativePlatform2011_ENs.pdf at 30.

91 *Ibid* at 20.

authority between the two levels of government. The concept is associated, in other words, with the "strict constructionism" of classical legal federalism,[92] and signals a retreat of federal authority from realms of traditional provincial jurisdiction, a decline in the use of the federal spending power, collaboration with the provinces where the exercise of federal jurisdiction has an impact on provincial domains, and remedying the fiscal imbalance. It also includes taking steps to enhance the economic union, typically in the sense of removing non-fiscal barriers to interprovincial trade. By 2006, "open federalism" included working collaboratively with the provinces to establish a common (not necessarily "national") securities regulator. It typically would *not* have involved exercising the general trade and commerce authority in provincial domains of responsibility — that is, until the Ministry of Finance took up the project of a national securities regulator. While "open federalism" hardly breaks the mould of the Canadian federalism tradition[93] — indeed, it rings hollow in light of recent refusals to negotiate with the provinces over the health care transfer — it signalled that new unilateral federal initiatives would not be pursued over the objections of the provinces. This helps to explain why the proposal for a national securities regulator appears antithetical to the brand of federalism that Harper has been promoting for some time. It also suggests a split within the Conservative government between the finance ministry and Bay Street financiers, on the one hand, and a populist brand of provincial-rights Reformers, on the other.

How might this explain the Court's apparent about-face in the *Securities Reference*? The government's repeatedly expressed preference for respect of traditional provincial jurisdiction has generated a supportive discursive environment for the Court's

92 Robert Young, "Open Federalism and Canadian Municipalities" in Keith G Banting et al, *Open Federalism: Interpretations, Significance* (Kingston: Institute of Intergovernmental Relations, 2006) at 17. Geoff Norquay, former director of communications to Stephen Harper in the Office of the Leader of the Opposition, declared Harper a "classic federalist" in Geoff Norquay, "The Death of Executive Federalism and the Rise of the 'Harper Doctrine': Prospects for the Next Health Care Accord" (December 2011–January 2012) Policy Options 46 at 47.

93 See Keith G Banting, "Open Federalism and Canada's Economic and Social Union: Back to the Future?" in Keith G Banting et al, *Open Federalism: Interpretations, Significance, ibid* at 81. See also James Bickerton, "Deconstructing the New Federalism" (2010) 4 Canadian Political Science Review 56 at 68.

revival of the tropes of classical legal federalism. This is not to say that members of the Court closely follow Conservative policy rhetoric or tactics (or even the election returns) — only that the Court's constitutional decisions are not made in a vacuum, and that there is an observable correlation between the federal government's views on intergovernmental relations and the reasons issued by the Court in the *Securities Reference*. For this reason, we might read the Court's ruling as giving voice to dominant values and norms — or those vying for dominance — and observe that political discourse is one resource available to the Court in discerning what those dominant norms are or should be. Even if the judiciary operates under a different logic than politics, it is not immune from these sorts of influences.[94]

D. Conclusion

The dominant legal consensus expressed profound disappointment with the Court's ruling.[95] Many contributors to this volume give eloquent expression to this sentiment. It has not been my intention to contribute to this smack down of the Court, or to outline a roadmap for a less expansive national security regime. Instead, my objective has been to try to identify factors that gave rise to the heightened expectations that the Court would declare intra vires the proposed *Securities Act*, and then to hypothesize about some of the reasons the Court resisted the "dominant tide" and preferred to send promoters of a national securities regime packing.

I have argued that there were sufficient doctrinal resources to uphold the scheme and trend lines that pointed in a direction favourable to the federal side. Nevertheless, there was much that was wrong with the federal strategy, as I discussed in Section C above. Preferring to embrace a discredited discourse associated with classical legal federalism (at least in English-speaking Can-

---

94 I make a similar sort of claim about the supportive context for Supreme Court decision making provided by dominant media accounts in "Social Rights and 'Common Sense': Gosselin Through a Media Lens" in Margot Young et al, eds, *Poverty: Rights, Social Citizenship, and Legal Activism* (Vancouver: UBC Press, 2007).

95 There were, nevertheless, dissenting voices in the legal academy. See the contributions in this volume by Jeffrey McIntosh and Stéphane Rousseau as representative of this viewpoint.

ada), the Court ironically embraced a provincial rights discourse espoused by the Harper government in the realm of federal–provincial relations. Conversely, the Harper government reversed course by adopting a national securities policy dissonant with its own policy pronouncements. If securing and enhancing Canada's economic union was a priority for the federal government, this would not be achieved, the Harper government declared, over the objections of the provincial premiers. Some will credit the Prime Minister for reviving this preoccupation with classical legal federalism and the accompanying political program of liberal individualism, with its "emphasis on smaller government, lower taxes and balanced budgets."[96] In light of the *Securities Reference*, it must be acknowledged that the government got at least an assist on that score from the Supreme Court of Canada.

---

96   Tom Flanagan, "Beware of Ottawa Bearing Gifts" *The Globe and Mail* (17 January 2012) A15.

CHAPTER 6

Reference Re Securities Act: Comment on Lee and Schneiderman

Mahmud Jamal[1]

It is a privilege to comment on the excellent papers of Professor Ian Lee[2] and Professor David Schneiderman[3] analyzing the Supreme Court's decision in *Reference Re Securities Act*.[4] I profited greatly from Professor Lee's outstanding paper in the *Canadian Business Law Journal* on securities regulation and the trade and commerce power,[5] as, apparently, did Dalphond JA of the Quebec Court of Appeal, who cited it in his dissenting reasons in *Québec (Procureure générale) c Canada (Procureure générale)*.[6]

I agree that with Professor Schneiderman that the Supreme Court's decision resists the "dominant tide" of constitutional interpretation favouring the operation of legislation of both levels of government. It certainly appears to be a departure from the

---

1   I represented the Canadian Bankers Association (CBA) as an intervener in the *Securities Reference*, supporting the position of the Attorney General of Canada on the constitutionality of the federal Act. The following comments, however, reflect my views alone and not necessarily those of the CBA.

2   See Chapter 4

3   See Chapter 5.

4   *Reference Re Securities Act*, 2011 SCC 66 [*Securities Reference*].

5   Ian B Lee, "Balancing and its Alternatives: Jurisprudential Choice, Federal Securities Regulation and the Trade and Commerce Power" (2011) 50 Can Bus LJ 72.

6   *Québec (Procureure générale) c Canada (Procureure générale)*, 2011 QCCA 591 at paras 400 and 500. [*Quebec Securities Reference*].

brand of win–win or non-zero-sum-game federalism that the Supreme Court has championed for much of the past decade.

One can see the Court's brand of cooperative, win–win federalism in recent cases such as *Canadian Western Bank v Alberta*,[7] where the Court restricted the application of the interjurisdictional immunity doctrine, which previously had allowed a wider scope for federal legislative jurisdiction. The Court said that the dominant tide "should favour, where possible, the ordinary application of statutes enacted by *both* levels of government. In the absence of conflicting enactments of the other level of government, the Court should avoid blocking the application of measures that are taken in furtherance of the public interest."[8] Would these comments not have supported the *Proposed Canadian Securities Act*[9]— a measure that, as framed, did not conflict with any provincial law and that was clearly taken in furtherance of the public interest?

Both Lee and Schneiderman are surely right that there probably were sufficient judicial resources for the Court to have found in the federal government's favour. The trade and commerce jurisprudence — particularly *General Motors of Canada Ltd v City National Leasing*[10] and *Kirkbi AG v Ritvik Holdings Inc*[11] — allowed enough "interpretive room" for the Court to uphold the *Proposed Act*. As Schneiderman notes, many noted Canadian constitutional experts from sea to sea — including Lee[12] — shared this view. On the law, at least, this case could have gone the other way.

So why did the federal side lose — and lose so badly?[13] Part of the answer lies in Schneiderman's suggestion that the Court was concerned about federal unilateralism. Part of the answer also lies in this being the wrong question — the federal side did not lose, and there is in fact much in the decision that recognizes

---

7   *Canadian Western Bank v Alberta*, 2007 SCC 22.
8   *Ibid* at para 37 [emphasis in the original].
9   Order in Council PC 2010-667.
10 *General Motors of Canada Ltd v City National Leasing*, [1989] 1 SCR 641 [*General Motors*].
11 *Kirkbi AG v Ritvik Holdings Inc*, 2005 SCC 65 [*Kirkbi*].
12 Lee, "General Trade," above note 2.
13 Of the nineteen appellate judges who considered the constitutionality of the federal Act (five in Alberta, five in Quebec, and nine in the Supreme Court), only one — Dalphond JA of the Quebec Court of Appeal — found that Parliament had legislative jurisdiction to enact the proposed legislation under the general trade and commerce power.

the scope for federal jurisdiction over securities regulation and charts the path forward.

First, consider the narrative of federal unilateralism, which seems to have carried all nine judges of the Supreme Court. Schneiderman observes that this must have been a significant factor in the Court's decision. The reasons do, of course, include several express descriptions of the *Proposed Act* as a "wholesale takeover" of the regulation of the securities industry.[14] But there is more. We can see this concern, for example, in the Court's description of the facts. Any litigator will tell you that how you present the facts is critical to the morality play of a case. So, in the early part of the decision, we see the Court setting out almost a century's worth of recommendations for a national securities regulator, not just by way of background and context but to highlight that most reform proposals since the Royal Commission on Price Spreads in 1935 have envisaged some form of federal–provincial cooperation.[15] As the Court noted, "[n]ot surprisingly, the proposals generally envisaged cooperation between the provinces and the federal government as the route to achieving national standards and regulation."[16] Translation: *This is the Canadian way.*

We can also see the concern about federal unilateralism in a brief section titled "Securities Regulation in Other Federal States," which reviews the experiences of Germany, Australia, and the United States and emphasizes that "power-sharing between the central and local levels of government in this area can succeed."[17] Translation: *Where there's a will, there's a way.*

The second part of my answer to why the federal side lost is to challenge the premise of the question. The Supreme Court's decision recognizes, for the first time, a significant role for the federal government in securities regulation, particularly in regulating systemic risk and Canada-wide data collection, which the Court described as "matters of undoubted national interest."[18] This is not a bare rump of federal jurisdiction, as some have suggested: Parliament now has not only the *jurisdiction* to regulate systemic risk but probably also the *obligation* to do so, because

---

14 *Securities Reference*, above note 4 ("complete takeover" at para 117; "wholesale takeover" at para 128).

15 *Ibid* at paras 11–28.

16 *Ibid* at para 11.

17 *Ibid* at paras 48–52.

18 *Ibid* at para 122.

the provinces lack this power. Any future regulatory shortcoming in relation to systemic risk will inevitably be laid at the federal government's feet. This suggests, to me at least, that after many, many years of debate, Canada will finally get a federal securities regulator. The question is, what kind?

There is perhaps the vaguest support for this suggestion that the federal side did not "lose" in Mr. Justice Binnie's recent interview with *The Globe and Mail,* following his retirement from the Court. Asked about the "legal potential for a national securities regulator now that the Supreme Court has rejected the federal government's bid," he replied, "I was part of the court that decided the securities reference. There is nothing I can add to what was said there, but *my wish is that more commentators would actually read the decision instead of simply the outcome. They will find in that decision a large part of the answer to your question."*[19]

As to the path forward, as Lee rightly notes, a redrafted federal law aimed at the macroeconomic rather than microeconomic aspects of securities regulation surely would be valid, even without a cooperative federal–provincial solution. Nonetheless, it is a shame that the Court found the federal Act invalid in part because the federal Act resembled provincial securities laws. Lee suggests that part of the problem with the federal position was its characterization of the Act as "comprehensive securities legislation." But surely it would have been a relatively small drafting matter to make the federal Act look cosmetically different while remaining substantively the same? The federal Act could have been drafted around what even the Court acknowledged are undeniable federal interests, such as systemic risk. But the federal goal was to provide for continuity in a transition from provincial regimes to a federal regime. Here, as elsewhere, it seems, no good deed goes unpunished.

Lee also rightly contends that the Court should not be viewed as having retreated from the "double aspect" doctrine. While the judgment states repeatedly that the federal arguments about the changed character of security markets from local to nation-

---

19 Jacquie McNish, "The Supreme Court's retired, but hardly retiring, Ian Binnie" *The Globe & Mail* (13 April 2012) [emphasis added]. Moreover, throughout the decision the Court is at pains to highlight that the only issue it is addressing is the first branch of trade and commerce. Other potential heads of federal jurisdiction — international trade and commerce, POGG, criminal law, companies with federal objects, etc. — all remain open: see *Securities Reference,* above note 4 at paras 5, 32, 47, and 91.

al lacked evidentiary support in the record,[20] many of the past studies on the need for a federal regulator were in fact before the Court — including the Wise Persons' Committee report, the *Crawford Report*, and the *Hockin Report*. It is not clear what more the Court wanted. The good news, however, is that the ruling on double aspect is firmly anchored in the particular record before the Court.

Let me close in the same way that the Court closed — on a note of mild optimism about the future of a cooperative national regulator. In the last part of its decision, the Court undertakes a rare foray into providing policy advice to the federal and provincial governments, urging a return to the bargaining table under the jurisdictional lines drawn by the Court:

> It is not for this Court to suggest to the governments of Canada and the provinces the way forward by, in effect, conferring in advance an opinion on the constitutionality of this or that alternative scheme. Yet we may appropriately note the growing practice of resolving the complex governance problems that arise in federations, not by the bare logic of either/or, but by seeking cooperative solutions that meet the needs of the country as a whole as well as its constituent parts.[21]

Translation: *We're all in this together, so let's get back to work.*

---

20 See e.g. *Securities Reference, ibid* at paras 116–117, 125, and 127.
21 *Ibid* at para 133.

CHAPTER 7

Can Canadian Federalism Be Relevant?

Lorne Sossin

A. Introduction

In this brief comment, I argue that the Supreme Court of Canada's decision in the *Reference Re Securities Act*[1] is mired in jurisdictional abstraction and fails to articulate an approach to Canadian federalism that is relevant to the realities of the twenty-first-century administrative state. While the goal of the decision appears to be to revive the historic role of the Court as a catalyst for federal–provincial, negotiated cooperative federalism, its effect may well be to set back that very project. What we need in settings such as national securities regulation, I suggest, is a focus on the public interest and a new commitment to "purposive federalism."

When I teach Canadian federalism, I begin by asking students about a trip to the emergency room of a hospital. The care they will receive turns on a host of legal and policy questions, from the balance between public and private services to the funding of facilities, from the regulation of nurses and physicians to the availability of appropriate technology and medication. I ask the students whether it matters which level of government is performing those functions and funding those services. No one puts up a hand. "What matters is patient care," one student responds,

---

1   *Reference Re Securities Act*, 2011 SCC 66 [*Securities Reference*].

when pressed; "federalism is about constitutional law — it isn't relevant to everyday life."

Traditionally, the Court has tried to reconcile federalism with the realities of everyday life. The classic examples involve the development of the welfare state. The nineteenth-century division of powers left the federal government with the means to address social and economic turmoil during the 1930s, but only the provinces appeared to have the constitutional jurisdiction to legislate in these areas. Rather than explore a creative interpretation that would have permitted "New Deal" programs, a narrower approach was taken. The Supreme Court of Canada and the Privy Council struck down the federal *Employment and Social Insurance Act* in the mid-1930s.[2] The Court's decision was inconvenient and arguably out of touch with the suffering of many Canadians (coming at the height of the Depression), but it served as a catalyst for a series of federal–provincial negotiations. In 1940, following the report of the Rowell-Sirois Commission on Dominion–Provincial Relations, an amendment to the *Constitution Act, 1867,* gave Parliament jurisdiction over unemployment insurance. Cooperative federalism was entrenched as the "dominant tide," to use Dickson CJ's term,[3] and that episode was hailed as an example both of federalism's success and of the important role of the Supreme Court as a catalyst for bringing together the Federal Government and the provinces to produce negotiated compromises.

That is clearly the role the Court wishes to play in the context of the *Securities Reference*. As is discussed in detail, and from a variety of perspectives, in this volume, the Court held that the federal government's scheme, under the proposed *Canadian Securities Act*, for a national securities regulator to which provinces could "opt in" was outside its constitutional jurisdiction — and particularly the federal trade and commerce power under section 91 of the *Constitution Act, 1867.*

The Court highlighted that national securities regulation is possible to achieve, notwithstanding its view on the government's proposed *Securities Act*, but that doing so would require further federal–provincial negotiation:

2   *Reference Re The Employment and Social Insurance Act,* [1936] SCR 427, aff'd (*sub nom Attorney General for Canada v Attorney General for Ontario*) [1937] AC 355 (PC).

3   From *OPSEU v Ontario (Attorney General),* [1987] 2 SCR 2 at 18, cited in *Securities Reference,* above note 1 at para 58.

It is open to the federal government and the provinces to exercise their respective powers over securities harmoniously, in the spirit of cooperative federalism. The experience of other federations in the field of securities regulation, while a function of their own constitutional requirements, suggests that a cooperative approach might usefully be explored, should our legislators so choose, to ensure that each level of government properly discharges its responsibility to the public in a coordinated fashion.[4]

The Court emphasized the availability of a "cooperative" approach, highlighting "the growing practice of resolving complex governance problems that arise in federations, not by the bare logic of either/or, but by seeking cooperative solutions that meet the needs of the country as a whole as well as its constituent parts."[5] The notion of *cooperative federalism* has been invoked to capture a general ethos of negotiated solutions in settings where the division of powers prevents a particular policy goal from being achieved by one level of government acting unilaterally.[6] It builds on what the Court characterized as the "constitutional creativity" and "cooperative flexibility" inherent in Canadian federalism.[7] Importantly, the Court linked such a cooperative approach to the obligation on each level of government to properly discharge its responsibilities to the public.[8]

Rather than focus on what would allow government to achieve the policy ends necessary for the public interest, however, the Court focused on what would maintain the jurisdictional balance:

> In summary, notwithstanding the Court's promotion of cooperative and flexible federalism, the constitutional boundaries that underlie the division of powers must be respected. The "dominant tide" of flexible federalism, however strong its pull may be, cannot sweep designated powers out to sea, nor erode the constitutional balance inherent in the Canadian federal state.[9]

---

4   *Securities Reference, ibid* at para 9.
5   *Ibid* at para 132.
6   See Christopher Hunter, "Cooperative Federalism & *The Securities Act Reference*, 2011 SCC 66: A Rocky Road" (13 January 2012), online: The Court www.thecourt.ca/2012/01/13/cooperative-federalism-the-securities-act-reference-2011-scc-66-a-rocky-road/.
7   See *Securities Reference*, above note 1 at para 58.
8   *Ibid* at para 9.
9   *Ibid* at para 61.

In my view, this approach risks unmooring Canadian federalism from its normative roots. Canadian federalism has been from the outset a normative project of cooperation, redistribution, and nation-building;[10] the question is whether cooperative federalism is enhanced more by the Court's asserting exclusivity in the division of powers or, alternatively, by the recognition of mutuality and the necessity for harmonization and enhancing policy outcomes. For example, recognizing shared federal and provincial jurisdiction over the protection of the environment is important precisely because this leads to more effective environmental protection. In my view, recognizing dual and overlapping jurisdiction through mechanisms such as the "double-aspect" and "necessarily incidental" doctrines of Canadian federalism produces the kind of federalism capable of addressing the policy challenges of the twenty-first-century administrative state. To regress to a period of "watertight" division of powers is not only to risk undermining the protection of the securities market but to risk the relevance of Canadian federalism itself.

B. Division of Powers and the Twenty-first-Century Administrative State

Canada's constitutional division of powers was the product of nineteenth-century political compromise, individual convictions, and historical accident.[11] It set the country on a course of principled pragmatism that has arguably been Canada's single most enduring characteristic.

This kind of principled pragmatism has guided the Supreme Court as much as any other political institution in Canada. It has led the Court to develop innovative solutions to the deficiencies of the *Constitution Act, 1867*, ranging from the recognition of Constitutional Conventions and unwritten constitutional principles to a "living tree" approach to interpreting the text of the division of powers. It has also led the Court to develop a "purposive" approach to Canadian federalism, particularly in areas — such as

---

10   For an elaboration of this stream and the alternatives, see Sujit Choudhry, Jean-Francois Gaudreault-DesBiens, & Lorne Sossin, eds, *Dilemmas of Solidarity: Rethinking Redistribution in the Canadian Federation* (Toronto: University of Toronto Press, 2006).

11   See Peter Russell, *A Constitutional Odyssey*, 3d ed (Toronto: University of Toronto Press, 2004).

securities regulation — which are not addressed in the text of the division of powers.[12]

We now associate purposive constitutional interpretation with the *Charter*.[13] Purposive federalism, however, recognizes that the dry words of the division of powers must be interpreted with particular normative ends in mind. One such end clearly is that the federal and provincial governments maintain distinct areas of responsibility; another end is that governments ought to be able to pursue the important policy goals in the public interest that they are best positioned to achieve. The national securities regulatory scheme proposed by the federal government appears consistent with both ends: it preserves provincial securities commissions where provinces so desire, which maintains both provincial and federal distinctive roles, and allows for a more effective regulatory framework.

Whereas the purposive approach is associated with judicial activism in the *Charter* context, it may well lead to greater judicial deference in the context of federalism. Exclusivity should be understood as the exception rather than the norm in Canadian federalism, and only egregious incursions beyond the competence of one level of government into the sphere of the other should attract judicial intervention. In my view, this would advance rather than stymie the principled pragmatism of the *Constitution Act, 1867*: While the federal government could play a role in areas where it hitherto has not (e.g., a national post-secondary education or mental health strategy), the provinces too could flex their muscles in areas that have in the past been reserved for the federal government (e.g., provincial trade and foreign investment strategies).

Contributions to this volume by Trebilcock and Iacobucci, among others, make clear that from the standpoint of effective public policy (and consistency with the analogy of competition regulation), the federal government's national securities scheme should have been upheld. Numerous commissions and studies have consistently made the point that effective regulation of

---

12 The phrase "purposive federalism" has been invoked in the Canadian context at least since David Smith, "National Political Parties and the Growth of National Political Community" in R Kenneth Carty & W Peter Ward, eds, *National Politics and Community in Canada* (Vancouver: UBC Press, 1986) at 82.

13 See *Hunter et al v Southam Inc*, [1984] 2 SCR 145.

securities requires a national regulatory scheme. However, as the Court clarified in the following passage, what is "optimum" as a matter of policy is not relevant to the discussion of what is "constitutionally permissible":

> We would add that, in applying the *General Motors* test, one should not confuse what is optimum as a matter of policy and what is constitutionally permissible. The fifth *General Motors* criterion, it is true, asks whether failure of one or more provinces to participate in the regulatory scheme would "jeopardize the successful operation of the scheme in other parts of the country". However, the reference to "successful operation" should not be read as introducing an inquiry into what would be the best resolution in terms of policy. *Efficaciousness is not a relevant consideration in a division of powers analysis* (see *Reference re Firearms Act* (Can.), at par. 18). Similarly, references in past cases to promoting fair and effective commerce should be understood as referring to constitutional powers that, because they are essential in the national interest, transcend provincial interests and are truly national in importance and scope. Canada must identify a federal aspect distinct from that on which the provincial legislation is grounded. *The courts do not have the power to declare legislation constitutional simply because they conclude that it may be the best option from the point of view of policy. The test is not which jurisdiction — federal or provincial — is thought to be best placed to legislate regarding the matter in question. The inquiry into constitutional powers under ss. 91 and 92 of the* Constitution Act, 1867 *focuses on legislative competence, not policy.*[14]

In my view these statements, which seek to disentangle policy from jurisdiction, miss the point of "purposive federalism." The passage from the *Firearms Reference* cited in the paragraph above bears repeating:

> Determining the legal effects of a law involves considering how the law will operate and how it will affect Canadians. The Attorney General of Alberta states that the law will not actually achieve its purpose. Where the legislative scheme is relevant to a criminal law purpose, he says, it will be ineffective (e.g., criminals will not register their guns); where it is effective it will not advance the fight against crime (e.g., burdening rural farmers with pointless red tape). These are concerns that were properly

---

14 *Securities Reference*, above note 1 at para 90 [emphasis added and citations omitted].

directed to and considered by Parliament. Within its constitutional sphere, Parliament is the judge of whether a measure is likely to achieve its intended purposes; efficaciousness is not relevant to the Court's division of powers analysis: *Morgentaler*, supra, at pp. 487-88, and *Reference re Anti-Inflation Act*, [1976] 2 S.C.R. 373.[15]

Principled federalism, then, is driven not by the *optimal* policy but, rather, by deference to each level of government's credible claims to effective policy. It is not for the Court to usurp the role of Parliament and the provincial legislatures in determining what is effective; but it is clearly relevant to the federalism analysis to understand and test claims of policy effectiveness.

The text of sections 91 and 92 includes words whose plain meaning could encompass narrow or broad swaths of jurisdiction — most significantly for the securities context, the "trade and commerce" provision of section 91 and the "civil rights and property" provision of section 92. Such breadth contemplates and even invites overlap. An interpretive position that begins from the assumption that these two spheres must be entirely distinct will be unworkable in the twenty-first-century administrative state. Rather, harmonization should be the point of departure for Canadian federalism. The Court can be an important catalyst for such harmonization (as has arguably been the case in the environmental context); but it cannot perform this role if it remains mired in jurisdictional abstraction.

Schneiderman makes the point that the *Securities Reference* decision may best be explained through a prism of the Court's own legitimacy concerns with respect to the public.[16] He may well be right. But if so, I suggest, the challenge for the Court is to keep in mind the needs of the public and the realities of public policy as it crafts the future of Canadian Federalism.

C. Conclusion

Federalism is, as the Court observes in the *Securities Reference*, an exercise in balance. This balance lies at the heart both of Canada's success and of its fragility. The Court's decision in the

---

15 *Reference Re Firearms Act (Can.)*, 2000 SCC 31 at para 18.
16 See Chapter 5.

Securities Reference was clearly motivated by the desire to preserve this balance, as highlighted in the overview to the decision:

> It is a fundamental principle of federalism that both federal
> and provincial powers must be respected, and one power may
> not be used in a manner that effectively eviscerates another.
> Rather, federalism demands that a balance be struck, a bal-
> ance that allows both the federal Parliament and the provincial
> legislatures to act effectively in their respective spheres. Ac-
> cepting Canada's interpretation of the general trade and com-
> merce power would disrupt rather than maintain that balance.
> Parliament cannot regulate the whole of the securities system
> simply because aspects of it have a national dimension.[17]

The "balance" of federalism must be not only between the two
levels of government and between two institutions — the Court
and Parliament — but also, as I have argued above, between
jurisdictional abstraction, on the one hand, and responsiveness to
the policy realities of everyday life, on the other. To come back to
the hospital scenario that I put to my students at the beginning
of this chapter, a purposive approach would allow (and, arguably,
compel) the Court to focus on patient needs and the reasons why
we need hospitals as part of the federalism analysis, and not just
on how best to draw bright lines around health in the context of
the *Constitution Act, 1867*. Indeed, arguably it is in health care
that such a balance has been most carefully struck: federal–provincial negotiations occur regularly precisely because of a shared
de facto jurisdiction over this area vital to the everyday lives of
Canadians.

When the *Securities Reference* was released, I commented in
the media that in contrast to Canada's model of living tree constitutional interpretation, the *Securities Reference* decision reflected
a model of federalism more likely to "wither on the vine."[18] It is
not just the Court's credibility on the line; the normative foundations of Canadian federalism also hang in the balance. The way
forward, as in the past, is principled pragmatism, and the realization that constructive collaboration is the only basis on which
a country like Canada can work.

---

17 *Securities Reference*, above note 1 at para 7.
18 Bill Curry, "Ottawa will not go ahead with securities plan: Flaherty" *The
    Globe and Mail* (22 December 2011), online: The Globe and Mail invest-
    db2.theglobeandmail.com/servlet/story/GI.20111222.escenic_2280314/
    GIStory.

～ PART 3 ～
Regulatory Structure

CHAPTER 8

Assuring Independence and Expertise in Financial Services Law: Regulatory Oversight in Light of the Supreme Court of Canada *Securities Reference* Judgment

Janis Sarra

A. Introduction

Any legal system is only as good as the mechanisms available to resolve disputes between stakeholders working within the system, and the capacity and willingness to effectively enforce regulatory requirements in a manner that fosters compliance. Equally important, the system must allow individuals harmed by illegal acts to seek effective redress. In the wake of the Supreme Court of Canada's decision in *Reference Re Securities Act*,[1] one under-appreciated issue is the need for a system for enforcing and adjudicating financial services law that is responsive to the immediate and long term needs of investors, issuers, and the public. The Canadian government could move now to establish such a system, drawing from and building on the findings of the Supreme Court's judgment.

The Supreme Court held that the proposed *Canadian Securities Act*, as drafted, was not valid under the general branch of the federal power to regulate trade and commerce.[2] The Court

---

1   *Reference Re Securities Act*, 2011 SCC 66 [*Securities Reference*].
2   *Ibid* at para 134 (not valid under the federal government's power to regulate trade and commerce under s 91(2) of the *Constitution Act, 1867*). Pursuant to s 53 of the *Supreme Court Act*, the Governor in Council sought an advisory opinion from the Court as to whether its proposed *Securities Act*, set out in Order in Council PC 2010-667, fell within the legislative authority of the Parliament of Canada. The proposed Act

held that the effect of the proposed Act was "in essence to duplicate legislative schemes enacted by provincial legislators exercising their jurisdiction over property and civil rights under section
92(13) of the *Constitution Act, 1867*."[3] The judgment, rather than
offering clarity, may have unwittingly exacerbated the already
fractious process of securities law regulation in Canada, given
a failure to be more precise about the scope of federal regulatory authority in this field and its failure to address several significant issues. However, the judgment does offer some direction,
albeit underdeveloped, which may create a way forward in the
seemingly endless discussion about a national securities regulator.

This chapter suggests the immediate creation of a national
regulatory authority, the Canadian Financial Services Regulatory Authority, with legislative responsibility for the regulation of
systemic risk and of financial and capital markets that cross national borders. The regulatory authority would be granted strong
investigation and enforcement powers, and the legislative scheme
would create a separate independent adjudicative tribunal, the
Canadian Financial Services Tribunal, to hear and determine
appeals from first instance administrative and enforcement decisions. The national authority and tribunal would offer a system
of national oversight and enforcement that would allow issuers
distributing securities in more than one jurisdiction to choose
to be covered under the authority. Equally, if not more, important, it would recognize that problems of systemic risk require
global collaboration and regulatory oversight, as well as much
deeper thinking in Canada than is allowed either by interprovincial negotiations or by wholesale adoption of the limited regulatory framework of the United States. Canada requires a national
regulator on the international policy stage, one that can be a leader in fashioning the framework going forward, not a fragmented
follower of narrow conceptual changes.

---

did not unilaterally impose a unified system, but would have permitted
provinces and territories to opt in, with the aim of creating a unified national securities regulation system. The Court held that the question was
whether the sum of its particular provisions, read together, falls within
the general trade and commerce power, *ibid* at para 91.

3   *Ibid* at para 101.

1) Some Key Elements of the Supreme Court of Canada Judgment

The Supreme Court of Canada's judgment in the *Securities Reference* has been analyzed in depth elsewhere in this volume.[4] However, several aspects of the judgment are relevant to the discussion here. Pursuant to its "pith and substance" analysis, the Court examined the purpose and effect of the legislation, which was to establish a single comprehensive scheme.[5] It found that the goal of investor protection, without more, has historically been a provincial responsibility under section 92(13), but that two other goals — to foster fair, efficient and competitive capital markets, and to contribute to the integrity and stability of Canada's financial system — do have a federal aspect.[6]

While acknowledging that the securities market is of great importance to modern economic activity, the Court wrote that it could not ignore that the provinces have been deeply engaged in its regulation for many years.[7] The Court observed that the federal government must establish that the Act, read as a whole, addresses concerns that transcend local, provincial interests, and concluded that "[t]he legislative facts adduced by Canada in this Reference do not establish the asserted transformation. On the contrary, the fact that the structure and terms of the proposed Act largely replicate the existing provincial schemes belies the suggestion that the securities market has been wholly transformed over the years."[8] According to the Court, the day-to-day regulation of securities within the provinces, the main thrust of the Act, remains essentially a matter of property and civil rights within the provinces, and the effect of the proposed legislation would be to duplicate and displace the existing provincial and territorial securities regimes and replace them with a new federal scheme

---

4   See Chapters 2 and 13.

5   *Securities Reference*, above note 1 at para 93. The two-step approach to determining the validity of the Act under the division of powers involves first characterizing the proposed statute and then determining whether the legislation, as characterized, falls under a head of constitutional power that can support it.

6   *Ibid* at para 97.

7   *Ibid* at para 115.

8   *Ibid* at para 116.

regulating, on an exclusive basis, all aspects of securities trading in Canada.[9]

The Court did acknowledge that the provinces, acting in concert, lack the constitutional capacity to sustain a viable national scheme aimed at genuine national goals such as management of systemic risk or Canada-wide data collection, and that such matters might be qualitatively different from what the provinces, acting alone or in concert, could achieve.[10] However, it held that the proposed Act reflected an attempt to go well beyond these matters of undoubted national interest and reach down into the detailed regulation of all aspects of securities within the provinces, including all aspects of public protection and professional competence, and thus overreached the legislative interest of the federal government.[11]

The Supreme Court also acknowledged that a number of the proposed provisions authorized adoption of regulations directed at systemic risk: the sections relating to derivatives, short-selling, credit rating, urgent regulations, and data collection and sharing, all of which, in the Court's view, fall under the federal trade and commerce power.[12] The Court found that the expert evidence supported the view of systemic risk as an emerging reality ill-suited to local legislation,[13] and held that "prevention of systemic risk may trigger the need for a national regulator empowered to issue orders that are valid throughout Canada and impose common standards, under which provincial governments can work to ensure that their market will not transmit any disturbance

---

9　*Ibid* at para 106. The Court held at para 117: "the record does not support a necessary link between the national interest in fair, efficient and competitive capital markets and the registration requirements applicable to a securities dealer in Saskatchewan or Québec. Viewing the Act as a whole, we conclude that it overreaches the proper scope of the general branch of the trade and commerce power descending well into industry-specific regulation. The wholesale displacement of provincial regulation it would effect is not justified by the national concerns that Canada raises."

10　*Ibid* at para 121, citing *General Motors of Canada Ltd v City National Leasing*, [1989] SCR 641 [*General Motors*].

11　*Securities Reference*, above note 1 at para 122.

12　*Ibid* at para 103, the Court, citing the proposed Act at ss 89–90 relating to derivatives, s 126(1) on short-selling, s 73 on credit rating, s 228(4)(c) relating to urgent regulations and ss 109 and 224 on data collection and sharing.

13　*Ibid* at para 104.

across Canada or elsewhere."[14] The Court concluded that the proposed Act's emphasis on nationwide data collection could similarly be seen as aimed at anticipating and identifying risks that may transcend the boundaries of a specific province.[15] The Court observed that provincial governments, acting in concert, lack the constitutional capacity to sustain a viable scheme aimed at genuine national goals related to fair, efficient and competitive markets and the integrity and stability of Canada's financial system, and on these matters, a federal regime would be qualitatively different from a voluntary interprovincial scheme.[16]

While the Supreme Court recognized that regulation of systemic risk is appropriately within the domain of federal legislative authority, and that such risks "can be evasive of provincial boundaries and usual methods of control,"[17] overall, the judgment underplayed the issue of managing systemic risk under securities law in a period when Canada and its closest financial and capital market partners have yet to fully recover from the most significant financial crisis of this century. More appropriate oversight of derivatives and credit rating agencies was glossed over in the judgment, notwithstanding their very direct and significant contributions to the profound losses suffered by investors and others during the financial crisis. The Court's own test of whether the provincial and territorial securities regulators, acting alone or in concert, would be "constitutionally incapable of enacting"[18] legislation to provide a national framework to reduce systemic risk ignored the history and difficulties to date in legislating in concert on matters such as derivatives and other structured financial products viewed as significant causes of the global financial crisis.

It is unclear whether the Court recognized that managing systemic risk requires regulatory oversight at multiple levels, given the pervasive nature of structured financial products in our financial and capital markets. It failed to recognize the importance of global public policy debate and the pressing need for coordinated international action to temper the activities of global capital as it rapidly moves its speculative products around the

---

14 *Ibid.*
15 *Ibid* at para 105.
16 *Ibid* at para 123.
17 *Ibid* at para 103.
18 *Ibid* at para 38, citing *General Motors*, above note 10.

globe. The current system of oversight in Canada leaves profound gaps, which create tremendous risks for market participants. While a measure of cooperation between authorities is necessary, there is also an urgent need for national oversight and international coordination if systemic risk is truly to be addressed in a meaningful way.

B. National Oversight of Systemic Risk

Systemic risk can set off a series of "negative economic consequences that pervade an entire financial system."[19] Historically, systemic risk was viewed as risk that can cause a chain reaction; hence the failure of one participant or a small segment of the financial market to meet its contractual or counterparty obligations could create a domino effect that called on other market participants' liquidity, ultimately contributing to financial difficulties across a market.[20] In fact, the relationships are not linear, but rather, highly interconnected. Systemic risk is created by the interaction of numerous market factors that interact in complex ways to compound transactional risks into more pervasive systemic problems. Increased systemic risk in recent years was exacerbated by the shift of the derivatives market from being primarily aimed at risk management to being highly speculative; the entry into the market of hedge funds and other market players that pressed for higher-risk, high-return products, shifting the nature of the credit default swap and other structured financial products markets; "covenant-light" lending in the period leading up to the crisis and the rise of securitization and syndication; the growth of multinational enterprises crossing both industrial and financial sectors and national borders; and the failure to develop and oversee effective, timely and transparent clearing and settlement systems for structured financial products.[21]

Systemic risk is not so much difficult to define as difficult to reduce to a single definition. That is because systemic risk

---

19 *Ibid*, citing *Securities Reference*, above note 1 (Record of the AG of Canada, Vol 1, Expert Report, Michael J Trebilcock, "National Securities Regulator Report" at para 26).

20 Bank for International Settlements (BIS), *64th Annual Report* (Basel: BIS, 1994) at 172–77.

21 Janis Sarra, "Risk Management, Responsive Regulation, and Oversight of Structured Financial Product Markets" (2011) 44 UBC L Rev 779.

manifests itself in a variety of ways, depending on the particular market, the market participants, and the degree of cross-sector contamination and cross-border impact. Multiple localized risks can together amplify overall risk such that it takes on a systemic quality. Institutions now operate across separate legal personalities, multiple sectors, and jurisdictional boundaries, and their financial market activities are now interconnected to a historically unprecedented degree. These risks are often opaque, thanks to the lack of a rigorous disclosure system and the highly complex nature of some of the products and market activities. It is precisely why systemic risk requires a concerted national and international strategy.[22]

While systemic risk has long been recognized within the financial sector, the degree of interconnectedness was under-recognized prior to the 2008–2009 financial crisis; specifically, the degree to which financial markets could destabilize real economic activity was not fully appreciated. Despite now recognizing the risks, Canadian securities regulators have not been able to respond effectively because of Canada's fragmented regulatory structure. The link between financial services and other economic activity is yet another rationale for according national regulatory attention to systemic risk, while still recognizing a role for regional securities regulators. The World Bank and other organizations now recognize that systemic risk can encompass financial shocks that can damage the "real economy."[23]

Derivatives, in particular, are a significant aspect of the financial landscape that requires better regulatory oversight. In the period leading up to the financial crisis, the complex nature of these products, such as credit default swaps (CDS), collateralized debt obligations (CDO), index trades and credit-linked notes,[24] shifted the market away from a strategy focused on risk

---

22   Miquel Dijkman, "A Framework for Assessing Systemic Risk" (World Bank Policy Research Working Paper 5282, April 2010). See also Olivier De Bandt & Phillip Hartmann, "Systemic Risk: A Survey" (European Central Bank Working Paper No. 35, November 2000).

23   Dijkman, *ibid* at 6. See also Sir Mervyn King, Governor, Bank of England, Speech to British Bankers Association, London, "Banking and the Bank of England" (10 June 2008), online: Bank of England www.bankofengland.co.uk/publications/speeches/2008/speech347.pdf; Nikil Chande, Nicholas Labelle, & Eric Tuer, "Central Counterparties and Systemic Risk" (Bank of Canada, Financial System Review, December 2010).

24   These products can be cash flow based or synthetic, bundled or housed within a variety of special purpose entities.

management to a highly speculative market approach in which risk was "commodified." Derivatives and swaps have existed for decades as risk management products without particularly harmful effects. However, the rapid introduction of new complex products in the five years leading up to 2008 created systemic risks to financial markets — and, in turn, to real economies — without the monitoring and discipline that exist for securities markets or traditional commercial lending activity. The lack of transparency of such products meant that counterparty risk was not well understood or appropriately priced.[25] With a complex interlocking set of claims, the financial system became increasingly interconnected, operating on a global scale and concentrated in a few key financial hubs. The over-the-counter (OTC) CDS market was ill equipped to deal with bank failures and "cascading swaps" as the market tried to settle the CDS.[26]

Derivatives continue to be a common financial and risk management tool for Canadian companies of all sizes and across a wide range of sectors. It is the use of derivatives as both risk management tools and speculative products that has shifted the nature of risks in financial markets. The Bank for International Settlements reports that from January 1991 to June 2011, the global OTC derivatives market grew by 780 percent, from just over US$80 trillion to more than US$707 trillion in notional amounts outstanding.[27] Interest rate contracts account for more than 62 percent of the total OTC derivatives market in each reporting year.[28] Foreign exchange derivatives contracts have ranked second in total notional amounts outstanding, but their proportion of the total outstanding contracts has decreased from

---

25 As Andrew Haldane, Executive Director of Financial Stability for the Bank of England, said in April 2009, "An investor in a CDO squared would need to read in excess of 1 billion pages to understand fully the ingredients." Quoted in M. Goldstein, "Derivatives and the Blizzard of Paperwork," online: May 15, 2009, Bloomberg Businessweek, www.businessweek.com/investing/wall_street_news.

26 In 2010, two years after Lehman Brothers failed, the swaps were still settling.

27 Bank for International Settlements, "OTC Derivatives Market Activity in the First Half of 2011" Bank for International Settlements (BIS), Monetary and Economic Department (November 2011), online: BIS www.bis.org. OTC derivatives market activity statistics are published semi-annually. Notional amount outstanding means the total amount referenced in the derivative contract.

28 *Ibid.*

22 percent to 10 percent over this period. Also significant are CDS and equity and commodities derivatives. A study commissioned by the Bank of Canada reports that Canada has approximately 2 percent, or approximately US$14 trillion, of the notional amount outstanding in the global OTC derivatives market and that foreign exchange contracts maintain a larger share in the Canadian OTC market than globally, at 23 percent of the total in 2010.[29]

The Bank of Canada estimates that in 80 percent of all Canadian OTC derivatives market activity, at least one side of the transaction is recorded in a foreign jurisdiction.[30] Because of the thin disclosure requirements, the exact amount of market activity in Canada is not known. However, the fact that Canada is implicated in derivatives contracts in the trillions of dollars, and that the overwhelming majority of derivatives transactions are made in foreign jurisdictions, is evidence that the need for regulatory oversight is important and immediate.

Moreover, structured financial products are not used only by financial services companies. The International Swaps and Derivatives Association (ISDA) reports that 94 percent of Fortune Global 500 companies use derivatives; the types used depend heavily on the sectors in which businesses operate.[31] While a portion of this derivatives activity is risk management and hedging against price and currency-exchange fluctuations, many companies also use derivatives to take active, speculative positions, which create the potential for over-exposure to swings in derivatives contract values, leading in turn to increased volatility in settlement payment obligations.[32]

---

29   Carolyn Wilkins & Elizabeth Woodman, "Strengthening the Infrastructure of Over-the-Counter Derivatives Markets" (Bank of Canada, Financial System Review, December 2010) at 35, online: Bank of Canada www.bankofcanada.ca, citing Canadian Foreign Exchange Committee (CFEC), "The Canadian Foreign Exchange Market: Developments and Opportunities" (2010), online: CFEC www.cfec.ca/files/developments.pdf.

30   Wilkins & Woodman, *ibid* at 36.

31   International Swaps and Derivatives Association (ISDA) News Release, "Over 94% of the World's Largest Companies Use Derivatives to Help Manage Their Risks, According to ISDA Survey" (23 April 2009) online: ISDA www.isda.org; Eraj Shirvani, ISDA Chairman and Head of Fixed Income for EMEA at Credit Suisse in *ibid* at para 6.

32   Christopher C Géczy, Bernadette A Minton, & Catherine M Schrand, "Taking a View: Corporate Speculation, Governance, and Compensation" (2007) 62:5 Journal of Finance 2405.

Securitization was also a problem that was not appropriately identified as creating potential systemic risk. Originally developed to transform credit risk into market risk by pooling loans and issuing tradable claims against the pool, securitization as a risk management tool relied on the liquidity of primary markets for placing asset-backed securities.[33] Securitization differs from traditional bank lending in that banks, after originating the loans, hold them for only a short time before the loans are sold or their associated risks are sliced into tranches, repackaged and then sold, often in public markets. When structured appropriately, securitization allows a bank to manage credit and other risks of its loan portfolio.[34] However, a negative feature of securitization by banks is that in many instances, once the bank has extracted fees on the original loan, the financial risk is passed along to various tranches of debt, often sold to multiple investors who are not made aware of the true risk of such products. Between 2008 and 2010, there was a failure by banking supervisors, financial services regulators, and governments to understand the incentive effects of this originate-and-distribute model of lending. CDO discouraged front-end assessment of borrowers' creditworthiness, as lenders were off-loading their risk almost immediately onto the market. The incentive effects were that banks' intermediation function, including screening and monitoring of borrowers, was severely impaired and CDO were mispriced.[35] Once securitization markets became illiquid, banks were vulnerable to heightened risk from exposures to credit risk — loans that could no longer be securitized, for example — and to market risk from changes in the mark-to-market value of the securitized assets.[36]

The problems associated with credit rating agencies included outdated assessment tools and conflicts of interest. Investors relied too much on credit ratings that failed to take account of liquidity risk and the lack of transparency regarding investments.[37] There were conflicts of interest in the way in which credit rat-

---

33 Mario Draghi, Chair, Financial Stability Board, "The Global Financial Crisis" (9 December 2009, remarks), online: BIS www.bis.org/review/r091216a.pdf?frames=0 at 2.

34 *Ibid* at 9.

35 Janis Sarra, "Prudential, Pragmatic and Prescient, Reform of Bank Resolution Schemes" (2012) 21 International Insolvency Review 17.

36 Draghi, above note 33 at 9.

37 Deb Pragyan et al, "Whither the Credit Ratings Industry?" Bank of England Financial Stability Paper No. 9 (March 2011).

ing agencies were compensated, creating disincentives to rigorous risk assessment and pricing for particular financial products. The "hardwiring" of credit ratings into a vast array of certification and marketing of products exacerbated these conflicts.[38] When the loan quality of US subprime mortgages worsened and the agencies belatedly downgraded their ratings of these mortgages and other asset-backed securities, investors began to shun such products, as they could not accurately price risk; there was a rapid spread of loss of confidence to other financial products and concerns emerged about the financial health of bank counterparties.[39] Yet Canadian securities regulators remain unable to hold credit rating agencies to any standards of conduct that protect retail investors in a meaningful way.

As noted above, derivatives products continue to be widely used by market participants. Issuers use forward contracts to limit their exposure on commodities or currency exchange;[40] banks and other financial lenders hedge risks associated with their credit decisions by purchasing CDS, securitizing their loans or participating in syndicated lending. Significant investors hedge the risk of equity investment through equity swaps; and recent events in the takeover market illustrate continuing regulatory oversight problems with respect to hedging and "empty voting" by hedge funds.[41] Structured financial products, therefore, must be viewed as both risk management tools and speculative products, which may require different kinds of oversight in the market. The tendency to lump all these products and their goals together masks their complexity and pervasiveness and the fact that there is a range of regulatory responses depending on the nature of the

---

38 *Ibid* at 5.
39 Basel Committee on Banking Supervision, "Findings on the Interaction of Market and Credit Risk" BCBS Working Papers No 16 (May 2009) at 10.
40 See the activities on the Montreal exchange for example.
41 See for example, TELUS. See also Henry Hu and Bernard Black, who observe that through the use of credit and other derivatives, and the growing share-lending market, investors are able to hold greater voting power than their economic ownership warrants, a phenomenon they term "empty voting." "Hidden ownership" results when the investor has sold the voting power but still holds an economic stake in the company. Henry TC Hu & Bernard Black, "Hedge Funds, Insiders, and Empty Voting: Decoupling of Economic and Voting Ownership in Public Companies" (2007) 13 Journal of Corporate Finance 343. See also Janis Sarra, "Dancing the Derivative Deux Pas, the Financial Crisis and Lessons for Corporate Governance" (2009) 32:2 UNSWLJ 447.

products, their objective, the nature of the market participants that may need to be monitored or protected, and the scope of the regulatory authority's mandate.

Arguably, systemic risk falls within the constitutional "double aspect" doctrine, in that systemic risk arising out of financial and capital markets activities is within the regulatory purview of all levels of government, and thus must be a matter of concern for all legislators.[42] Systemic risk engages securities law but also financial services law, banking law and monetary law, and thus falls under jurisdiction of federal regulators and the central bank.[43] Given its nature, systemic risk arguably falls primarily, although not exclusively, to the federal government. Rousseau, in his contribution to this volume, observes that the decentralized model has been characterized by a combination of competition and collaboration among regulators, endorsing the Supreme Court's conclusion that one cannot ignore that the provinces have been deeply engaged in the regulation of securities markets for many years.[44] He argues that analysis is needed to understand the perimeters of systemic risk and the negative externalities associated with it.[45] Such a project, I suggest, is an ongoing challenge, given the dynamic nature of derivatives markets and the fact that most market players do not fully understand the nature and implications of many products and the scope of the associated risks. Yet derivatives products continue to exist, and at multiple levels of market activity, in both the financial and securities markets. The Bank for International Settlements and the International Organization for Securities Commissions (IOSCO) have both described systemic risk as having macro-prudential elements and thus a need to protect the financial system overall, and micro-prudential elements, more focused on market efficiency.[46] Yet Canada's provincial and territorial governments appear "constitutionally incapable" of effectively regulating these elements of the market,

---

42 The federal law pursues an objective that in pith and substance falls within Parliament's jurisdiction, while the provincial law pursues a different objective that falls within provincial jurisdiction; *Canadian Western Bank v Alberta*, 2007 SCC 22 at para 30.

43 See *Office of the Superintendent of Financial Institutions Act*, RSC 1985, c 18 (3rd Supp); *Bank Act*, SC 1991, c 46.

44 Rousseau, above note 4.

45 *Ibid* at 7.

46 IOSCO, 2010 report and Bank for International Settlements, 2009.

given their uneven capacities to understand the challenges and their inability to resolve political and normative differences.

1) Why Continue to Pursue a National Regulator for Systemic Risk and Cross-Border Securities?

Three years after the height of the financial crisis, Canada lacks a coherent national framework for oversight and management of systemic risk. Cooperative negotiation toward a national regulatory authority may not be possible in the next short period, as several provincial governments are awash in their constitutional success at having persuaded the Supreme Court to find the draft legislation constitutionally invalid, which in turn has created tensions within the Canadian Securities Administrators (CSA) and a lack of political will to cooperate on much of anything. Since the *Securities Reference*, the CSA, despite its good intentions, has been in some chaos, lacking leadership and foresight. It is therefore timely and important for the federal government to move to fill the governance and oversight gap, particularly in the area of systemic risk.

A national regulatory authority would considerably enhance the effectiveness of oversight and mitigation of systemic risk. Resources could be allocated more effectively, targeting systemic risk on the basis of nature and type of risk and probability of occurrence.[47] A national authority could improve Canada-wide cooperation in investigation and evidence gathering, particularly in the context of investigating and prosecuting criminal offences,[48] and would reduce unjustified variation among the provinces and territories in enforcement priorities and investor protection.[49] As the Wise Persons Committee observed, it would minimize the costs of duplication and make Canada's capital markets more competitive and attractive to issuers and investors by eliminating the additional costs and administrative hurdles posed by thirteen individual regulators.[50]

---

47 Wise Persons' Committee to Review the Structure of Securities Regulation in Canada, *It's Time* (Ottawa: Department of Finance, 2003) at 27 [WPC].

48 *Ibid* at 28. See also *Securities Reference*, above note 1 (Factum of the AG of Canada at para 32).

49 WPC, above note 47 at 28.

50 *Ibid* at 33.

The Supreme Court of Canada has previously sanctioned the jurisdiction of provincial securities commissions, both within their provincial boundaries and beyond those boundaries where their jurisdiction extends to impacts on market participants outside a particular province.[51] It is also evident that different jurisdictions have moved in different ways toward more rules-based regulation or more standards/outcomes-based approaches, offering retail investors and issuers a different view of models.[52] The creation of a national securities regulator need not detract from these historically recognized functions. Markets have changed dramatically, however, in respect of issuers, underwriters, and registrants and in respect of retail investors, creating qualitatively different risks. It is here that the judgment in the *Securities Reference* failed to undertake a more dynamic analysis of federal-provincial authority based on a living constitutional approach, which recognizes the seriousness of the risk to large numbers of individuals now implicated in national and international markets.

For example, hedge funds remain largely unregulated in Canada, and the pervasiveness of their activities in both the securities and financial markets has direct implications for retail investors, who pay the price for the upside value generated by the opaque and highly speculative activities of these market actors. Hedge funds, while increasingly notorious, are not the only example. There is currently a tremendous lack of transparency with respect to the way in which sophisticated market players can "game" the system through various market exemptions while staying out of reach of regulators. Aside from issues of systemic risk, there is also a pressing issue of regulatory oversight of market players that move from one Canadian jurisdiction to the next, engaging in either illegal practices or "sharp practices."

As noted in the introduction, the federal government could move immediately to create a Canadian Financial Services Regulatory Authority (CFSRA), with a separate independent Canadian Financial Services Tribunal (CFST). Such a move would respond to the continuing need for national regulatory oversight in the areas of financial services, large issuers and cross-border market players. It would preserve and enhance the stability and integrity of Canada's financial and capital markets. Its mandate would be the markets, but the emphasis on "services" signals that its over-

---

51 *Securities Reference*, above note 1 at para 43.
52 See for example the approach of the BC Securities Commission.

all purpose is to protect both investors and the Canadian public from the systemic risks associated with these markets. The national regulatory authority and the tribunal, as the second check on the system, would be aimed at ensuring the integrity, transparency and stability of the financial system and the protection of market participants and the Canadian public. The national regulatory authority would have the capacity to monitor developments, provide leadership in conceptualizing and implementing responses, evaluate market and regulatory changes, and adjust the system appropriately.

One of the CFSRA's primary mandates would be to address systemic risk, which would include a coordinated and independent regulatory look at the myriad types of derivatives and other structured financial products, including risk management products, highly speculative products, and a range of risk profiles that call for different types and degrees of regulatory response. There needs to be a much more comprehensive understanding of the benefits of these products and of the negative consequences of leaving them unchecked or only lightly regulated. A national regulator would have the resources to seriously analyze the available policy choices, rather than simply following the lead of the United States, which has really only tinkered at the edges of the derivatives market in its efforts at regulatory reform.

The mandate of the CFSRA would include identifying and overseeing systemic risk and developing appropriate responses, including appropriate preventive responses and early intervention mechanisms. The need for such oversight has been recognized globally, given the interconnectedness of financial services firms and their products and the pro-cyclical nature of financial market behaviour, which in turn generates its own risk.[53]

The CFSRA would work with provincial securities regulators, as well as the Bank of Canada, the Office of the Superintendent of Financial Services (OSFI), the Canadian Deposit Insur-

---

53 Group of Thirty, *Enhancing Financial Stability and Resilience: Macroprudential Policy, Tools, and Systems for the Future* (Washington DC: The Group of Thirty, 2010), online: Group of Thirty www.group30. org/images/PDF/Macroprudential_Report_Final.pdf at 30–32; IOSCO, "Mitigating Systemic Risk: A Role for Securities Regulators" (IOSCO Discussion Paper OR01/11, February 2011), online: IOSCO /www.iosco. org/library/pubdocs/pdf/IOSCOPD347.pdf.

ance Corporation (CDIC), and Assuris.[54] Each of these structures or organizations has particular mandates — the stability of the monetary system, financial services, protection of depositors' or policy holders' interests, early intervention where risk is identified, etc.[55] There are numerous reasons why Canada did not have a banking crisis in the same manner that many jurisdictions experienced, including the existence of a federal system to identify risks to capital adequacy and liquidity and to intervene at very early stages where such a risk was identified.[56] The CFSRA could build on the strength of federal banking regulatory approaches to provide oversight of financial services and capital markets, drawing on the expertise and participation of these entities in crafting policy responses to emerging and continuing risks to the financial system. This system is not unconnected to provincial securities laws, and the CFSRA could provide a coordinating and leadership role in ensuring that securities commissions consider how their regional and local oversight meshes with national efforts to reduce systemic risk.

While Canada did not experience a banking crisis, it has experienced its own market failures, which highlight the urgent need for a national regulatory authority. For example, the $32 billion third-party asset-backed commercial paper (ABCP)

---

54 Assuris is the equivalent of the CDIC for the Canadian life insurance sector. OSFI has oversight of the viability of Canadian financial institutions, including an early intervention program.

55 See, for example, the new European Systemic Risk Board as one example of an oversight body with the mandate to manage systemic risks to financial markets in the EU. EC, *Regulation (EU) No 1092/2010 of the European Parliament and of the Council of 24 November 2010 on European Union macro-prudential oversight of the financial system and establishing a European Systemic Risk Board*, [2010] OJ, L 331/1; EC, *Council Regulation (EU) No 1096/2010 of 17 November 2010 Board conferring specific tasks upon the European Central Bank concerning the functioning of the European Systemic Risk*, [2010] OJ, L 331/162.

56 Other reasons include the conservative capital requirements for banks in place prior to the crisis; the conservative nature of our banks; and our system of early intervention in the insurance sector. Janis Sarra & Gordon Dunning, "Assuring the Future: Reform of the Insolvency Framework for Insurance Companies and Other Financial Institutions Under the Canadian *Winding-Up and Restructuring Act*" in Janis Sarra, ed, *Annual Review of Insolvency Law 2010* (Toronto: Carswell, 2011). See also Anita Anand, "Canada's Banks: Conservative by Nature" *The Financial Post* (31 March 2009), online: The Financial Post www.financialpost.com.

market experienced freezing and collapse in 2008. Third-party ABCP conduits were thought to be selling these products only to highly sophisticated investors that could appropriately assess risks of loss and could afford to lose their investment. The market had been exempted from securities regulation under National Instrument 45-106, which meant that investors did not receive prospectus-level disclosure on the nature of the products and the associated risks.[57] While ABCP issued by banks was subject to prudential oversight rules, third-party issuers of such products were not regulated in the same manner, and it was this part of the market that collapsed. The conduits held pools of commercial paper, and their sponsors, a range of financial entities, ostensibly provided the standby liquidity. Credit rating agencies — paid by the conduits, their sponsors, or the underwriters — rated the products as safer than they were, underestimating and consequently underpricing the risk.[58] Because of the nature of the financial institutions sponsoring the conduits and the exemptions granted by securities regulators, third-party ABCP conduits and sponsors were not back-stopped by capital adequacy requirements that banks are required to provide for similar products.[59] Moreover, the contamination effects of the third-party ABCP market collapse meant that bank commercial paper, even if the conduits were off-balance sheet or if they were benefiting from back-stopping of capital requirements of the banks, were at risk of significant losses unless the market failure was not addressed in a timely manner.

Thus, the combination of lack of regulatory oversight of the ABCP third-party market, including conduits, sponsors, and credit rating agencies; the failure to appropriately assess, disclose, or price risk; and the exempt market approvals created the conditions for the liquidity crisis once calls started being made on the contractual obligations. When banks, governments, and others cooperated to form the Pan-Canadian Investors Commit-

---

57 National Instrument 45-106, s 2.35, which allowed credit rating agencies to approve commercial paper without meeting prospectus requirements if the commercial paper matured within a year of date of issue.

58 Janis Sarra, "Restructuring of the Asset-Backed Commercial Paper Market in Canada" in Janis Sarra, ed, *Annual Review of Insolvency Law 2008* (Toronto: Thomson Carswell, 2009) at 346 [Sarra, "Restructuring"].

59 The banks reported their sponsorship as off-balance-sheet activities under Canadian GAAP, which meant that ABCP was not subject to the prudential requirements under which banks operate.

tee for Third Party Structured Asset-Backed Commercial Paper, it was discovered that almost 2,000 retirees had invested their life savings in the ABCP market, as had countless small businesses, venture start-ups, municipalities, and school boards.[60] While the dollar amount of sales to this market was less significant than that of sales to large investors, the impact was far greater. Retirees risked losing their entire life savings until the banks, the government, and other market players intervened to assist the most vulnerable investors on a "hardship" basis. Small businesses and public entities were not so fortunate and lost millions.

2) A National Regulator Could Create National Standards for Investor Protection

The sale of ABCP to retail investors and retirees is yet more evidence that the "know your client" standard to which financial advisors are currently held is inadequate to protect vulnerable investors. Advisors did not appreciate the risks and had no fiduciary obligation to their clients — retail investors — to satisfy themselves that by recommending such products they were acting in their clients' best interests.[61] It is evidence of a need for a new regulatory approach to financial services, one that creates consistent standards across Canada and recognizes the changing nature of financial markets.

Interestingly, the Supreme Court held that the need to respond to systemic risk may support federal legislation, "but it does not alter the basic nature of securities regulation that, as shown, remains primarily focused on local concerns of protecting investors and ensuring the fairness of the markets through regulation of participants."[62] The judgment emphasized the protection of regional and local investors but ignored the fact that the majority of securities offerings are in multiple jurisdictions in Canada and the United States, while the secondary trading market is national. The current system also largely ignores investors who invest nationally and imposes financial and physical barriers to

---

60 Sarra, "Restructuring," above note 58 at 346.
61 Investment Industry Regulatory Organization of Canada, "Regulatory Study, Review and Recommendations Concerning the Manufacture and Distribution by IIROC Member Firms of Third-Party Asset-Backed Commercial Paper in Canada" (October 2008).
62 *Securities Reference*, above note 1 at para 128.

seeking remedies in other jurisdictions. Finally, the *Securities Reference* judgment ignored the issue of the tremendous growth in numbers of "financial citizens": citizens that are implicated in capital markets, whether or not they want to be. Given the rapid decline in company-sponsored defined benefit pension plans, there has been huge growth in self-directed retirement and economic security investment by individuals, with concomitant risk of loss. Yet the current securities regulatory structure was designed for investors who could afford the losses associated with market participation; it is not adequate to the needs of new investors implicated in the market through their self-directed investments, mutual funds, and other investments.

Financial advisers should be held to a higher standard than "know your client." Lawyers must act in their clients' best interests, just as doctors and teachers do. It is reasonable that market registrants giving financial advice should also be held to a standard of acting in their clients' best interests. Their failure to do so generates another type of systemic risk, this time to the system of long-term financial planning and financial security of older citizens. The Court's "investor protection, without more" finding ignores the changing challenges of investor protection when there is no national framework in place. The ABCP example discussed above demonstrates the need for federal resolution mechanisms: parties had to use Canada's insolvency framework to address the ABCP market problems because securities law proved woefully inadequate to the task.

A national regulator could enhance protection of investors against particular market risks and design policy to reflect the changing nature of the market and the need for national standards of protection. The national regulator could also bring the system for resolution of disputes between consumers and providers of financial services within its own purview, replacing the voluntary, non-binding and non-enforceable system now in place. The current Ombudsman for Banking Services and Investments (OBSI) for the banking and investment industry relies on voluntary participation by banks, and two of Canada's four major banks have opted out. The OBSI lacks authority, and if a company has not complied with any resolution it suggests, the information is simply posted on the Internet; there are no enforceable remedies for the complainant.[63] Yet a complaints system is only as good as its ability to fairly determine the merits of claims and to effectively enforce any remedies that are appropriate in the circumstances.

The proposed CFSRA could be given regulatory oversight of protection of such investors, as well as responsibility for regulation of credit rating agencies. It could be authorized to address national issues such as short-selling; undertake urgent national regulation where necessary; engage in nationwide data collection; and monitor capital markets to identify potential systemic risk. In other words, it would have regulatory oversight of financial products and financial investors as a keystone concept, including effective enforcement mechanisms. It could generate a much-needed discussion about the possibility of restricting availability of some products such as contracts for difference to particular investors and the issue of standards of investment advice. The fact that provincial securities authorities have to date been unable to agree on national legislation is telling;[64] the *Securities Reference* underplayed the public-interest role that a national securities regulator would play in this regard.

At present, it is almost impossible to influence public policy; most individuals and many companies have insufficient resources

---

63   IIROC and MFDA require membership, but RBC is not a participating firm for banking services and TD has also opted out, leaving the OBSI's future uncertain. The OBSI had 386 complaints in 2010, but no jurisdiction to investigate or enforce.

64   Only Québec has enacted legislation, Québec *Derivatives Act*, RSQ c I-14.01, although there are a growing number of discussion documents: Canadian OTC Derivatives Working Group, "Reform of Over-the-Counter Derivatives in Canada: Discussion Paper from the Canadian OTC Derivatives Working Group" (26 October 2010), online: Bank of Canada www.bankofcanada.ca/wp-content/uploads/2010/10/reform.pdf; Canadian Securities Administrators Derivatives Committee (CSADC), "Consultation Paper 91-401 on Over-the-Counter Derivatives Regulation in Canada" (2 November 2010), online: Ontario Securities Commission www.osc.gov.on.ca/documents/en/Securities-Category9/csa_20101102_91-401_cp-on-derivatives.pdf; Canadian Securities Administrators (CSA), Consultation Paper 91-401 and Consultation Paper 91-402, "Derivatives: Trade Repositories" (23 June 2011); CSA, Consultation Paper 91-403, "Derivatives: Surveillance and Enforcement" (25 November 2011); CSA, Consultation Paper 91-404, "Derivatives: Segregation and Portability in OTC Derivatives Clearing" (10 February 2012). It is not to suggest that no action is occurring. Canadian securities administrators were able to agree on liquidity provisions for market mutual funds that mirror new US requirements, requiring 5 percent liquidity.

to work with all thirteen regulators, which leaves policy design and development in the hands of government employees, with, at best, a marginal effort at a democratic policy process. A national regulatory authority could build in consultation mechanisms meaningful to issuers, market participants, retail investors and others who currently have no access to public policy development. Such mechanisms would need to include resources to reduce information asymmetries and barriers to participation, as well as allowing for discussion among various interests during policy deliberations.

C. Creating Certainty and Accessibility for Issuers

One topic extremely relevant to national oversight is that the *Securities Reference* judgment largely ignored the issuer side of the purpose of the draft legislation. Issuers that distribute in more than one province or territory, or distribute in Canada and the United States or another country, do not have the benefits of a streamlined national regulatory structure or its protection internationally. Yet the Court's multiple references to the fact that the federal government did not rely on its interprovincial trade and commerce power[65] suggest that the federal government could craft a national regulatory structure that offers issuers operating in markets that cross provincial and national borders the option to be under the regulatory oversight of a national authority. Such a system would still respect local and regional securities authority, but would recognize the need for a national option.

The issue of giving issuing companies access to the option of filing nationally is more than just addressing the costs of multiple filings, which in itself is highly significant. Also at issue are the barriers to the market that the current system represents for venture and other companies that are trying to grow their businesses and do not have the resources and infrastructure to comply with multiple policy nuances across jurisdictions. The search

---

65 The SCC mentions five times in the judgment that the government did not rely on the federal interprovincial trade authority. See e.g. *Securities Reference*, above note 1 at para 47, in which the Court held "Canada bases its argument that the proposed Act is constitutional entirely on the s. 91(2) general trade and commerce power. It does not rely on the s. 91(2) power over interprovincial trade which gives Parliament the power to legislate on interprovincial and international aspects of securities."

for capital is national and international for many companies, and the regulatory oversight structure needs to recognize that reality. While the CSA has gone some way toward harmonizing regulatory oversight through national instruments, change is very slow and not particularly responsive to the need for protection of issuers and investors. Moreover, the CSA is now in a highly fractious period, such that achieving consensus on any issue is difficult.[66] The Court's admonition to the federal government to cooperate with the provinces and territories ignores its own lengthy earlier description of failed efforts to come to any consensus on a national framework.

Under the model proposed here, companies distributing in more than one jurisdiction would be allowed to opt for a national securities regulator. Such a structure allows issuers a choice of regulator and a choice to deal with a single regulator rather than multiple securities commissions. It would align securities law with corporate law, in terms of choice for companies, given that Canadian registered companies in Canada can choose whether to incorporate under the federal *Business Corporations Act* or the provincial corporations statute where they are located. Regional offices of the national securities regulator would ensure access for local investors. Such an approach leaves provincial and territorial commissions intact for local and regional securities, and where issuers operating across provincial borders so opt. Such a model would meet the fourth and fifth elements of the *General Motors* test.[67] The Supreme Court's warning that both federal

---

66 Moreover, the public discourse and the Supreme Court's judgment ignore the elephant in the room, which is the fact that these services are revenue generators for the provinces precisely because they are so costly for parties, both in actual costs and in forgone market windows; the drivers of non-agreement frequently have more to do with this issue than with protecting investors.

67 The *General Motors*, above note 10, test, frames the inquiry into whether a legislative scheme falls within the general trade and commerce power in terms of the following non-exclusive indicia: (1) Is the law part of a general regulatory scheme?; (2) Is the scheme under the oversight of a regulatory agency?; (3) Is the law concerned with trade as a whole rather than with a particular industry?; (4) Is the scheme of such a nature that the provinces, acting alone or in concert, would be constitutionally incapable of enacting it?; (5) Would failure to include one or more provinces or localities in the scheme jeopardize its successful operation in other parts of the country?, cited in *Securities Reference*, above note 1 at para 108. The Court held that the first three *General Motors* were met. In respect of the third question, the Court held "We accept that preservation of

and provincial powers must be respected is observed in a structure that gives issuers a choice. Such a structure does not "eviscerate" provincial authority;[68] arguably, it allows regulators at both levels to offer quality and timeliness of regulatory oversight that will make them the jurisdiction of choice for companies.

D. Enforcement

An important issue largely ignored by the Court's judgment in the *Securities Reference* was the lack of an effective national enforcement system. There have been difficulties in documentation and enforcement of both regulatory non-compliance and criminal behaviour, as well as difficulties in coordinating evidence gathering in support of such enforcement activities. A market participant sanctioned in one province can simply recommence the same practice over the provincial border, often to the detriment of new sets of vulnerable retail investors. Numerous studies have observed that the existing fragmented system of securities regulation allows offenders to simply move across provincial borders to escape enforcement actions.[69] Coordination difficulties have impeded investigations, leading to multiple proceedings that are inefficient and sometimes unfair to market participants.[70] Levels of investor protection are uneven and inequitable, and in the *Securities Reference*, the Court underplayed what many believe to be a significant lacuna in the current system — the fact that there is not an effective national enforcement system and an arm's-length independent tribunal to adjudicate on securities and financial matters.

---

capital markets to fuel Canada's economy and maintain Canada's financial stability is a matter that goes beyond a particular "industry" and engages "trade as a whole" within the general trade and commerce power as contemplated by the *General Motors* test. Legislation aimed at imposing minimum standards applicable throughout the country and preserving the stability and integrity of Canada's financial markets might well relate to trade as a whole. However, the proposed Act reaches beyond such matters and descends into the detailed regulation of *all* aspects of trading in securities, a matter that has long been viewed as provincial: *Securities Reference, ibid* at para 114.

68 *Securities Reference, ibid* at para 7.
69 WPC, above note 47 at 28.
70 *Ibid* at 11.

The urgent need for a national enforcement structure was put most eloquently by the Canadian Coalition for Good Governance (CCGG) in its factum to the Supreme Court in the *Securities Reference*:

> Capital market abuse knows no boundaries. Provincial securities regulators, on the other hand, do — the *Constitution Act, 1867* prohibits them from stepping outside their provincial boundaries. This asymmetry between multi-jurisdictional "crime" and jurisdictionally-limited "punishment" has serious implications for the enforcement of securities law in Canada. Offenders whose abuses can harm Canadians in multiple provinces are typically prosecuted and sanctioned in only one, as administrative prosecutions are rarely co-ordinated with similar prosecutions in other provinces. Administrative prosecutions in a province are even less frequently co-ordinated with federal criminal prosecutions.[71]

The CCGG documented numerous instances of "jurisdiction-hopping," in which sanctions for egregious market conduct or fraud in one province allowed the market actor to simply set up shop elsewhere and perpetrate tremendous harms to investors in other provinces.[72] As the CCGG observes, "even when reciprocal orders are pursued, in less than 4% of orders, they are plagued by 'delays, administrative inconsistency, and complexity.'"[73] That such harms are entirely preventable, and yet securities regulators have failed to take meaningful action to date, speaks volumes about the need for a national enforcement system.

The CFSRA could be given authority to prosecute all cases of securities law violations, financial services violations, and fraud wherever the alleged conduct is perpetrated across a provincial or national boundary. The defendant may be covered under either provincial or federal laws, but the national regulator would have a mandate to bring one proceeding, with national effect, to determine the scope of any violations and the appropriate sanctions. The federal legislation could extend the protections and benefits

---

71 *Securities Reference*, above note 1 (Factum of the Canadian Coalition for Good Governance, at para 1).

72 *Ibid* at paras 9–14, including, Micheal Mitton's history of fraudulent and abusive trading; RJ Smith's multiple acts of fraud; and Vernon Smith's multi-jurisdictional fraudulent scheme.

73 *Ibid* at para 12, citing *Securities Reference*, above note 1 (Record, Report of the Canadian Bankers' Association, Affidavit of Marion Wrobel, Exhibit 1 at paras 8–18).

of both criminal and administrative sanctions in a co-ordinated manner to Canadians in all provinces.

The CFSRA could offer a coordinated enforcement regime for all alleged violations that cross a provincial boundary and for all criminal conduct relating to securities and financial services violations. It would have the expertise to investigate and prosecute alleged harms, while the CFST would have the expertise and authority to adjudicate appeals, as discussed below, allowing an integrated and more effective national enforcement system. Arguably, frauds perpetrated on market participants move beyond provincial borders, are national in nature, and require a careful and systematic national response in terms of both sanctions and deterrence.

National enforcement of securities and financial services law will benefit issuers as well. Most issuers comply with the law, yet suffer the effects of a regulatory system that allows bad actors to flourish and ultimately increases the cost of capital, discourages investor participation, and increases both specific and systemic risk. Capital markets can be regional, national or international in scope. While provincial securities commissions may be well suited to and have a deep history in regional oversight,[74] they depend on cooperation to undertake enforcement beyond provincial boundaries. Political will and resources significantly affect, and in some instances undermine, such cooperative efforts. Issuers as well as investors suffer from this result.

E. Independent Arm's-Length Adjudication

Critically important to the design of a national securities regulatory authority is the creation of a national, independent, and impartial adjudicative tribunal. The Expert Panel on Securities Regulation has criticized the current regime's adjudicative process, saying that it has often been perceived to be unfair and lacking in independence and impartiality.[75]

---

74 *Securities Reference*, above note 1 (AG of Alberta, Record Volume XVIII, Affidavit of William Rice, Chair, Alberta Securities Commission at 8 [AG of Alberta]), which specified that its mandate is to protect investors within the Province of Alberta.

75 Expert Panel on Securities Regulation, *Creating an Advantage in Global Capital Markets: Final Report and Recommendations* (Ottawa: Depart-

The creation of the Canadian Financial Services Tribunal (CFST) would respond to concerns about the need for independence in adjudication of financial services. It would eliminate the perceived bias inherent in the current integrated commission structure, where the commission bringing the case has a vested interest in the outcome, which can create a perception of unfairness for the parties affected by the proceeding and make a "fair" hearing difficult to achieve. Orders of the CFST would have national authority, which would eliminate the necessity for applications for enforcement in other Canadian jurisdictions, aid in preventing market players from exploiting interjurisdictional limitations, and would provide an integrated approach encompassing both criminal and administrative sanctions.[76]

The CFST would create greater efficiency in the adjudicative process by avoiding a multiplicity of hearings by different commissions. When issuers or their agents are subject to multiple prosecutions and multiple investigations, multiple proceedings can be very costly to defend. Given our legal system's presumption of innocence, we should not maintain unnecessary barriers to effective defence against allegations. The opportunity to bring the matter before a single tribunal with the authority to determine all allegations, charges, or orders would create greater fairness and efficiency and would ensure uniform enforcement and sanctions where appropriate.

Appropriately resourced, the CFST's hearings could be held in a timely and accessible manner, with the tribunal sitting in the region where most parties are located and offering teleconferencing and other services where appropriate. The decisions rendered would provide greater consistency — including their reasoning, sanctions, and remedies — which would give market participants greater certainty in understanding the scope of acceptable conduct.

The CFST would allow for independent review of CFSRA decisions on alleged statutory violations or failures to comply with regulatory requirements. It would strengthen the integrity of the process in that tribunal members would not be trying to enforce unarticulated policy considerations or informal directions from

---

ment of Finance, 2009), online: Expert Panel www.expertpanel.ca/eng/documents/Expert_Panel_Final_Report_And_Recommendations.pdf

76 AG of Alberta, above note 74 at 3 and 4.

their administrative superiors.[77] Bifurcation of the policy, enforcement, and adjudication processes would create incentives for the CFSRA to clearly articulate policies that underlay its regulatory choices, such that the parties and the CFST have transparent and certain standards against which to assess impugned conduct. The CFST would interpret and apply the statutes and their regulations. Moreover, it would afford the CFSRA a greater ability to set enforcement priorities.[78]

In addition to adjudicating on matters of financial market risk and securities in respect of cross-border issuers, and assuming that the appropriate expertise and resources were given to the CFST, it could also adjudicate securities criminal matters, pursuant to the *Criminal Code*, where the expertise of the tribunal is important to determination of the charges. The CFST could be vested with authority to adjudicate some offences under the *Criminal Code*, such as securities fraud and fraud that affects public markets;[79] fraudulent manipulation of stock exchange transactions;[80] insider trading;[81] indictable offences such as intent to make gain or profit by the rise or fall in price of the stock by entering into a sale or purchase agreement without the bona fide intention of acquiring or selling the shares;[82] the indictable offence of a broker who, while employed by any customer to buy and carry shares on margin, reduces the amount of those shares below what the broker should be carrying for all customers by selling on his or her own account where, among others, the broker or his firm has an interest in the shares;[83] and the offence of providing a materially false prospectus, statement, or account to induce others to become shareholders, to defraud/deceive shareholders or other parties related to a company such as creditors, or to induce one to enter into any security for the company's benefit, or entrust or advance anything to the company.[84] Specialized expertise could be developed and applied, reducing inconsistencies

---

77 Coulter A Osborne, David J Mullan & Bryan Finlay "Report of the Fairness Committee to the Ontario Securities Commission" (5 March 2004) at 12–20.
78 *Ibid* at 22.
79 *Criminal Code*, RSC 1985, c C-46, s 380.
80 *Ibid*, s 382.
81 *Ibid*, s 382.1.
82 *Ibid*, s 383.
83 *Ibid*, s 384.
84 *Ibid*, s 400.

arising out of different provincial and criminal court determinations.

An independent tribunal to adjudicate Canadian securities violations would help to protect both investors and market integrity, assist in reducing systemic risk, offer consistency in decision making, and address perceived biases inherent in the current integrated commission structure. In Québec, the *Bureau de décision et de révision en valeurs mobilières* serves as an independent adjudicative tribunal under the provincial *Securities Act*,[85] offering an example of an independent expert tribunal that is arm's length from the first instance enforcement regulator.

The impartiality of the CFST would ensure that it is "fair and seen to be fair" in its adjudication of disputes arising under the national securities legislation. Since the tribunal is not promulgating the policy being adjudicated, market participants can have some confidence that any challenges brought will be given due consideration. Similarly, since the CFST is not part of the enforcement body that initially enforced regulatory violations or other alleged misconduct, it will consider the evidence and submissions by all parties before it and render a judgment without pressure to conform to its own first-level enforcement decisions.

The CFST would be vested with authority to hear all appeals or reviews of the national legislation, but it could also be given authority to hear and determine cases involving more than one provincial securities commission. Such authority could be enshrined in the legislation where national questions of investor protection or integrity of the markets are involved, and could also be allowed on an optional basis where securities commissions agree. The adjudicative structure could encompass a mechanism whereby parties to a provincial commission decision agree to have a matter within their jurisdiction that has provincial cross-

---

85 The *Autorité des marchés financiers* ("AMF") has responsibility for the supervision of financial markets, the protection of investors and the public, and the regulation of securities trading. It administers the Québec *Securities Act*, RSQ c V-1.1, with rule- and regulation-making authority. The AMF can conduct investigations, take steps to ensure compliance with the Act or regulations and impose fines. However, its decisions can be reviewed by the Bureau. Stéphane Rousseau, *The Québec Experience with an Independent Administrative Tribunal Specialized in Securities: A Study of the Bureau de décision et de révision en valeurs mobilières: A Research Study Prepared for the Expert Panel on Securities Regulation in Canada* (Ottawa: Expert Panel on Securities Regulation, 2008) at 3 and 11.

border implications determined by the CFST. In such cases, there would need to be some sensitivity as to where hearings were held and the type of videoconferencing facilities available to parties elsewhere. There are also other potential circumstances in which parties could bring a dispute to the national tribunal, such as investor harm in more than one provincial jurisdiction or issues concerning issuers or investors outside Canada as well as within Canada. The CFST could also provide a mechanism to appeal or ensure compliance with findings regarding consumer investment and banking services complaints, creating a dispute resolution mechanism that has actual power to enforce substantiated complaints and resultant orders. Access could be assured by having the tribunal conduct regional hearings where the parties are located or wherever the greatest harm to investors appears to have occurred.

Concerns about aligning policy goals of the CFSRA with the independent tribunal can be addressed by clear statutory language and clarity in regulations. Tribunal members would be appointed on the basis of their expertise in securities, financial markets, accounting, business regulation, securities law, and adjudication, as well as on the basis of regional representation. Like many administrative tribunals in Canada, the CFST would be vested with quasi-judicial powers, including the ability to summon witnesses, require production of disclosures, and determine the scope and admissibility of expert and first-hand evidence. Its authority would address problems that currently exist for provincial securities commissions' capacity to enforce subpoena when dealing, for example, with parties or witnesses in other provinces. The tribunal would operate under a strong statutory privative clause, which would make its rulings binding on all parties, and challenges to its authority would be limited to complaints regarding conflict of interest, denial of natural justice, or constitutional overreach.[86] The CFST could have a role in approving

---

86 The structure of the CFST could reflect national and regional expertise and experience. The CFST Chair could be nominated by the federal finance minister, and in turn could recommend a short list of potential adjudicators, full and part time, based on experience, expertise and regional representation; terms would be three to five years, renewable once. The tribunal could sit in panels of one to three, and be vested with powers of superior courts to summons witnesses and compel production of records and documents, where failure to comply would be enforced by

cross-border protocols for cooperation among tribunals and international tribunals or regulators.

There would be greater consistency in decisions and remedies, ultimately improving protection of investors and effectiveness of capital markets, and greater efficiency in the adjudicative process through an avoidance of a multiplicity of proceedings. The CFST would strengthen the integrity of the hearing process by eliminating the potential for unarticulated policy considerations to inform sanction hearings. Such a tribunal would be consistent with the Supreme Court's reasoning, as it would not infringe on provincial involvement in the day-to-day regulatory functions of local and regional securities.

F. Conclusion

Appropriately conceived and well resourced, a national regulatory authority and independent adjudicative tribunal would have the expertise and the legal capacity to create a comprehensive code for addressing systemic risk, protecting investors nationally, establishing standards of conduct for multiple market participants, ensuring a harmonized approach to securities enforcement, and facilitating the creation of a national consumer complaints mechanism.

A national regulatory authority could significantly contribute to the creation of accessible, timely, and clear disclosure obligations, recognizing different types of investors. It could take a leading role in setting national policy on corporate governance guidelines, which provincial regulators have to date failed to do. In addition, it would have a significant role in public interest oversight and protection, both at the regulatory/policy stage and at the enforcement and appeal stages.

Ford and Gill argue elsewhere in this volume that data collection could become a substantive regulatory tool, drawing on scholarship regarding the notion of a federal information clearinghouse that can provide the basis for more cogent policy decisions and suggesting that a "clearinghouse regulator" could set broad goals and regulatory requirements for disclosure while al-

---

the federal court or a superior court. Decisions would be rendered in writing, with reasons where appropriate.

lowing local processes to determine how to meet those goals.[87] Whether this model or another is adopted, the important point is that the current regulatory gaps are exacerbated by the lack of transparency of products, their market concentration, and their effects in the market; and that the collection, organization, evaluation and application of data can offer a powerful means of understanding markets and retooling policy choices in light of such understanding.

As discussed above, in addition to immediate authority over managing systemic risk and the above oversight, the CFSRA and CFST could be granted authority over all securities matters for issuers cross-listed on Canadian and international exchanges, so that where issuers are operating concurrently domestically and outside Canada, they would fall automatically under the scope of the national regulator. If operating across provincial or territorial boundaries, issuers would have the choice of coming within the regulatory oversight of a provincial commission or of the CFSRA.

The national regulator could be given specific public interest authority where the number of investors affected across Canada creates a threat to the stability of the financial system or seriously undermines the goals of investor protection.

The CSA would still be the vehicle for negotiation of national policy and instruments for the securities commissions in terms of their securities activities, and CFSRA would be involved in working toward consistency in development of securities law. Where enforcement issues touch on both federal and provincial/territorial regulators, there would have to be development of new channels of communication and cooperation, perhaps more possible with a clearer delineation of constitutional authority. The SCC has previously held that the provinces and federal government may delegate their powers to a single regulator;[88] other jurisdictions have also created systems for delegation, Australia being a case in point.[89]

---

87 See Chapter 9.
88 *Reference Re Agricultural Products Marketing Act*, [1978] 2 SCR 1198; *British Columbia (Milk Board) v Grisnich*, [1995] 2 SCR 895.
89 Australian Securities and Investment Commission (ASIC), online: ASIC www.asic.gov.au. ASIC has regulatory responsibility for finance brokers, trading on licensed equity, derivatives, and futures markets, consumer protection in superannuation, insurance, deposit taking, trustee companies, and consumer credit.

As discussed briefly above in the context of systemic risk, the CFSRA would represent Canada in international policy development. More than merely a single national voice at the international table, the CFSRA would have the capacity to fashion a Canadian analysis and perspective on issues that will influence decision makers around the world. It is no surprise that the Bank of Canada has been such an influential presence internationally in the banking context: a combination of liberal policies that adopted a fairly aggressive approach to fiscal responsibility and capital adequacy, an effective early intervention program, and the concentration of bank capital have allowed Canada to play a leadership role in the public policy discussion moving forward. It is equally evident from the discussion documents issued by the CSA to date that there is a fragmented understanding of the issues relating to systemic risk and securities law and far too much unquestioning acceptance of regulatory choices by Canada's largest trading partner, the United States. Important issues such as the scope and oversight of central counterparty clearing facilities and the appropriateness of offering some structured financial products to retail investors need a strong and insightful national voice as these significant policy choices are being debated internationally.

Policy deliberations at IOSCO and the Financial Stability Forum demand thoughtful and innovative thinking about regulatory choices. Such discussions require not only technical expertise, but also a broader public policy interest that shapes the framework to take account of broader interests and to examine and remedy externalities created by the current system. As noted earlier, systemic risk is multifaceted and requires equally multifaceted and coordinated responses. In this respect, securities law and financial services law have changed fundamentally from the time when provincial securities regulators established their jurisdiction over property and civil rights.

The G20 commitment to overhaul the infrastructure of the OTC derivatives market involves increased standardization of OTC derivatives products, including trading on exchanges or electronic platforms, central clearing within projected deadlines, new reporting requirements to trade repositories, and higher capital requirements where contracts are not centrally cleared. Each of these issues raises a number of public policy concerns in which Canada should be fully engaged. Only through a national regulatory authority that has the best interests of a broad range of stakeholders as its focus, will Canada be able to ensure that international developments protect local investors and issues to the maximum extent possible.

CHAPTER 9

A National Systemic Risk Clearinghouse?

Cristie Ford and Hardeep Gill

In *Reference re Securities Act*,[1] the Supreme Court of Canada allocated to the federal level of government responsibility for two things: data collection and the management of systemic risk. The path forward now presumably entails cooperative federalism and negotiation between the federal and provincial governments around the relationship between these responsibilities and those of provincial securities regulators. In view of these negotiations, and in the interest of protecting Canadian investors, taxpayers, and capital markets from systemic risk in particular, this essay considers what exactly falls within the newly defined scope of federal responsibility.

Our claim is that the Reference can be seen as an invitation to create a meaningful and ambitious national systemic risk regulator, and one deeply connected to the securities markets and securities regulators. Regulating systemic risk requires deep information channels into local markets. Systemic risk has always been a function of myriad smaller, more localized risks, but over the last few decades financial innovation has embedded systemic risk even further into the daily operations of capital markets. In other words, it is simply not possible to manage systemic risk at some metaphysical distance from the day-to-day operations of the securities markets themselves. The day-to-day operations of

---

1   2011 SCC 66 [*Securities Reference*].

issuers, registrants, and regulators in the capital markets are *constitutive* of systemic risk.

The Reference opens the possibility that the federal government can create not an overlapping fourteenth securities regulator, but a different kind of regulatory capacity at the federal level. In giving data collection responsibilities to the federal government, the Reference is giving it a potentially significant and valuable tool, and one that complements the federal responsibility for managing systemic risk. This essay will argue that the combination of systemic risk and data-collection responsibilities could generate not a twentieth-century-style frontline regulator but an active "clearinghouse" regulatory body, as envisioned by some scholars in law and organizational theory. As we describe further below,[2] a regulatory clearinghouse is an institution that sets broad goals and regulatory requirements, while leaving detailed implementation of regulation to more local units. Crucially, such a clearinghouse would have the data analysis capacity and the authority to require more local regulatory units to produce information, and to demonstrate their compliance with the centrally-defined goals. This is not the path that the federal government would have chosen, and it is not a straightforward path. Nevertheless, with some creative thinking, it may have some advantages. A commitment to meaningful systemic risk management and data collection gives the federal government a principled way to imagine a coherent role for itself in Canadian securities regulation.

A. The *Reference* Decision and the Scope of Federal Authority

The Supreme Court of Canada delivered the Reference on 22 December 2011. Its contents are thoroughly analyzed throughout this volume; this essay focuses only on the two areas of responsibility the Court allocated to the federal government. The first, and most significant, is responsibility for preventing systemic risk:[3]

---

2   See Part C, below in this chapter.

3   "Manage" is probably a better term than "prevent," since systemic risk cannot be prevented even if acute systemic risk *crises* can be averted. This essay uses the term "manage," except when referring specifically to particular paragraphs in the Reference.

Prevention of systemic risk may trigger the need for a national regulator empowered to issue orders that are valid throughout Canada and impose common standards, under which provincial governments can work to ensure that their market will not transmit any disturbance across Canada or elsewhere. . . .

We accept that preservation of capital markets to fuel Canada's economy and maintain Canada's financial stability is a matter that goes beyond a particular "industry" and engages "trade as a whole". . . . Legislation aimed at imposing minimum standards applicable throughout the country and preserving the stability and integrity of Canada's financial markets might well relate to trade as a whole.[4]

The Court suggested, "without attempting an exhaustive enumeration," that some of the proposed federal Act's provisions on derivatives, short-selling, credit rating, urgent regulations, and data sharing seemed to be directed at systemic risk.[5] These provisions do not collectively constitute a coherent mandate. The Court apparently intended them as broadly illustrative, and we should take seriously the caveat that this list of topics is not exhaustive. For many observers familiar with how capital and financial markets operate, the larger problem is that one cannot actually manage systemic risk without having substantially more authority than these provisions provide over the myriad incremental, local decisions that create systemic risk in the first place.

---

4   *Securities Reference*, above note 1 at paras 104 and 114.
5   *Ibid* at para 103. The provisions the Supreme Court identified are s 73 (designation of credit rating organizations and other organizations), s 89 (prohibiting the sale of exchange-traded derivatives except on designated exchanges), s 90 (prohibiting the sale of designated derivatives unless a prescribed disclosure document has been filed and delivered), s 126(1) (requiring the declaration of short positions), ss 109 and 224 on data collection and sharing (requiring respectively that market participants keep records and produce them to the Chief Regulator where required; and prohibiting persons from representing that the Tribunal has provided any merit-based approval of persons, products, or the adequacy of disclosure), and s 228(4)(c) (permitting the Canadian Securities Regulatory Authority to make regulations without first publishing a notice, in urgent situations). The definitional distinctions between the Canadian Securities Regulatory Authority, the Tribunal, and the Chief Regulator (as head of the Authority's regulatory division) are no longer particularly relevant given the likelihood that the envisioned regulatory architecture will not come to pass.

Parsing the language of the Reference, responsibility for managing and responding to systemic risk does seem to include the power to engage in at least two distinct regulatory acts. First, the national regulator has the power to *issue orders* that are valid throughout Canada. Second, it has the power to impose *common standards* (or, elsewhere, "minimum standards") designed to ensure that one market will not "transmit any disturbance across Canada" and that the stability and integrity of Canada's financial markets are preserved.[6] Moreover, these powers are clearly and exclusively within federal jurisdiction. This is not something the provincial governments can accomplish simply by working together:

> The provinces' inherent prerogative to resile from an interprovincial scheme aimed for example at managing systemic risk limits their constitutional capacity to achieve the truly national goals of the proposed federal Act. The point is not that the provinces are constitutionally or practically unable to adopt legislation aimed at systemic risk *within* the provinces. Indeed, some provincial securities schemes contain provisions analogous to the ones aimed at systemic risk found in the proposed Act. The point is simply that because provinces could always withdraw from an interprovincial scheme there is no assurance that they could effectively address issues of national systemic risk and competitive national capital markets on a sustained basis.[7]

The second responsibility the Reference allocates to the federal level of government relates to data collection:

> The emphasis in the proposed Act on nationwide data collection may similarly be seen as aimed at anticipating and identifying risks that may transcend the boundaries of a specific province. By analogy with Statistics Canada, it might be argued that broad national data-collecting powers may serve the national interest in a way that finds no counterpart on the provincial plane.

The Court left open precisely how national data-collection powers could serve the national interest. As Ed Iacobucci notes in this volume, the Court's analysis of data collection must have been based on the efficacy of collecting data at the federal level (even though the Court held policy efficacy to be an irrelevant consider-

---

6   *Ibid* at paras 103 and 114.
7   *Ibid* at para 120.

ation in determining federal jurisdiction overall).[8] The analogy
to Statistics Canada does not address whether the data-collection
powers of a national securities regulator would be equivalent in
size, scope, or mandate to those of Statistics Canada.

The Court concludes,

> Aspects of the Act, for example those aimed at management
> of systemic risk and at national data collection, appear to be
> directly related to the larger national goals which the Act pro-
> claims are its *raison d'être*.[9]

This essay looks at these two constitutional spheres of authority in turn. Part B, immediately below, tries to illuminate the
nature of systemic risk. It makes the point that systemic risk
does not operate on a separate plane from the day-to-day operation and regulation of securities markets. On the contrary, systemic risk is a function of multiple smaller risks, combined and
interacting in interconnected national, and international, markets. What this means is that in order to manage systemic risk,
the federal government must be able to assess risks arising out
of underlying architectural elements of capital markets (such as
clearinghouses) as well as issuers, securities (not just derivatives),
registrants, exchange trading rules, retail investment products
such as money-market mutual funds, and capital markets players
such as hedge funds. Although frontline regulatory responsibility for the securities markets would remain with the provinces, a
national systemic risk regulator would have to be in a position to
require detailed information from those provinces, and it would
have to have the power to oversee how provincial regulators collect and manage data. Part B also considers the undeniable connections between domestic and international securities markets
and between securities regulation and financial regulation more
broadly.

Part C considers recent scholarship in law and organizational
studies to highlight the fact that data collection can be an important regulatory tool and, moreover, one that is especially well
suited to regulating fast-moving environments such as the capital markets. It considers whether, in granting the federal government the power to impose standards concerning systemic risk,

---

8   Edward M Iacobucci, "Competition Policy, Efficacy and the National
    Securities Reference," in this volume.
9   *Ibid* at para 117.

the Reference has actually granted the federal government the power to enact some form of principles-based or outcome-oriented regulation around systemic risk. Part D concludes.

B. Systemic Risk

1) What is systemic risk?

Systemic risk is the aggregate of multiple smaller risks. As Anita Anand has noted, systemic risk involves "the risk of breakdown among institutions and other market participants in a chain-like fashion that has the potential to affect the entire financial system negatively."[10]

Systemic risk can be a function of several conditions.[11] Institutions that are *"too big to fail"* cannot be permitted to fail because their size makes them systemically important. Institutions may also be *"too interconnected to fail"* because of the number and overlapping nature of their mutual obligations and covenants. Interconnectedness through credit default swaps played a major role in creating the recent financial crisis.[12] Global institutions that are involved in multiple sectors, as AIG was (providing insurance, offering asset-management financial services, and participating in many parts of the capital markets), spread and exacerbate systemic risk. *Concentrated* markets like Canada's, in the financial sector and elsewhere, are more systemically vulnerable if a risk in that sector crystallizes. The *correlation of expos-*

---

10 Anita I Anand, "Is Systemic Risk Relevant to Securities Regulation?" (2010) 60 UTLJ 941 at 942 [Anand].

11 See generally Staff of the International Monetary Fund and the Bank for International Settlements, and the Secretariat of the Financial Stability Board, "Guidance to Assess the Systemic Importance of Financial Institutions, Markets and Instruments: Initial Considerations," *Report to the G-20 Finance Ministers and Central Bank Governors* (October 2009), online: Financial Stability Board. www.financialstabilityboard.org/publications/r_091107d.pdf [*Report to G-20*].

12 Sheri Markose et al, "Too Interconnected to Fail: Financial Contagion and Systemic Risk in Network Model of CDS and Other Credit Enhancement Obligations of US Banks", *Paper prepared for ECB Workshop on Recent Advances in Modelling Systemic Risk Using Network Analysis* (5 October 2009), online: Agent-based Computational Economics and Financial Modelling www.acefinmod.com/docs/TooInterconnectedTo-Fail_15112009.pdf.

ures between industries that depend on each other also tightens causal connections and generates systemic risk. Finally, *opacity and complexity* exacerbate systemic risk because they increase interconnectedness while also making linkages harder to identify and contagion effects harder to predict.

Metaphorically, we could describe systemic risk in different ways. The first would be to see it as a chain, as in Anita Anand's formulation. The chain imagery effectively evokes the dynamic cause-and-effect process by which systemic risk spreads. Like a line of dominoes, the movement of one piece affects all other pieces that touch it. At a greater level of complexity, and still consistent with the Anand formulation, the metaphor of the "chain reaction" explosion evokes a more exponential multiplier effect: the first explosion kicks off not one additional explosion but several, which in turn kick off still more in subsequent rounds.

While the chain-reaction imagery captures the *mechanism* of systemic risk, the analogy of sedimentary geologic layers may capture the *nature* of systemic risk. Arguably, it is the sedimentary, accretive nature of systemic risk for which the Reference does not account. Each individual layer of decision-making may be relatively innocuous, but taken together the layers build up to a potentially dangerous height. What this image suggests is that if the federal level of government cannot have some degree of timely oversight over the incremental decisions that issuers and securities market participants make in their operations, it will not be able to regulate systemic risk.

Beyond the metaphors of systemic risk as chain reaction or sedimentary layers is recent work done by network economists on the underlying structure of global financial markets.[13] The realization that interconnectedness can produce systemic risk derives significantly from this work.[14] Network studies map the various links among institutions and examine the ways in which risk, including systemic risk, is a function of these links. As an important report prepared for G-20 finance ministers and central bank governors in 2009 insists,

> In order to assess the systemic importance of a financial institution, it is not enough to assess the *initial impact* a financial institution could have on other financial institutions in the face of credit and liquidity shocks. It is crucial to also track *second*

13 See e.g. *ibid.*
14 *Report to G-20*, above note 11 at 24–28.

round effects. . . . In subsequent rounds of contagion, these
cumulative effects could lead to significant capital impairment
and/or failures of other institutions in the network. It is also important to analyze financial instruments which represent *con-
tingent extended links* between institutions that can increase
the range of contagion such as credit default swaps.[15]

Although network analysis so far has tended to focus on banks
and financial institutions, securities markets generally are also
susceptible to systemic risk. Five examples below seek to demonstrate how lower-level risks — that is, a series of individually
unremarkable decisions — can aggregate into systemic risk in
the securities markets in particular.[16]

2) Systemic Risk and the Securities Markets

a) Canadian Issuers, Derivatives, and Interconnectedness

Canadian issuers are linked to each other, and internationally,
through multiple mechanisms. These links are vectors along
which risk, including systemic risk, travels.

Issuers and their distributions are linked to other issuers and
other distributions through their underwriters, their creditors,
their debt holders, the registrants that sell their products, and
their investors (including institutional investors and venture
capitalists). There are also business-based or industry-based connections between issuers. Some are self-evident: The Canadian
banking industry is highly concentrated, as are other industries
such as telecommunications. Others are correlated in terms of
risk: the fates of extractive industry issuers, their service providers, and other ancillary businesses, for example, are linked
together, and collectively they are linked to relevant global commodity prices and other phenomena. Concentration risk and the
correlation of exposures within particular industries generate
systemic risk.

Just as important, but more opaque, are the complex and
hard-to-track ways in which risks associated with seemingly
uncorrelated issuers can be correlated through their reliance

---

15 *Ibid* at 24 [emphasis added].
16 The discussion is broadly complementary to Anand, above note 10, and to
Anita Anand, "After the Reference: Regulating Systemic Risk in Canadian Financial Market," in this volume.

on structured finance. Financial engineering innovations have radically increased and made more complex the ways in which issuers, investors, markets, industries, and even economies are interconnected. That engineering has increased systemic risk while at the same time making that risk harder to track.[17]

Issuers in multiple industries now use derivatives to hedge the risks associated with their businesses (to say nothing of individuals and organizations that use them for the purpose of speculating). Entities doing work across borders, including banks and international mining companies, manage foreign-exchange exposure through derivatives. Resource companies — mining companies, forestry companies, and oil and gas companies — manage risks related to commodity price changes through derivatives. Small businesses use derivatives to manage risks associated with changing costs of supplies. Lenders such as credit unions use derivatives to manage risks associated with having long-term fixed obligations, like residential mortgages, while offering variable rates of return on deposits.[18]

Modern derivatives practice has also "shattered the atom" of the corporate share itself. A share's constituent elements (for present purposes, primarily its voting right and the positive economic interest the shareholder is meant to have in the corporation's success) can be disassembled and recombined in novel and inscrutable ways, including by parties with opaque or counterintuitive motives.[19] Corporate risk can be sliced ever more finely and parcelled out to parties willing to purchase it, rather than allocated to shareholders in a lumpen fashion in the form of equity.[20] Nor are equity and debt instruments really distinct anymore, thanks to innovations such as "reverse exchange securities" (which create assets that are half share, half bond),

---

17　Patricia A McCoy, Andrey D Pavlov, & Susan M Wachter, "Systemic Risk through Securitization: The Result of Deregulation and Regulatory Failure" (2009) 41 Conn L Rev 1327.

18　We are indebted to Paul Bourque for this list of examples.

19　Henry TC Hu & Bernard Black, "The New Vote Buying: Empty Voting and Hidden (Morphable) Ownership" (2006) 79 S Cal L Rev 811.

20　Ronald J Gilson & Charles K Whitehead, "Deconstructing Equity: Public Ownership, Agency Costs, and Complete Capital Markets" (2008) 108 Colum L Rev 231.

and securitization generally (which creates securities out of aggregate pools of debt, including consumer debt).[21]

These decisions are often innocuous, and may even be highly beneficial, for an individual issuer. But because multiple issuers are hedging risks in the over-the-counter derivatives markets, and their shares are being deconstructed in multiple ways, issuers' fates and their financial instruments — including their common shares — may be interconnected in significant but non-obvious ways. This interconnectedness creates systemic risk. The complexity and opacity inherent in these transactions means that the risk is harder to address. It is also noteworthy that the issuers distributing the most complexly structured instruments tend to be banks. Banks are systemically important in Canada not only because they are also depository banks (as if that were not sufficient in itself) but because financial services make up such a large portion of Canadian listed equities markets.[22]

Structured finance does not reduce risk, of course. It transfers it. Determining to whom it is transferred can be very complex and non-transparent. Nevertheless, we know from the recent financial crisis that risk can be concentrated in unexpected quarters, such as American insurer AIG's London-based Financial Products Division.[23] The catastrophic systemic risk that AIG's collapse would surely have produced meant, in turn, that the counterparty risk associated with those hedging transactions was borne by American taxpayers and others.

b) Long-Term Capital Management and Hedge Funds

Hedge funds and other specialized trading firms are ubiquitous in global financial systems, and the manner in which these com-

---

21 Tamar Frankel, "New Financial Assets: Separating Ownership from Control" (2010) 33 Seattle UL Rev 931 at 945–46.

22 The financial services sector is the largest single sector listed in Canada in terms of market capitalization. As of 29 February 2012, it constitutes 23 percent of Toronto Stock Exchange market capitalization and 22 percent of the combined market capitalization of the TSX and the TSX-V. TMX Market Intelligence Group, "Current MIG Report: What's Listed on TSX and TSX Venture Exchange as at February 29, 2012" (29 February 2012), online: TMX Group www.tmx.com/en/mig/index.html.

23 See e.g. Gretchen Morgenson, "Behind Insurer's Crisis, Blind Eye to a Web of Risk" *New York Times* (27 September 2008), online: The New York Times Company www.nytimes.com/2008/09/28/business/28melt. html?pagewanted=all.

panies interact with the other financial institutions can bring about significant systemic risks. Canada has a sizable hedge fund industry, which in 2004 held approximately $20 billion in assets.[24] Many of the safeguards in place to protect the economy from risks posed by the activities of banks and other types of funds do not apply to hedge funds and specialized trading firms.

Hedge funds account for approximately 1 percent of total funds held by financial institutions,[25] yet they pose risks for the entire financial industry through their operation. The primary reasons for this are the interconnected nature of large financial institutions and the comparative lack of regulations on the function of hedge funds. This situation is best illustrated by the near failure of the American hedge fund Long-Term Capital Management (LTCM) in 1998. The fund employed as principals some of the luminaries of the financial world, including two Nobel Prize winners in economics and numerous Harvard business professors. For this reason, among others, LTCM was able to achieve a high level of leverage, and had a functional debt-to-equity ratio of approximately 25:1. At its prime, it held $4.7 billion in equity, placing it in the upper echelon of hedge funds in size. The fund also held off-balance-sheet positions of approximately $1 trillion in derivatives such as swaps.[26]

The Russian financial crisis of 1998 crystallized losses by LTCM totalling $500 million in the bond arbitrage market and forced it to close out its positions in other sectors at a loss to gain liquidity.[27] This rush to liquidity ultimately brought about its downfall. The counterparties to LTCM — many large financial institutions on Wall Street — worried that a default by LTCM

---

24 See the "AIMA Canada Hedge Fund Primer" (June 2004), online: Alternative Investment Management Association Canada http://aima-canada.org/doc_bin/AIMA_Primer.pdf; the industry has been growing steadily since 2004, having approximately doubled in size according to the "Scotiabank Asset Weighted Canadian Hedge Fund Index" (March 2012), online: Scotiabank www.scmonline.com/analytics/reports/SCH-FPI_monthly.pdf.

25 See e.g. Hedge Fund Facts.org, "Hedge Funds: How They Serve Investors in the US and Global Markets" (August 2009), online: Coalition of Private Investment Companies www.hedgefundfacts.org/hedge/wp-content/uploads/2009/09/Hedge_Funds.pdf.

26 Roger Lowenstein, *When Genius Failed: The Rise And Fall Of Long-Term Capital Management* (New York: Random House, 2000) at 191.

27 See Roger Lowenstein, *ibid* at ch 8 for a very good account of these events.

could bring about a catastrophic chain of defaults, potentially leading to a shortening of investment capital and a meltdown of the economy. To keep this from happening, the Federal Reserve Bank of New York organized a private bailout by the major counterparties of LTCM totalling approximately $3 billion.

The President of the Federal Reserve Bank of New York testified before the US House of Representatives that if LTCM had been allowed to default, its major counterparties would have lost billions of dollars.[28] He went on to state,

> [T]here was a likelihood that a number of credit and interest rate markets would experience extreme price moves and possibly cease to function for a period of one or more days and maybe longer. This would have caused a vicious cycle: a loss of investor confidence, leading to a rush out of private credits, leading to a further widening of credit spreads, leading to further liquidations of positions, and so on. Most importantly, this would have led to further increases in the cost of capital to American businesses. . . . [I]t was my judgment that the American people, whom we are pledged to serve, could have been seriously hurt if credit dried up in a general effort by banks and other intermediaries to avoid greater risk.[29]

The fact that hedge funds like LTCM are substantially unregulated is what creates this form of systemic risk. One of the principals of LTCM, Eric Rosenfeld, during an address to a business class at MIT, indicated that although the bankruptcy of LTCM was not predictable at any particular time, it could not continue to operate over a long period of time because of its very high leverage and speculative investment methods.[30] Therefore, by allowing such a fund to persist unregulated, the economy admitted the systemic risk that its collapse would eventually be sure to pose. The implication for present purposes is clear: Funds like LTCM create systemic risk, the management of which is now the *federal* government's responsibility in Canada.

---

28 See Statement, William J McDonough, President Federal Reserve Bank of New York (1998), online: Federal Reserve Bank of New York http://newyorkfed.org/newsevents/speeches/1998/mcd981001.html.

29 *Ibid.*

30 Eric Rosenfeld, MIT Tech TV Presentation (19 February 2009), online: MIT http://techtv.mit.edu/videos/2450-eric-rosenfeld-15437-presentation-21909.

c) The ABCP Crisis, Disclosure, and the Role of Registrants

As is well known, the Canadian asset-backed commercial paper (ABCP) market crashed in August 2007 when conduits were no longer able to "rollover" (resell) their maturing notes.[31] ABCP is short-term debt (maturing in less than one year, and often in 170 days) that is backed by a pool of longer-term loans such as residential mortgages, car loans, credit card debt, student loan debt, and credit derivatives. Conduits are specialized trusts that hold the underlying assets and issue the commercial paper backed by those assets to investors. Since the maturity of the underlying assets is long-term and the commercial paper issued is short-term (a situation known as a "maturity mismatch"), a conduit needs to reissue (or "rollover") notes for the same set of assets several times before the underlying assets mature.

ABCP in Canada is not subject to the same level of prudential oversight as regular bank lending. Assets held on a bank's balance sheet are subject to capital requirements, while those being securitized through conduits into ABCP are not. Nor is ABCP subject to full prospectus-level disclosure under securities regulation. ABCP was offered under the short term debt exemption in section 2.35 of National Instrument 45-106, which covered any security with a maturity date not more than one year from the date of issuance, so long as it had an "approved credit rating" from an "approved credit rating organization". This meant that any disclosure about ABCP was voluntary. IIROC-regulated broker dealers then marketed and sold ABCP to some 1,800 retail investors. Retail investors vastly outnumbered sophisticated institutional investors in this market, though they collectively held only a fraction of what the institutional investors (primarily the banks) held.

The ABCP Crisis was triggered by the realization that much of the commercial paper issued by Coventree Inc., the largest third-party (that is, non-bank) dealer of ABCP, had been exposed to the increasingly shaky US subprime mortgage market. In November 2006, Dominion Bond Rating Service (DBRS), the only ratings agency in Canada for non-bank ABCP products, had indicated to

---

31 See John Chant, "The ABCP Crisis in Canada: The Implications for the Regulation of Financial Markets", Research Study prepared for Expert Panel on Securities Regulation (2009) online: Expert Panel on Securities Regulation www.expertpanel.ca/eng/reports/research-studies/index.html at 4.

Coventree that it would take a more stringent approach in rating some of their transactions.[32] In January 2007, DBRS notified Coventree that it would refuse to rate some of their transactions unless Coventree met additional liquidity requirements.[33] Coventree could not roll over its maturing commercial paper, and banks, as emergency liquidity providers, did not step in to help. In August 2007, the ABCP market as a whole froze. No ABCP conduits could roll over their maturing notes, and investors could not access their investments.

In his review of the crisis, Professor John Chant splits its causes into pre- and post-crisis influences. Among the pre-crisis influences are an unstable business model (in that any business model based on a maturity mismatch is subject to "runs"), overly favourable credit ratings, over-leverage and the under-pricing of risk, the exemption of ABCP from the prospectus requirements, and investors' own eagerness for a higher rate of return.[34] Another issue was that non-bank-sponsored ABCP, which was based on assets from other markets such as the US subprime mortgage market, had grown to account for almost 50 percent of the entire market by the end of 2006.[35]

Post-crisis, the crisis was magnified by a lack of transparency on the part of arrangers and conduits, conditional liquidity arrangements, and "mark to market" accounting.[36] The lack of transparency in the set-up of sponsors, conduits, and various intermediaries meant that investors could not differentiate between conduits that were saddled with toxic assets and those that were not. Therefore, when the conduits set up by Coventree could not roll over their notes, other conduits had a similar problem. The fact that ABCP was not subject to the same levels of prudential regulation as other bank operations meant that banks could earn revenue from assets while simultaneously reducing

---

32 Paul D Davis, Stephen Genttner, & Matthew Langford, "Timely disclosure obligations – *Coventree* decision outlines guiding principles" (November 2011), online: McMillan www.mcmillan.ca/timely-disclosure-obligations--coventree-decision-outlines-guiding-principles.

33 "Credit crisis 'made in Canada'" *The National Post* (27 September 2007), online: Postmedia Network Inc. www.canada.com/nationalpost/financial-post/story.html?k=63868&id=3f92dc01-2dce-41a1-8035-358121a6725a.

34 Chant, above note 31 at 20–22.

35 *Ibid* at 20.

36 *Ibid* at 23.

the amount of capital they had to keep on hand.[37] But when the ABCP Crisis unfolded, the conduits held by banks were affected to the same degree as non-bank conduits. Banks then realized that in order to retain their reputation and keep the crisis from affecting their on-balance-sheet business adversely, they would need to provide assistance to the investors in their conduits. In this way, the off-balance-sheet activities of banks ended up being indemnified by their on-balance-sheet activities.

The Bank of Canada characterized the ABCP Crisis as having the potential to profoundly affect the Canadian economy. David Dodge, then governor of the Bank of Canada, told the *Financial Post* that the crisis had "stymied activity in the credit markets with would-be buyers not able to secure the necessary loans," and that were a collective restructuring agreement not reached, "the problems could make their way to so-called Main Street."[38] The same *Financial Post* story indicates that the Bank of Canada considered "[s]olving the ABCP problem [to be] in the public interest, certainly in the interests of the functioning of the financial markets . . ."[39] In other words, the Bank of Canada itself considered that leaving the ABCP Crisis unaddressed could pose a systemic risk.

The ABCP Crisis also highlights the particular role of registrants in safeguarding investors against systemic risk. Registrants have an obligation to "know their clients" and to not sell them assets that are ill-suited to them. Given the fundamental flaws underlying the ABCP market, it seems reasonable to assume that ABCP was not well-suited to at least some of the retail investors to whom it was marketed. The problem was exacerbated by the prospectus exemption, which meant that registrants did not even have access to prospectus-level disclosure on ABCP products. A credit rating agency that gives unwarranted high ratings to complex financial products contributes to systemic risk. Likewise, a registrant that markets and sells such complex wholesale financial products downstream without understanding what they are also contributes to systemic risk.

---

37 *Ibid* at 33.
38 Opinion, "TD May Join the ABCP Bailout" *The Financial Post,* online: National Post www.financialpost.com/opinion/story.html?id=d7eefab7-9dc6-44c4-93e5-b6b5ee3761f8.
39 *Ibid.*

The fact that registrants can generate systemic risk — a point made by David Johnston and Kathleen Rockwell before the financial crisis[40] — illustrates how foundational and unavoidable systemic risk is in Canadian securities markets. Issuers and investors are linked to each other, through registrants. This is the justification for capital reserve and risk management requirements in National Instrument 31-103, but the ABCP Crisis suggests that registrants can also be vectors for systemic risks by means of their sales practices. The relationship between wholesale product originators and registrants, and registrants' potential incentives to market particular products to their clients, can contribute to spreading systemic risk.

Some of the factors listed above, such as Coventree's holding subprime assets and subsequently failing to disclose pertinent information to its shareholders, the behaviour of the ratings agencies, the lack of transparency of conduits, and the eagerness of investors, derive from smaller decisions that in isolation might not have been consequential. Together, however, they created the conditions for the ABCP Crisis to occur and thus contributed to the systemic risk already present through the operation of a market built upon a fragile business model.

d) The Flash Crash of 2010 and High-Frequency Trading

The so-called "Flash Crash" of 2010 exemplifies a different type of systemic risk presented by investment firms — one in which the way they operate has a negative effect on the day-to-day operation of the markets. At approximately 2:45 pm ET on March 6, 2010, the S&P 500 dove an unprecedented 900 points (6 percent), subsequently recovering about 600 points before closing. During a period already characterized by heightened volatility resulting from the emerging Greek sovereign debt crisis, an extraordinarily large sell order of E-mini S&P contracts (valued at approximately $4.1 billion) was initiated by a mutual fund complex.[41] An E-mini S&P contract is a futures contract worth 50 times the value of the S&P 500 stock index. The sell-off triggered an enormous amount of sell pressure on the market and a shortage of liquidity (i.e., a

---

40 Most recently see David Johnston & Kathleen Rockwell, *Canadian Securities Regulation,* 4th ed (Markham: LexisNexis, 2006) at 10.

41 Andrei Kirilenko et al, "The Flash Crash: The Impact of High Frequency Trading on an Electronic Market" (2011), online: The Q Group http://q-group.org/pdf/Kyle-paper-Q-group_flash_crash_01182011_small.pdf.

shortage of buyers),[42] as the number of E-minis in supply greatly exceeded the number in demand.

Noting the extraordinary sell pressure, high-frequency trading (HFT) firms, which are firms that use algorithmic (computer-automated) trading strategies to trade in the market, reacted quickly. HFT firms are technical traders, not value-based traders. They typically hold positions for mere seconds or milliseconds, and often function as de facto "market-makers" by providing liquidity and relying on the bid–offer spread to make a profit. In other words, HFT firms buoy market volume and provide liquidity by engaging in large numbers of transactions, even though the overwhelming majority of those transactions are cancelled within milliseconds of being entered into. Unlike other market-makers such as broker-dealers, however, HFT firms retain the freedom to withdraw from the market when conditions become unfavourable.

Because HFT firms can query markets across very short time intervals, they sensed market abnormalities soon after the March 6 sell order was placed. They quickly sold their inventories of E-mini's before traditional traders could react,[43] thus benefitting from the valuations before the sell-off, and then substantially disengaged from the market.[44] The additional sell-off by HFT firms led to what appeared to be a further shortage of liquidity on the markets — that is, a massive buyer shortage resulting from the fact that HFT firms accounted for a large percentage of trade volume and were not buying. The precipitous drop in stock markets was thus exacerbated by the activity of the HFT firms.

Because of the volume of trading they engage in, HFT firms have a stabilizing influence on the markets and contribute to their efficient operation. The sudden withdrawal of HFT firms can exacerbate any decline in the market. Thus, their ability to exit the markets in unfavourable conditions produces systemic risk[45] by increasing the potential magnitude of a negative market shock, and thereby increasing the probability that a chain of market or institutional failures will be triggered.

---

42 *Ibid* at 36.

43 *Ibid.*

44 Harald Malmgren & Mark Stys, "The Marginalizing of the Individual Investor", *The Magazine Of International Economic Policy* (2010) online: The International Economy www.international-economy.com/TIE_Su10_MalmgrenStys.pdf at 24.

45 *Ibid* at 25.

A second criticism of HFT firms is that they obscure what has traditionally constituted market liquidity, since most of their trades have a net-zero effect on the market, even though they account for a significant percentage of total volume. This effect tends to obscure thinning of volume originating from "normal buyers," and can thus hide possible risks.[46] HFT firms worsen the risks associated with momentum-driven price movements — that is, they tend to exacerbate price declines and hasten price increases — which is thought to undermine "value investing," or buy-and-hold strategies that rely on company fundamentals.[47] The greater the divergence of investing strategies from fundamentals, the greater the eventual market corrections that must take place, and the greater the systemic risks associated with those market corrections.

e) Investors and Money-Market Mutual Funds

Investors themselves are linked through the large pension and investment funds that are the main vehicle for most Canadians' participation in the securities markets. Particularly relevant to systemic risk concerns are the money-market mutual funds.

The Money Market Fund (MMF) marketplace is another example of an established financial sector that is susceptible to contagion effects and runs. Together with the size of the market and its position in the economy as the single largest commercial lender, this means that MMFs pose a significant systemic risk to the US economy in particular, but also to Canada's economy. The United States Securities and Exchange Commission is well aware of that risk, since the freezing of the credit markets in 2008 was largely due to MMF activity.

Background on MMFs: An MMF is a special type of mutual fund that, in many ways, operates similarly to a bank deposit. Like other mutual funds, an MMF carries a net asset value (NAV) ratio, which describes the rate of return on the investment on any given day. The NAV for a mutual fund is calculated by taking a weighted average of the assets held by the fund over the number of outstanding shares. The distinguishing feature of MMFs is that their NAV ratio is fixed at 1.00, which means that when an investor (or shareholder) wishes to redeem shares, the amount

---

46　*Ibid* at 46.
47　*Ibid* at 46–47.

of money returned by the fund must be the same as the principal. The mechanism that allows MMFs to achieve this is called amortized cost accounting, which means that the daily value for each asset held by the fund is assumed to be the value at maturity. This type of calculation allows the fund to constantly balance its assets such that the NAV ratio comes out at or very near 1. The assumption made by the funds is justified, provided that the assets held are sufficiently short-term and safe enough that they can be counted on to have an actual (mark-to-market) value that is very close to the value at maturity. The catch in all of this is that MMFs are not required to have an external insurance provider to cover any losses that occur.

The American MMF industry holds approximately $3.2 trillion, or approximately 30 percent of the entire mutual fund market. About one third of investors in this market are "retail" investors, who essentially treat MMFs as if they were as stable as deposit accounts while still taking advantage of their relatively high rate of return. MMFs oblige these investors by providing chequing privileges, an open withdrawal policy, and other bank-like services. The other two-thirds of MMF investors are institutional or corporate investors, who effectively outsource much of their cash management operations to MMFs.[48] Even hedge funds and other financial institutions place money in MMFs as short-term, low-risk investments.[49]

MMFs function as short-term corporate lending vehicles because they hold significant high-grade commercial paper. For example, if a trustworthy corporation needs a short-term loan in order to reorganize some of its operations or pay its employees, then it might sell commercial paper to an MMF to obtain the necessary funds. It could repay the money with interest at the time the paper matures. Corporations often prefer selling short-term commercial paper to an MMF to taking a loan from a bank, since it is less costly.

The 2008 credit crunch: Although investors are warned, on the prospectus or the US registration statement, that MMFs are not

---

48   Jonathan Macey, "Reducing Systemic Risk: The Role of Money Market Mutual Funds as Substitutes for Federally Insured Bank Deposits," John M. Olin Center for Studies in Law, Economics, and Public Policy No. 422, online: Yale Law School http://digitalcommons.law.yale.edu/cgi/viewcontent.cgi?article=3100&context=fss_papers at 9.

49   *Ibid* at 8–9.

guaranteed to be completely safe, few actually seem to believe it. Professor William Birdthistle attributes this primarily to the fixed NAV, which gives MMFs the appearance of being unaffected by market fluctuations, and to the ways in which they are advertised: fund managers reportedly tout the stability offered by MMFs.[50]

When Lehman Brothers collapsed in September 2008, its commercial paper became worthless. The Reserve Primary Fund, which held much of that paper, lost approximately $785 million, or 1.2 percent of its total value.[51] Because the fund was not insured and the fund managers could not cover such a large loss through their own reserves, the NAV ratio of the fund was forced to vary from the fixed value of 1 to a new value of 0.97. This devaluation phenomenon has been colloquially termed "breaking the buck," and it was virtually unprecedented in MMF history: The only other time it had happened was in 1994, when a much smaller fund had its NAV ratio recalculated to 0.96. When the buck broke for the Reserve Primary Fund, it came as a severe shock to investors, not only because they had lost 3 percent of their holdings but because they had lost it in an investment they had assumed was virtually riskless.[52]

The initial consequence of breaking the buck was a run on the Reserve Primary Fund. This is because the interest in an MMF is a "demand equity,"[53] meaning that investors are entitled to get back their principal, not just the proportion of the fund that their share represents. A loss of 3 percent in value therefore meant that the last 3 percent of investors to get out of the fund would lose out completely, since the other 97 percent would have taken their principal. Typical mutual funds are not demand equities (they are "demand debts"),[54] and so are not vulnerable to runs in the same way.

The run on the Primary Fund forced it to go through the capital it had on hand and then sell off its assets at a discount in order to meet the withdrawal demands of its investors. As investors in other MMFs watched the collapse of the Primary Fund, they

---

50 William Birdthistle, "Breaking Bucks in Money Market Funds" (2010) 5 Wisc L Rev 1155 at 1187.
51 *Ibid* at 1177.
52 *Ibid.*
53 Macey, above note 48 at 51.
54 *Ibid* at 51.

also looked to redeem their investments. In preparation for a run on their funds, managers of the other funds reserved extra cash rather than reinvesting it. Corporate sellers of commercial paper consequently lost access to a large source of capital that they typically used to fund day-to-day operations.[55] It was not the initial Reserve Primary Fund run itself but this effect on corporate borrowing that was of real significance: It affected the economy as a whole, and prohibited growth.

This type of behaviour is especially noteworthy in that starting the run (and thus the systemic crisis) required only a few very risk averse investors to withdraw from the fund before others determined that it was becoming too risky to stay in, and subsequently decided to exit themselves. In this way, like a Depression-era bank run, the fund dynamics after the breaking of the buck resembled a large-scale prisoner's dilemma.

The Canadian Connection: Canadian MMFs exist, and mirror their US counterparts in make-up. The market in Canada is smaller, however: it held approximately $39.4 billion at the end of 2010, a 6.4 percent share of the total mutual fund market, compared with 30 percent in the US.[56] These numbers are trending slowly downwards, from a high in early 2009. This trend may be accounted for by the combination of the current low interest rate environment, and competition from bank accounts offering similar yields. This is not to say that in a different economic environment the MMF marketplace would not see a revival. As demonstrated in the United States, these markets can grow very rapidly.[57]

Recently, the various Canadian securities regulators modified their regulations for MMFs, such that these funds are now required to have greater liquidity available in the event of a severe loss. The precise provision is that 5 percent of assets must be cash or cash-equivalents available within a day, and 15 percent must be cash or cash-equivalents ready within a week.[58] This in-

---

55 Birdthistle, above note 50 at 1180.

56 Investment Funds Institute Monthly Report, online: The Investment Funds Institute of Canada http://statistics.ific.ca/english/Reports/MonthlyStatistics.asp.

57 Macey, above note 48 at 16.

58 *Annex C, Amendments to National Instrument 81-102 Mutual Funds* BCSC Notice (9 February 2012), online: BCSC www.bcsc.bc.ca/uploadedFiles/securitieslaw/policy8/81102_[NI_Amendments_Advance_No-

creased liquidity should have the effect of halting runs on funds. The new rule is clearly aimed at limiting the systemic risk posed by MMFs, and hence is now directly under the federal rather than provincial purview.

3) The New Scope of Federal Systemic Risk Authority

Professor Steven Schwarcz has discussed the challenge of complexity in the financial markets in a way that helps shed light on what "systemic risk" entails today.[59] He describes complexity in the assets that underlie modern structured financial products — for example, variability in property values, interest rates, mortgage terms, and the creditworthiness of individual mortgagees[60] — overlayered with complexity in the design of the structured products themselves — for example, in the design of synthetic products so complex that adequate disclosure to investors was virtually impossible[61] — and exacerbated by complexity in modern financial markets (including indirect holding systems and the widespread use of complex mathematical risk modelling).[62] Schwarcz examines how these multiple complexities can lead to inappropriate lending standards, failures of disclosure, and a lack of transparency and even of comprehensibility.[63] Perhaps the most difficult problem to manage is that they also create a complex system characterized by intricate causal relationships and a "tight coupling" within credit markets, in which events tend to amplify each other and move rapidly into crisis mode.[64] The financial crisis illustrates beyond doubt the myriad interrelated ways in which complexity can generate systemic risk and impair both markets and financial regulation.

In allocating to the federal level of government the responsibility for managing systemic risk, the Reference has given it a daunting task. Certain market players establish the underlying

tice]_(Annex_C).pdf *National Instrument 81-102* BCSC (30 April, 2012), online: BCSC www.bcsc.bc.ca/uploadedFiles/securitieslaw/policy8/81-102[NI]_Apr30-2012.pdf.

59 Steven L Schwarcz, "Regulating Complexity in Financial Markets" (2009) 87 Wash UL Rev 211.

60 *Ibid* at 216–20.

61 *Ibid* at 220–30.

62 *Ibid* at 231–36.

63 *Ibid* at 236–38.

64 *Ibid* at 245–58.

architecture that allows the capital markets to function, and regulating them is necessary in order to regulate systemic risk. Specifically, exchange trading rules would need to be regulated in terms of their potential systemic risk effects. Clearinghouses would also need to be regulated, because the failure of a clearinghouse could bring down the entire domestic securities market and affect international markets as well. Capital adequacy and risk management for registrants, as envisioned in National Instrument 31-101, are also fundamental to mitigating systemic risk in key parts of the Canadian capital markets.

In addition, to manage the systemic risk produced by modern and complex capital markets, the federal government will need at least some degree of oversight and jurisdiction over three further layers of risk, which broadly track the three levels of complexity identified by Schwarcz. First, a federal systemic risk regulator will need jurisdiction over the systemic risks associated with underlying issuer securities under particular conditions. As described above, issuer securities whose risks are correlated, or which operate in concentrated markets, are susceptible to systemic risk. More than this, however, a systemic risk regulator would need to have visibility into and jurisdiction over the degree to which issuers are interconnected through their hedging (and speculative) behaviour in the derivatives markets.

Second, issuers that securitize underlying assets and bundle them into consolidated debt obligations, ABCP, MMFs, or other securities generate and spread systemic risk, particularly when these products make it into the retail market without any of the prudential adequacy rules (or the CDIC insurance) that deposits would attract. As was the case with ABCP, the nature and degree of risk can be hard to identify *ex ante*. In the United States, the new SEC Rule AB enforces asset-level disclosure and tagging of assets precisely in order to improve visibility into such instruments.[65] Other systemic risks are generated by the waterfall agreements and risk modelling assumptions built into such securitized assets, and still more are generated by registrant conduct in the marketing and sale of such products, particularly

---

65 United States Securities and Exchange Commission, "Final Rule: Issuer Review of Assets in Offerings of Asset-Backed Securities," Release No. 33-9150 (28 March 2011) [17 CFR Parts 229 and 230], online: SEC http://www.sec.gov/rules/final/2011/33-9176.pdf.

when those products are developed by the wholesale arms of their own institutions.

Third, as the LTCM and Flash Crash examples suggest, a systemic risk regulator would have to be able to grapple with the role played by hedge funds, HFTs, and similar players in generating and exacerbating systemic risk.

The Bank for International Settlements (BIS) identifies a series of ways to deal with systemic risk.[66] In general, these strategies are aimed at reducing contagion effects, and sometimes at increasing visibility. They include increasing market robustness by raising prudential standards and capital and liquidity buffers; developing an orderly resolution regime for institutional failure; examining financial industry structure for features such as "too big to fail" institutions; developing a more robust market infrastructure, for example by requiring that derivatives be exchange-traded or cleared with a central counterparty; and, finally, supervising financial institutions more fully and more proactively.

The BIS model assumes (except perhaps in its last point) that regulators already have the capacity to see what is going on in the markets. This is not currently the case in Canadian securities regulation, however, and it is certainly not the case at the federal level. A Canadian national systemic risk regulator would have to be in a position to know what emergent problems and linkages characterize the Canadian capital markets landscape and to map out network linkages and other sources of systemic risk.

This requires that the federal government have detailed issuer-related, distribution-related, and market-related data. Assuming that the path forward involves cooperative federalism, this data would presumably come from frontline regulators at the provincial level. Being able to compare data across jurisdictions in terms of both *disclosure* and *methods* is essential to ensure that data from the various provinces is comparable. That is, the federal systemic risk regulator would have to be in a position to oversee what information provincial regulators require in their jurisdictions and what methods they use to gather it. The modern capital markets call for a systemic risk regulator that is in a

---

66 Jaime Caruana, "Systemic Risk: How to Deal with It?" (February 2010), online: Bank for International Settlements www.bis.org/publ/othp08.htm.

position to deal with the complex ways in which fast-moving and complex financial products can generate systemic risk.

We should remember that international regulatory arbitrage contributed significantly to the development of the recent financial crisis. Regulatory arbitrage across Canadian jurisdictions would be extremely detrimental, and to the extent that it contributed to systemic risk it would be the federal government's responsibility. We should also recall that a lack of comparability between particular financial products contributed to that crisis, and that some institutions intentionally avoided making products comparable in order to stymie regulatory oversight.[67]

Of course, systemic risk is not generated only in the securities markets. The federal systemic risk regulator envisioned here would also have to be at least well connected to (if not integrated with) institutions addressing systemic risk posed by banks, insurers, payment systems, and accounting practices. To be clear, what is called for is a broader systemic risk remit than the Office of the Superintendent of Financial Institutions (OSFI) currently exercises.

Canada's financial system is closely interconnected with all of the world's major economies,[68] and exogenously generated systemic risk is therefore also a clear risk for domestic capital and financial markets. Several overlapping forums, both political and technocratic, are seeking to play a role in international financial regulation going forward. Many of the gaps in international systemic risk regulation, including those around hedge funds, exchange-traded derivatives and central counterparties for OTC derivatives, and credit rating agencies, fall partly within the mandate of the International Organization of Securities Commissions (IOSCO).[69] A Canadian systemic risk regulator would therefore have to possess the formal capacity to speak for Canada at IOSCO, to complement positions taken by Canada's Department of Finance, the Governor of the Bank of Canada, and OSFI

---

67 United Kingdom Financial Services Authority, *The Turner Review: A Regulatory Response to the Global Banking Crisis* (London: Financial Services Authority, 2009), online: Financial Services Authority www.fsa. gov.uk at 47.

68 Camelia Minoiu & Javier A Reyes, "A network analysis of global banking: 1978-2009"International Monetary Fund Working Paper WP/11/74 (April 2011), online: IMF www.imf.org/external/pubs/ft/wp/2011/wp1174.pdf.

69 See e.g. Chris Brummer, *Soft Law and the Global Financial System* (New York: Cambridge University Press, 2012) at 213–27.

in forums such as the Financial Stability Board (FSB), the BIS, and the G-20.[70]

If Canada can develop a comprehensive federal-level systemic risk regulator that can incorporate information from the local level in a particularly effective way, it may be able to take a leadership role in the ongoing international conversation about systemic risk. Section C below, which addresses the possibilities inherent in the federal government's responsibility for data collection, describes one means of developing such a regulator within the scope of federal power under the Reference.

C. Data Collection and the Systemic Risk Clearinghouse

This essay argues that "data collection," as the term is used in the Reference, can in fact be a substantial regulatory tool. We draw on the notion of the "regulatory clearinghouse," developed by new governance and experimentalist scholars in law and organizational theory, to animate one model of regulation that uses data collection as a central mechanism.

What is a clearinghouse? The *Canadian Oxford Dictionary* defines it as follows:

> **1.** a bankers' establishment where cheques and bills from member banks are exchanged, so that only the balances need be paid in cash.
>
> **2.** an agency for collecting and distributing information, materials, etc.[71]

The institution of the financial clearinghouse is well understood by anyone with an interest in banking or securities regulation. The idea of an "information clearinghouse," which is our focus here, may be more familiar in academic or scientific circles. Our claim is that there are advantages to introducing the second, broader notion of the clearinghouse into securities regulation as a means of responding to the Reference.

---

70 On the political mandate of the G-20, see David T Zaring, "International Institutional Performance in Crisis" (2010) 10 Chicago J Int'l L 447.

71 *The Canadian Oxford Dictionary*, 2d ed, *sub verbo* "clearing house". The COD considers "clearing house" to be two words, not one, but this essay follows the academics in presenting it as one word.

Scientists and policy researchers deploy information clearing-houses as part of an evidence-based policy strategy. Examples include the What Works Clearinghouse (WWC) in the United States, which, as the name suggests, tries to look at what works in education policy.[72] Evidence-based policy development proceeds by a series of steps: determining the criteria for evaluating the effectiveness of a particular policy; establishing a framework for that evaluation; undertaking content analysis — that is, looking at what data is generated — and doing comparative studies; and, finally, building in constant revision to the analytical process based on learning generated through the evidence-based process itself. On this model, the clearinghouse is a central body that aggregates data. In its simplest incarnation, it is not much more than a repository for data, which can then be used by others. Online clearinghouses are many, and many of them limit themselves to the circumscribed, but still useful, function of putting as much information as possible about a particular topic in one place, to reduce search time costs for dispersed potential users of that information.

There is another, more ambitious version of the information clearinghouse. It is still underpinned by and fundamentally concerned with data collection, the second major function that the Reference allocates to the federal level of government. We argue that this more ambitious version of the information clearinghouse offers a promising way forward for securities regulation in the wake of the Reference. Drawing on some scholarly literature in the "experimentalist" or "new governance" vein, we can imagine a clearinghouse with more robust information-forcing and accountability powers.

Over the last two decades or so, regulatory practice and scholarly work in regulation studies have undergone something of a conceptual revolution. Regulation is a much more complex thing than it was thirty years ago. Moreover, in North America, Europe, Australia, and the UK, old-fashioned, bureaucratic "com-

---

72 But see Jere Confrey, "Comparing and Contrasting the National Research Council Report *On Evaluating Curricular Effectiveness* with the What Works Clearinghouse Approach" (2006) 28 Educational Evaluation and Policy Analysis 195 (critiquing the WWC's empirical methodology).

mand-and-control" regulation has given way to what has come to be known as "flexible regulation."[73]

As the name suggests, "flexible regulation" seeks to develop more flexible, context-sensitive, nuanced regulatory strategies across a variety of subject matter areas. Forms of flexible regulation have been applied in areas as diverse as international labor standards,[74] workplace safety and domestic labor law,[75] EU governance,[76] environmental regulation,[77] and securities and

---

73 See e.g. Ian Ayres & John Braithwaite, *Responsive Regulation: Transcending the Deregulation Debate* (Oxford: Oxford University Press, 1992); Eric Orts, "Reflexive Environmental Law" (1995) 89 Nw UL Rev 1227; Julia Black, *Rules and Regulators* (Oxford: Oxford University Press, 1997); Michael C Dorf & Charles F Sabel, "A Constitution of Democratic Experimentalism" (1998) 98 Colum L Rev 267; Neil Gunningham, Peter Grabosky, & Darren Sinclair, *Smart Regulation: Designing Environmental Policy* (Oxford: Oxford University Press, 1998) [Gunningham]; Malcolm K Sparrow, *The Regulatory Craft: Controlling Risks, Solving Problems, and Managing Compliance* (Washington, DC: Brookings Institution, 2000); Christine Parker, *The Open Corporation: Effective Self-Regulation and Democracy* (New York: Cambridge University Press, 2002); Cary Coglianese & David Lazer, "Management-Based Regulation: Prescribing Private Management to Achieve Public Goals" (2003) 37 Law & Soc'y Rev 691; Orly Lobel, "The Renew Deal: The Fall of Regulation and the Rise of Governance in Contemporary Legal Thought" (2004) 89 Minn L Rev 342; Gráinne de Búrca & Joanne Scott, eds, *Law and New Governance in the EU and US* (Oxford: Hart, 2006).
74 Lucio Baccaro & Valentina Mele, "Pathology of Path-Dependency? The ILO and the Challenge of 'New Governance'" (5 October 2010) paper prepared for MIT Institute for Work and Employment Research Seminar, online: MIT Sloan http://mitsloan.mit.edu/iwer/pdf/Lucio_Baccaro-IWER_paper_20101005.pdf.
75 Cynthia Estlund, *Regoverning the Workplace: From Self-Regulation to Co-Regulation* (New Haven: Yale University Press, 2010); Orly Lobel, "Interlocking Regulatory and Industrial Relations" (2005) 57 Admin L Rev 1071.
76 David M Trubek, & Louise G Trubek, "New Governance and Legal Regulation: Complementary, Rivalry, or Transformation?" (2007) 13 Colum J Eur L 539; Gráinne de Búrca & Neil Walker, "Law and Transnational Civil Society: Upsetting the Agenda?" (2003) 9 Eur LJ 387; Jonathan Zeitlin, "The Open Method of Coordination in Action: Theoretical Promise, Empirical Realities, Reform Strategy" in Jonathan Zeitlin, Philippe Pochet, & Lars Magnusson, eds, *Open Method of Coordination in Action: The European Employment and Social Inclusion Strategies* (Brussels: Presses Interuniversitaires Européennes-Peter Lang, 2005).
77 Orts, above note 73.

financial regulation.[78] While there are a number of versions of flexible regulation,[79] all share the conviction that old-style, one-size-fits-all prescriptive regulation is a starkly limited tool. In its place, proponents of flexible regulation advocate a restructured and more collaborative relationship between the state and regulated entities, one that incorporates private and non-state parties' experience and expertise.[80]

Because flexible regulation is premised on a decentralized, information-based, flexible and collaborative approach, scholars have had to consider what role a central state regulator (or a regional one, or in some cases a transnational body) still can and ought to play.[81] Among the various scholarly perspectives, the one characterized by the deepest commitment to incrementalism and pragmatism, and which has most fully imagined what a regulator should look like in order to permit this, is the "experimentalist" perspective. Its chief proponents are Charles Sabel at Columbia Law School and his coauthors, including Michael Dorf, Joshua Cohen, and William Simon. Many other versions of flexible regulation have a great deal to recommend them in various contexts, and several explicitly agree on the need for a centralized data management regulatory clearinghouse.[82] Experimentalism is

---

78 Black, above note 73; Cristie Ford, "Toward a New Model for Securities Law Enforcement" (2005) 57 Admin L Rev 757; Cristie Ford, "New Governance, Compliance, and Principles-Based Securities Regulation" (2008) 45 Am Bus LJ 1 [Ford 2008]; Robert F Weber, "New Governance, Financial Regulation, and Challenges to Legitimacy: The Example of the Internal Models Approach to Capital Adequacy Regulation" (2010) 62 Admin L Rev 783.

79 See e.g. Mary Condon, "The Walter S. Owen Lecture: Canadian Securities Regulation and the Global Financial Crisis" (2009–2010) 42 UBC L Rev 473; Sharon Gilad, "It Runs in the Family: Meta-Regulation and Its Siblings" (2010) 4 Regulation & Governance 485.

80 Parker, above note 73; Gunningham, above note 73; Peter Drahos, "Intellectual Property and Pharmaceutical Markets: a Nodal Governance Approach" (2004) 77 Temp L Rev 401.

81 See e.g. Drahos, *ibid*; Gregory Shaffer & Mark Pollack, *Transatlantic Governance in the Global Economy* (Lanham, MD: Rowman & Littlefield, 2001); Adrienne Héritier & Dirk Lehmkuhl, "Introduction: The Shadow of Hierarchy and New Modes of Governance" 28 J Pub Pol 1.

82 See also e.g. Bradley C Karkkainen, "Collaborative Ecosystem Governance: Scale, Complexity, and Dynamism" (2002) 21 Va Envtl LJ 189 (advocating that different levels of government "pool" their information in order to "build a richer collective understanding . . . of [a] problem" at 222–25); Susan P Sturm, "New Governance and the Architecture of

especially useful here, however, because it speaks to the specific task of trying to imagine what the federal level of government in Canada could do with authority over data collection.

The experimentalist clearinghouse is a centralized regulatory institution charged with aggregating multiple decentralized regulatory interactions into a systematic regulatory structure. Sabel and his colleagues have written about experimentalist structures in a variety of contexts, ranging from American constitutional and administrative law through drug treatment courts, EU governance, and transnational governance regimes.[83] In brief, the clearinghouse regulator operates differently from a traditional regulator in that it sets broad goals and regulatory requirements, but it allows more local, context-specific experiments to determine the best means by which to meet those goals. The clearinghouse regulator has "information-forcing" powers, meaning the capacity to require that local units generate and produce comprehensive data and to require that that information be produced in consistent and comparable forms so that it can be usefully aggregated. Using substantive principles-based, outcome-oriented, or similar analytical methods, it assesses local units' success in meeting centrally established regulatory expectations. Although the central clearinghouse is operating at a somewhat greater remove from day-to-day operations, this does not mean that it needs fewer resources. On the contrary, thorough and incisive analysis of meta-level information requires more, not less, regulatory capacity than straightforward command-and-control regulation would.[84]

Learning, Mobilization, and Accountability: Lessons from Gender Equity Regimes" in de Búrca & Scott, above note 73; Sparrow, above note 73 (expressing a desire for agencies to "organize the lessons they learn and to make the accumulated knowledge readily available" at 167–68).

83   See primarily Dorf & Sabel, above note 73; Michael C Dorf & Charles F. Sabel, "Drug Treatment Courts and Emergent Experimentalist Government" (2000) 53 Vand L Rev 831; Charles F Sabel & Jonathan Zeitlin, "Learning from Difference: The New Architecture of Experimentalist Governance in the EU" (2008) 14 Eur LJ 271; Charles F Sabel and William H Simon, "Minimalism and Experimentalism in the Administrative State" (2011) 100 Geo LJ 53.

84   Julia Black, Martyn Hopper & Christa Band, "Making a Success of Principles-Based Regulation" (2007) 1 Law & Fin Markets Rev 191; Cristie Ford, "Principles-Based Securities Regulation in the Wake of the Global Financial Crisis" (2010) 55 McGill LJ 257 at text accompanying note 119 [Ford 2010].

Based on its analysis of the information being generated, the clearinghouse monitors local units' compliance with centrally defined goals, primarily through benchmarking and comparative analysis. Particular local units' successes in meeting regulatory goals become "benchmarks." The central clearinghouse has the capacity to challenge local units' strategies, outcomes, or overall performance in meeting regulatory goals by reference to other local units' performance benchmarks. Like Brandeisian "multiple laboratories for democracy,"[85] the clearinghouse structure permits parallel learning. It also builds in some flexibility for local units to devise their own context-appropriate mechanisms for addressing regulatory problems, so long as they demonstrably meet the overall standards set by the central clearinghouse regulator.

The spectre of the "race to the bottom" can be a risk of competitive federalist models. This argument is not infrequently made with regard to state-level corporate law in the United States.[86] Regulatory competition and arbitrage also very likely played a role in the run-up to the financial crisis, because global financial institutions were in a position to play London and New York against each other.[87] Under the experimentalist model, such a race to the bottom is avoided through the presence of a central standard-setting clearinghouse regulator — something not present either in US corporate law or in international financial regulation pre-crisis. The clearinghouse regulator can also generate incentive structures to reward leaders (for example, with more autonomy) and punish laggards (for example, with closer oversight).

A subtler but still pernicious problem is the possibility of a "race to the middle," a concern expressed by Professor Andrew Green in his contribution to this volume.[88] In this case, the vari-

---

85 *New State Ice Co v Liebmann*, 285 US 262 (1932), Brandeis J, dissenting ("It is one of the happy incidents of the federal system that a single courageous State may, if its citizens choose, serve as a laboratory; and try novel social and economic experiments without risk to the rest of the country" at 311).

86 Most famously, see William L Cary, "Federalism and Corporate Law: Reflections upon Delaware" (1974) 83 Yale LJ 663.

87 See e.g. Shaun French, Andrew Leyshon & Nigel Thrift, "A Very Geographical Crisis: The Making and Breaking of the 2007–2008 Financial Crisis" (2009) 2 Cambridge J Regions Econ Soc 287.

88 Andrew Green, "Effectiveness, Accountability and Bias: Some Concerns about a Quasi-National Securities Regulator," in this volume.

ous local actors lack any incentive to become practice leaders, and standard practice across local units coalesces at a mimetic, complacent, suboptimal level.[89] Experimentalism's prescription for this problem is for the clearinghouse regulator to set its comparative benchmarks based on *best practices* to emerge from local units, not just industry standards. In their original article on the subject, Dorf and Sabel describe this as "rolling best practices rulemaking."[90]

Among the perceived advantages of experimentalism is the idea that experimentalism makes sense as a commitment to a deeply pragmatic, evidence-based, learning-by-doing mechanism. The central clearinghouse is responsible for setting broad goals within the scope of its mandate. The precise details of how to meet those goals, however, are determined based on experience at the more local level. Moreover, means and ends are interrelated: the federal government's precise understanding of the nature and origins of systemic risk will evolve through actual experience in trying to manage it and this, in turn, may generate revised expressions of the original goal. This is only a partial answer to the problems of complexity and uncertainty that bedevil financial markets regulation in general and systemic risk regulation in particular. The question we should be asking ourselves is not whether an evidence-based, learning-by-doing mechanism will be flawless under such challenging conditions, but whether there are reasons to think that relative to other real-life options, they might stand a better chance of being effective under those conditions.

In the context of Canadian securities regulation and the federal/provincial division of powers in the wake of the Reference,

---

89 On the tendency of institutions to imitate each other, see Paul J DiMaggio & Walter W Powell, "The Iron Cage Revisited: Institutional Isomorphism and Collective Rationality in Organizational Fields" in Walter W Powell & Paul J DiMaggio, eds, *The New Institutionalism in Organizational Analysis* (Chicago: University of Chicago Press, 1991).

90 Dorf & Sabel, above note 73 at 350–54; on rolling best practices rulemaking in the context of principles-based securities regulation in Canada, see Ford 2008, above note 78 at pages 41–45; Cristie Ford, "Principles-Based Securities Regulation" (2009) Research Study prepared for Expert Panel on Securities Regulation (2009), online: Expert Panel on Securities Regulation www.expertpanel.ca/documents/research-studies/Principles%20Based%20Securities%20Regulation%20-%20Ford.English.pdf at 21–22.

a federal regulatory clearinghouse along experimentalist lines could look something like the following:

- The federal government establishes a clearinghouse regulator. The Reference tells us that "[l]egislation aimed at imposing minimum *standards* applicable throughout the country and preserving the stability and integrity of Canada's financial markets might well relate to trade as a whole."[91] Thus empowered, the clearinghouse articulates broad goals and sets minimum standards around systemic risk (including systemic risk with international origins or implications) and data collection. Whether it does so in the language of principles, outcomes, or processes matters less than that it does so in language cast at a high enough level of generality that the goals can cover the full range of Canada's experience with systemic risk. Principles-based or outcome-oriented measures are the likeliest candidates here.[92]

- Experimentalism's "local units" here are primarily provincial and territorial *regulators*, not issuers or registrants. Provincial and territorial regulators are responsible for generating comprehensive, fine-grained, top-quality data from issuers, registrants, exchanges, clearinghouses, and others. The federal government's responsibility for data collection implies influence over, and perhaps even oversight of, national transaction reporting infrastructure such as exchanges, clearinghouses, trade repositories, data consolidators and processors, and trade surveillance.[93] These are required to produce data in aggregable form to the federal systemic risk regulator. Beyond question, as the Canadian Securities Transition Office's pre-Reference plan also recognized, maintaining local

91 *Securities Reference*, above note 1 at para 114.
92 One of the authors' own understandings of principles-based regulation has been most recently described at Ford 2010, above note 84 at 262–78.
93 Under current Canadian law, provincial securities regulators delegate some statutory authority to the self-regulating registrant bodies, IIROC and the MFDA, as well as to the clearinghouse, CDS, the exchanges (collectively owned by the TMX Group), and so on. With respect to SROs such as IIROC, the important point here is that data on any systemic risk posed by its membership makes its way up to the federal clearinghouse regulator. There may be reason to consider establishing direct federal-to-SRO (and -exchange, -clearinghouse, etc.) information channels around systemic risk-related issues, distinct from the delegated statutory authority that flows from provincial authorities to SROs.

regulatory offices has clear benefits. A local regulatory presence improves the chances of effectively pulling local, context-sensitive knowledge into the central clearinghouse. It also enhances access and communication channels for local securities market participants, improves compliance and enforcement intelligence, and provides a formal, institutional voice for distinct provincial and local securities constituencies. Indeed, in keeping with the spirit of cooperative federalism described in the Reference, it serves many of the purposes that the Supreme Court's *Reference re Secession of Quebec* held the constitutional principle of federalism to serve within Canadian confederation as a whole.[94] As we know, the provinces and territories are not capable of addressing systemic risk challenges or of developing a comprehensive data collection function on their own. Combining provincial or territorial frontline securities regulators with a national clearinghouse permits a degree of local or regional diversity without compromising centralized overall systemic risk management.

- The federal government's responsibility for data collection, combined with the provinces' and territories' continued responsibility as frontline securities regulators, means that the federal government must have the ability to mandate extensive disclosure requirements from provincial and territorial securities regulators. It must require that provinces and territories push fine-grained, high-quality information upward, in forms capable of being aggregated, on all matters that concern systemic risk.[95] The federal government can set clear requirements around the generation and form of that information, as is necessary to allow the federal government to manage systemic risk. In contrast to the high-level standards established around systemic risk in general, some requirements around data collection should be more detailed and process-based. Good regulatory design always requires a mix of more detailed and more principles-based provisions. On some topics, the advantages that detailed, prescriptive rules provide in terms of certainty and limiting discretion will outweigh the advantages that more principles-based drafting

---

94 *Reference re Secession of Quebec*, [1998] 2 SCR 217 at paras 43 and 55–60.

95 See Section B(2), above in this chapter.

offers in terms of flexibility and context-sensitivity. A federal-level legislator concerned with ensuring that the information flowing from provincial/territorial to federal level is highly comparable will want to establish detailed, process-based requirements around the forms of information being generated and produced at the provincial and territorial level.

• The federal systemic risk regulator may also want to consider mandating particular operational processes for provinces and territories, if those processes are likely to produce better quality data. For example, experimentalist scholars argue that broad stakeholder participation improves the quality of information produced by ensuring that a broader and more contextually-grounded range of perspectives go into the deliberative process. On this basis, the federal systemic risk regulator could decide that provinces should establish consumer or investor panels, like Ontario's or the FSA's, to ensure the explicit incorporation of a fuller range of stakeholder voices into the data-generating architecture at the provincial and territorial level.[96]

• The clearinghouse regulator monitors the provinces' and territories' comparative successes and challenges in meeting federally defined broad goals on matters bearing on systemic risk. It benchmarks the provinces' and territories' accomplishments in accordance with evidence-based policy development principles. It determines criteria for evaluating effectiveness, establishes a framework for that evaluation, undertakes content analysis, and engages in comparative analysis. This kind of process is not unknown to the federal government: a version of evidence-based policymaking is embedded in the Cabinet Directive on Streamlining Regulation, which sets out the standards that apply whenever the federal government embarks on regulation-making.[97]

---

96 The Hon Tom Hockin's Expert Panel on Securities Regulation recommended that such panels be established. Expert Panel on Securities Regulation, *Final Report and Recommendations* (2009), online: Expert Panel on Securities Regulation www.expertpanel.ca/eng/documents/Expert_Panel_Final_Report_And_Recommendations.pdf at 36-37.

97 Government of Canada, *Cabinet Directive on Streamlining Regulation* (2007), online: Treasury Board of Canada Secretariat www.tbs-sct.gc.ca/ri-qr/directive/directive-eng.pdf.

- The federal clearinghouse needs both the technical (data-analysis) and legal capacity to engage in meaningful comparative benchmarking. This requires sophisticated powers of data analysis. The clearinghouse would expect provinces to learn "in parallel," to consider the utility of innovations developed in other provinces, and to justify their own decisions in reasons-based ways. It may choose to develop "rolling best practices rules" (which are not inconsistent with the ability to set "minimum" standards, in the Reference's terms).[98] It may decide to establish any number of positive and negative incentives for provincial and territorial regulators. The clearinghouse must also be able to analyze data also across time, for example to develop an historical context for current levels of leverage or degrees of interconnectedness. Such longitudinal information could help to track and respond to behavioural cascades, such as the cascade toward excessive leverage that characterized investment banking in the United States in the run-up to the financial crisis.

- In the context of Canadian federalism, there would have to be a mechanism for resolving disputes between the federal and provincial/territorial levels of government around systemic risk management. Accountability mechanisms, too, would have to be developed. As Andrew Green has noted, a problem with multijurisdictional regulatory structures is that it may leave no jurisdiction accountable.[99] Presumably, if the federal government intends to assert that systemic risk and therefore its own jurisdiction is broad in scope, then it must also be accountable for failures within that scope. Where the political will to hold regulators accountable does not exist — another risk that Professor Green identifies — then accountability will be compromised, in this model and inevitably in every other model too.

- The clearinghouse regulator would be in a position to help coordinate action between provinces and territories in a way that the non-binding forum of the Canadian Securities Administrators cannot. The clearinghouse would be able to require provinces to coordinate and to meet performance standards set by other provinces, in the interest of managing

---

98 Ford 2008, above note 78 at 41–45.
99 See Green, above note 88.

systemic risk. Its capacity for data analysis allows it to focus on evidence-based and reasons-based justifications for taking particular steps to manage systemic risk.

• Finally, in keeping with an evidence-based, learning-by-doing approach and with the dynamic nature of securities market regulation, the clearinghouse would have to build in the capacity for constant revision to its own analytical processes, based on learning generated through its own experience and that of the provinces and territories. A national clearinghouse of Canadian capital markets data would make possible sophisticated data mining and industry- and product-specific predictive analytics, which ought then to be ploughed back into the standard-setting and oversight processes themselves.

Professor Jeffrey MacIntosh argues in this volume that in advocating a federal securities clearinghouse, we misconstrue the meaning of the Reference.[100] In our view, an energetic reading of the federal powers is needed to address the very real and pervasive problem of systemic risk. While it is certainly possible to read the Reference in a way that prizes cooperative federalism over actual policy effectiveness,[101] this subject matter is too important not to try to read it in a way that creates a workable regime for protecting Canadian investors and the Canadian public, and that permits each level of government to actually discharge the responsibilities it has been given.

What we propose is a form of cooperative federalism that takes seriously the responsibility the Supreme Court has allocated to the federal government. The purpose of the examples in Part B above is to demonstrate that systemic risk is inextricable from, and flows from, the day to day operations of the securities markets. If the federal government is to discharge the responsibilities the Court allocated to it, it must have some authority over those aspects of the securities markets that constitute that risk. By analogy, an engineer who is responsible for the safety and soundness of a new building must have some authority to direct the quality and use of the materials that comprise the building. This is particularly true where none of the building's subcontractors

---

100 Jeffrey G MacIntosh, "A National Securities Commission? The Headless Horseman Rides Again," in this volume.

101 We share Professor Iacobucci's concerns in this regard. See Iacobucci, above note 8.

is responsible for safety and soundness, where the subcontractors collectively do not have the capacity to ensure the building's
safety and soundness, and indeed where each subcontractor may
stand to gain by reducing his or her own safety standards relative to others'.[102]

Contrary to Professor MacIntosh's assessment, what we propose is not a "command-and-control" regime; quite the opposite.[103]
Nor does the establishment of a federal systemic risk clearinghouse make the provinces into federal "agents", any more than
a European Union harmonization directive makes European
member states "subjects" or "operatives" of the EU.[104] A national securities clearinghouse designed to respond to this unique
jurisdictional environment will not open the floodgates, or engen-
der federal incursions into corporate law, contract law, or health
law. What is contemplated here is a model of federal-provincial
cooperation that may be unprecedented in Canada, but that flows
logically from the unavoidable fact that regulating systemic risk
cannot be excised from regulating mundane securities market
operations. It would be a grave mistake to fetishize existing
understandings of cooperative federalism, if the cost is that the
federal government is not actually capable of managing systemic
risk.

In addition to charting a path forward by which the federal
government will be able to take care of its responsibilities for
systemic risk and data collection, the clearinghouse model has
a few potential advantages relative even to a conventional national securities regulator. First, this is an evidence-based model
that may be especially well suited to securities regulation. Pragmatic, comparative learning-by-doing is a reasonable response
to the uncertainty generated by complexity and volatility in the
financial markets. Second, this model may help provincial and
territorial regulators by establishing a mechanism for system-
atically learning from their own experiences and from those of
their peer regulators. Finally, this is not a duplicative fourteenth
securities regulator. It is a regulator with a different mandate,
skill set, and perspective, designed around the responsibilities
for collecting data and managing systemic risk that the Supreme
Court of Canada found the federal government to possess.

---

102 See Green, above note 88.
103 See sources, above note 73.
104 See sources, above note 76.

D. Conclusion

Following on the Reference, the Supreme Court of Canada envisioned a negotiated, cooperative federal arrangement.[105] In proceeding in this direction, the federal government should begin from a position of confidence about what its powers over systemic risk and data collection permit. We have sought to demonstrate that powers over systemic risk and data collection are not in fact inconsequential. These issues are too important to be regulated in a piecemeal fashion. Both the likelihood and the magnitude of systemic risk events are far greater today than they were in at the time of the Kimber Commission in 1965, or even at the time of the Wise Persons' Committee in 2003.

While we may, in the abstract, applaud the Supreme Court's reaffirmation of cooperative federalist principles, it is somewhat harder to do so in this context, when we consider the enormous danger that systemic risk presents for Canadian investors, taxpayers, and capital markets. In this essay we have tried to envision a federal systemic risk and data collection regulator that will still have the information base and capacity to manage these serious risks. Moreover, there may be a silver lining to the Court's decision, in that it opens the door to the potential creation of an entirely new kind of federal regulator — one that may, through its focus on data collection, actually be in a particularly promising position to regulate a phenomenon as dispersed and dynamic as the securities markets.

Our claim in this essay is that a federal systemic risk clearinghouse is consistent with the Reference, and that it can be built out in an ambitious way without creating a fourteenth regulator. Although developed in other regulatory contexts, the clearinghouse concept may actually be particularly appropriate for managing systemic risk arising from the securities markets. Unlike other parts of administrative law, in which the government takes a more engaged, merit-based position *vis-à-vis* industry actors,

---

105 *Securities Reference*, above note 1 at para 132 ("It is not for the Court to suggest to the governments of Canada and the provinces the way forward by, in effect, conferring in advance an opinion on the constitutionality on this or that alternative scheme. Yet we may appropriately note the growing practice of resolving the complex governance problems that arise in federations, not by the bare logic of either/or, but by seeking cooperative solutions that meet the needs of the country as a whole as well as its constituent parts").

securities regulation has always taken a bottom-up, de-centred, and information-forcing (i.e., disclosure-oriented) approach. The complexity, global interconnectedness, and speed of innovation that characterize modern financial markets also demand a regulator that is evidence-based, well-informed, well-resourced, and nimble. The federal government would never have opted for this kind of structure at first instance. The fact that the *Reference* gives it so few choices, however, also opens up new opportunities for creative thinking. The experimentalist securities regulation clearinghouse, based on data-collection powers and a mandate for managing systemic risk, may be a promising path forward.

CHAPTER 10

Effectiveness, Accountability, and Bias: Some Concerns about a Quasi-National Securities Regulator

Andrew Green

A. Introduction

Governance institutions and instrument choice are at the core of the problem of risk regulation, including how to address the risks arising from securities markets. The Supreme Court of Canada took the federal government's national securities regulator proposal off the table in its recent Reference decision.[1] The federal government had sought to establish a single national regulator, but the Supreme Court pointed toward a more cooperative approach, with some indication of areas that could be under national regulation such as information collection and the regulation of systemic risk. In this volume, papers by Cristie Ford and Hardeep Gill and by Janis Sarra offer an optimistic view of how such a partial role for a national regulator may actually be beneficial for addressing risk from the securities market.[2] However, while these authors raise excellent points about how this combination of federal and provincial regulation could operate effectively, the quasi-national regulatory system they propose raises concerns about how well systemic risk will actually be regulated and whether this regulatory model can overcome the difficulties of the current system.

---

1 *Reference Re Securities Act*, 2011 SCC 66.
2 See Chapters 8 and 9.

In *Reference Re Securities Act*, the Supreme Court noted "the growing practice of resolving the complex governance problems that arise in federations, not by the bare logic of either/or, but by seeking cooperative solutions that meet the needs of the country as a whole as well as its constituent parts."[3] Yet despite a long-standing discussion about the value of a national regulator, only partial cooperation has been achieved through the "passport" system. The possible reasons for this lack of a more complete cooperative agreement point to concerns with a quasi-national regulatory model.

The first explanation for the failure to reach a more complete agreement rests on the assumption that both federal and provincial governments want the same thing — to increase public welfare.[4] The difficulty arises because each provincial government focuses on the welfare of the residents of its own province, which creates the potential for a province to maximize its citizens' welfare by externalizing the costs of its decisions on individuals in other provinces or countries. For example, preventing systemic risk is in the nature of a public good: all residents of Canada would benefit from regulatory measures taken by a province that reduce such risk. However, steps taken to reduce systemic risk can be costly (either directly or indirectly through reduced economic growth) and a province may wish to delay or reduce regulation, thereby obtaining gains for which it faces only a portion of the costs.

The result is a classic Prisoner's Dilemma-type problem in which all provinces would likely be better off if every province took steps to address such risks, but each has incentive not to regulate but instead to free-ride on the actions of others. One solution to such a problem is cooperation among the actors. While they may wish to cooperate, however, they may also have different views of the optimal form of cooperation, as each seeks a cooperative agreement that benefits individuals or industries within its own jurisdiction (such as small issuers as opposed to large issuers). The lack of agreement on the form of coordination

---

3   Above note 1 at para 132.

4   For a fuller discussion of these two explanations, see Anita I Anand & Andrew J Green, "Why Is This Taking So Long? The Move towards a National Securities Regulator" (2010) 60 UTLJ 663 [Anand & Green (2010)]; Anita I Anand & Andrew J Green, "Side-Payments, Opt-Ins and Power: Creating a National Securities Regulator in Canada" (2011) 51:1 Can Bus LJ 1[Anand & Green (2011)].

may hinder cooperation.[5] The alternative of federal regulation imposing a coordinating solution was taken off the table, for the most part, by the Reference decision.

The second explanation arises not because provincial or federal regulators cannot agree on public-interested solutions but because these regulators are not seeking public-interested solutions to begin with. Provincial opposition to or support for a national regulator, on this view, stems from a range of parties seeking to further their own interests. These parties may include legislators, regulators (such as provincial securities commissions), professional bodies or issuers and industry.[6] For example, regulators may seek to augment both their employment prospects and their power (through the number and size of firms within their jurisdiction or the volume of trading) by opposing or supporting particular regulatory models. Federal legislators or potential regulatory officials may similarly support a national regulator in order to enhance political support or in pursuit of other self-interested benefits. Such a self-interested explanation for the lack of support for a national regulator raises concerns both about how to bring about a cooperative solution and about the form of any such solution.

Both of these explanations — the welfare story and the self-interest story — raise issues about the design of institutional structures attempting to regulate the securities market in Canada, as well as about the choice of instruments through which to undertake such regulation. These concerns relate to the effectiveness and accountability of Ford and Gill's proposal for a national systemic risk clearinghouse; they also underlie questions of bias and lack of independence with respect to Sarra's proposal for a Canadian Financial Services Tribunal.

B. Effectiveness and a Clearinghouse Model

Ford and Gill argue that regulating systemic risk cannot be done at "some metaphysical distance from the day-to-day operations of the securities market"; these operations, they write, are "constitutive of systemic risk."[7] For Ford and Gill, the result of the

---

5   Anand & Green (2010), above note 4.
6   Anand & Green (2011), above note 4.
7   Chapter 9.

Supreme Court Reference is that the federal government will be able to create a "clearinghouse" regulatory body, whose powers would be based on the federal government's jurisdiction, as laid out by the Court, to regulate systemic risk and collect information. The federal government will be able to gather information on how different provincial bodies are dealing with risks and create benchmarks that will lead to more effective regulation of risk.

Ford and Gill are correct that national data collection will aid in controlling systemic risk. As mentioned above, controlling systemic risk is a public good. Provincial regulators will underinvest in information, as they bear the costs of information gathering and analysis while other provinces (and countries) reap at least some of the benefits. Federal collection and dissemination of information will help overcome this problem and could aid in building regulatory structures to reduce systemic risk.

However, information gathering and dissemination seems unlikely to be sufficient. Even under the welfare story of non-cooperation, there remain positive externalities that arise when any province reduces risk in the securities markets; provinces will underinvest not only in information but in control since, as noted, regulatory measures are costly and no province faces the entire cost of not taking action (or, conversely, reaps the entire benefit of acting) to reduce systemic and other types of risks that may spill across borders. Similarly, on the self-interest story, there will continue to be political pressure for regulatory measures that benefit local interest groups. The increased information does not necessarily spur sufficient action, though it may increase pressure for regulatory action to the extent that it makes the costs of non-regulation salient to parties who are harmed.

Information, therefore, may not be sufficient to induce optimal regulation in a decentralized system. As a result, Ford and Gill call for benchmarking — for the central authority to choose certain provinces' policies or outcomes as measures against which to compare other provinces' progress. However, even if information provision creates some pressure toward comparison across provinces, the movement may not necessarily be in optimal directions; there is of course the danger of a "race to the bottom" in which regulators attempt to attract economic activity or political support by demonstrably lowering their regulatory bars relative to other jurisdictions.

While there may be some political support for controls (that is, being clearly at the bottom of the distribution in terms of regulatory standards would be politically disadvantageous), the result may be not a race to the top but a race to the middle. Provinces may be unwilling to be either a clear leader or a laggard, but content to satisfy any appetite for regulatory measures by ensuring that their controls are neither the strictest nor the weakest. There is some evidence of such a "race to the middle" in how provinces set minimum wage levels.[8]

The solution, for Ford and Gill, is for the central authority to choose "best practices" for meeting centrally determined goals as the source of the benchmarks. Such benchmarks have the potential to aid provinces that seek to improve their policies. Further, as Ford and Gill argue, if the central regulator updates these benchmarks on a "rolling" basis, it will have some grounds for rulemaking based on experience. There is, of course, the prior difficulty of knowing what the overall goals should be in the context of systemic risks that are characterized by "complexity and opacity."[9] In such a context, it is difficult to know what the goal should be or what counts as "effective," although, the adaptability and learning that Ford and Gill advocate may aid in identifying and adjusting to new threats over time.

Further, such benchmarking works only for those areas over which the central authority has clear jurisdiction to make rules — such as, following the Supreme Court's decision, systemic risk. For areas over which the federal government does not have jurisdiction (any risk regulation creating externalities other than systemic risk), the benchmarks may simply provide evidence for the provincial regulators that they are within the desired middle range. To improve regulation in these areas, the federal government must either seek cooperative agreements or attempt to expand its regulatory authority, using its powers over systemic risk as a Trojan Horse.

---

8 David Green & Kathryn Harrison, "Races to the Bottom Versus Races to the Middle: Minimum Wage Setting in Canada" in Kathryn Harrison, ed, *Racing to the Bottom? Provincial Interdependence in the Canadian Federation* (Vancouver: University of British Columbia Press, 2006) 193.

9 Chapter 9, Section B(2)(a).

C. Accountability in a Clearinghouse Model

A further difficulty with the clearinghouse model, as an attempt to coordinate provincial and federal regulation of risks, is that it may weaken accountability, in that the public may have a reduced ability to hold any particular government to account in the event that harmful risks do materialize. First, there is a concern about the well-known collective action problem, as the harms are spread across a diffuse public. It is difficult enough, at times, for the public to recognize that a harm has occurred, or at least it is often too costly for individual members of the public to act given the relatively small individual harms. Adding on a dual regulatory structure may make it very difficult to hold either level of government to account. As in the area of the environment in Canada (where jurisdiction is split across both levels of government), the provincial and federal governments may "pass the buck," each shifting blame to the other level at times of crisis. Moreover, again as with environmental regulation, it may be that when the salience of financial risk is low for the public, neither level of government will regulate, each hoping that the other level will bear the political and direct costs of regulation.[10]

Further, having more regulatory agencies is not necessarily preferable. Concentrated interests such as large issuers or even particular financial professional groups already have more power than the public in terms of resources. When there are more regulatory bodies to access, there are more opportunities for investors and the public to influence policy, but also more avenues for concentrated interests. If responsibility is spread across more institutions, it is even harder for the public to respond. Their resources are more thinly spread in trying to influence the agencies or to monitor and offset the influence of industry groups. There may be a "critical mass" needed to be effective, and if this is the case, creating more points of access as opposed to a more national model may not be the optimal solution.

The clearinghouse model does have the potential to increase accountability to the extent that it increases the amount of information on how the markets are operating and how successfully regulatory agencies are meeting whatever goals are set by the federal government. However, as noted previously, such ac-

---

10 Kathryn Harrison, *Passing the Buck: Federalism and Canadian Environmental Policy* (Vancouver: UBC Press, 1996).

countability could be good or bad. To the extent that information and benchmarking exposes rent-seeking by industry, they may increase the public's ability to pressure regulatory agencies for regulation or enforcement, thereby reducing risks. Conversely, however, if either the public do not care about externalities (that is, they are content that the provincial regulator does not impose the cost of addressing externalized risks) or industry groups are better able to monitor whether regulators are maintaining agreements not to regulate according to "best practices," information may lead to reduced regulation.[11]

Accountability under a clearinghouse system, therefore, can be a difficult issue.[12] The responsibility may be diffused over different regulators, making it harder both for the public to identify who should be held to account for a lack of action and for the public to actually take action to offset industry rent-seeking. Further, the impact of information and transparency depends on the underlying structure of political accountability.

D. Bias and Independence of a Quasi-national Tribunal

The partial nature of the institutional structure of any national agency will also be central to how effective it is at creating and enforcing risk regulation, either systemic or otherwise. Sarra advocates the creation of two bodies. The Canadian Financial Services Regulatory Authority (CFRA) would be a rule-making and enforcement agency. It would provide rules for issuers cross-listed on Canadian and international exchanges, as well as for any company distributing in more than one province that opts to be regulated by the Authority. The Canadian Financial Services Tribunal (CFST) would hear applications relating to cross-border issues, along with providing "a mechanism to appeal or ensure

---

11 Adrian Vermeule, *Mechanisms of Democracy: Institutional Design Writ Small* (Oxford: Oxford University Press, 2007) (discussing good and bad forms of accountability).

12 Accountability is of course not only a concern for the clearinghouse model. It is already an issue for securities regulators in Canada, particularly where the regulator has broad public interest and rule-making powers. It will therefore be important to examine how the accountability concern differs across different governance and instrument choices.

compliance with findings regarding consumer investment and banking services complaints."[13]

One of the key attributes of the CFST, for Sarra, is that it will be independent, eliminating some of the perceived bias of provincial regulatory tribunals, which are often part of the securities commission. In addition to the efficiency benefits, independence has the advantage of "strengthen[ing] the integrity of the hearing process by eliminating the potential that unarticulated policy considerations inform sanction hearings."[14]

Sarra has two institutional suggestions for achieving this independence and integrity. First, the members of the CFST would be "appointed on the basis of their expertise in securities, financial markets, accounting, business regulation and securities law, adjudication, as well as regional representation."[15] There would therefore be a mix of expertise and regional representation. Second, the CFST would be protected by a strong privative clause, but, to ensure alignment of its policy goals with the CFRA, there would be "clear statutory language and clarity in regulations."[16]

Such a tribunal would have some benefits. Staffing the CFST with experts may help to increase the accuracy and quality of decisions concerning securities regulations. Moreover, independence from political or "unarticulated" local policy considerations could also increase the welfare-enhancing aspects of decisions. Further, the privative clause may increase the likelihood that an expert, independent tribunal, as opposed to the generalist courts, will make the ultimate decision, which some would argue may minimize errors.

However, the suggestion by Sarra (and in some cases by the federal government) that regional representation should be a factor in the staffing of the CFST raises some concerns about the institutional design. Since the Supreme Court has blocked a unilateral move by the federal government to impose a national regulator, the federal government may "buy" provincial support through regional representation.[17] Politically, then, such representation may make sense, but it may also undermine the benefits sought from the CFST.

---

13   Chapter 8, Section E.
14   *Ibid.*
15   *Ibid.*
16   *Ibid.*
17   Anand & Green (2011), above note 4.

One possibility is that regional representation will not make any difference in the decisions of the CFST. Its principal benefit, therefore, would be the political one of distributing rents from the creation of the CFST, in the sense of symbolic recognition of regional importance. However, it seems unlikely that provinces would wish to have representatives on the CFST for symbolic reasons alone; they believe that the members of different regions will decide matters differently. A key concern is that these members would have different policy preferences — that is, that they would be appointed because they wish to promote regional interests rather than to use a particular form of expertise. The value of the independent, expert tribunal would then be reduced, if not lost. It seems unlikely that the "regional" nature of CFST members would increase the accuracy or welfare-enhancing nature of their decisions, unlike other areas of regulation or law where differences in values seem more stark and more central to the welfare benefits of a decision.

Moreover, a move away from the independence and expertise of the members toward regional representation enhances the benefits of allowing judicial review. While generalist judges may not have the expertise of CFST members, they may be able to act as a check on tribunal members who seek to decide on policy preferences that are not contemplated by the legislation or regulations. The underlying institutional structure may require the courts to have a policing function in order to temper regional interests, which would reduce the benefits of the strong privative clause that Sarra proposes.

E. Conclusion: Elements of Hope

Both Ford and Gill's and Sarra's papers seek solutions for securities regulation in the Supreme Court Reference. Ford and Gill have developed an interesting model of national securities regulation as a clearinghouse, adapting to new information and new risks; Sarra seeks to reduce the influence of bias in securities adjudication. Their proposals are thoughtful and bring forward important avenues for exploring the possibilities of a national role in the wake of the *Securities Reference*.

However, because of the *Securities Reference*, each moves toward a quasi-national regulatory model. Ford and Gill limit the scope of regulation governed by the regulator, while Sarra tempers independence and expertise with regional representation on the Tribunal. These partial solutions provide some hope for a more effective regulatory structure in Canada, but we must attend to the risk that the "cooperative" model put forward by the Supreme Court will push us back toward the problems with the existing model.

~ PART 4 ~
# Moving Forward

CHAPTER 11

After the Reference: Regulating Systemic Risk in Canadian Financial Markets

Anita Anand[1]

A. Introduction

Since the onset of the financial crisis in 2007, regulators have been preoccupied with the notion of systemic risk in financial markets, believing that such risk could cause the markets that they oversee to implode. At the same time, they have demonstrated a certain inability to develop and implement a comprehensive policy to address systemic risk. This inability is likely due not only to indeterminacy inherent in the term "systemic risk" but also to existing institutional structures which, because of their existing mandates, ultimately make it difficult to regulate risk across an entire economic system. These two concepts — defining risk and developing appropriate institutional structures — are central to the current inquiry. In this chapter, using the Supreme Court of Canada's recent decision in the *Securities Reference* case as a springboard,[2] I analyze and clarify the term "systemic risk" as it has been used in the policy context following the financial crisis. I then propose the creation of a systemic risk regulator for Canada, the Financial Market Regulatory Authority (FMRA).

1   Thanks to Jeff MacIntosh for very helpful comments and to Grant Bishop, Adam Curran, and Chava Schwebel for excellent research assistance funded by the Social Sciences and Humanities Research Council of Canada.
2   *Reference Re Securities Act*, 2011 SCC 66 [*Securities Reference*].

The main holding in the *Securities Reference* case is the rejection of the federal government's proposed statute[3] as a whole because it falls outside the general trade and commerce power in the Constitution.[4] The Court further held, however, that specific aspects of the proposed statute fall within the general trade and commerce power and are therefore constitutional. The Court reasoned that with respect to these matters — explicitly identified as including systemic risk and national data collection — the provinces lack the constitutional capability to sustain a viable national scheme. With the Supreme Court's endorsement of the federal government's jurisdiction in regulating systemic risk, questions arise: What is systemic risk, and how (if at all) should it be regulated?

The term "systemic risk" inspires ambiguity, despite the volumes of academic writing in this area.[5] While many agree that "systemic risk" refers to the interconnectedness of financial institutions such that the failure of one may lead to the failure of others, they disagree about specifics, including the extent to which the risk should be crystallized and whether the contemplated collapse relates to financial institutions only or to the entire economic system.[6] This chapter weeds through various

---

3 Proposed Canadian Securities Act (25 May 2010), online: Department of Finance Canada www.fin.gc.ca/drleg-apl/csa-lvm.pdf [proposed Act].

4 *Securities Reference*, above note 2; *Constitution Act, 1867* (UK), 30 & 31 Vict, c 3, s 91(2), reprinted in RSC 1985, App II, No 5.

5 This writing is reviewed and discussed in Steven Schwarcz, "Systemic Risk" Duke Law School Legal Studies Research Paper No 163 (March 2008) [Schwarcz]. See also Anita Anand, "Is Systemic Risk Relevant to Securities Regulation?" (2010) 60 UTLJ 941 [Anand]; Miquel Dijkman, *A Framework for Assessing Systemic Risk* (World Bank Policy Research Working Paper 5282, April 2010) [Dijkman]; Olivier De Bandt & Philipp Hartmann, *Systemic Risk: A Survey* (European Central Bank Working Paper No 35, November 2000); George G Kaufman & Kenneth E Scott, "What Is Systemic Risk, and Do Bank Regulators Retard or Contribute to It?" (2003) 7:3 The Independent Rev 371 [Kaufman & Scott]; John Taylor, "Defining Systemic Risk Operationally" in George Shultz, Kenneth Scott & John Taylor, eds, *Ending Government Bailouts As We Know Them* (California: Hoover Press, Stanford University, 2003) at 33–57 [Taylor]; João AC Santos, *Bank Capital Regulation in Contemporary Banking Theory: A Review of the Literature* (Bank of International Settlements (BIS) Working Paper, No 90, September 2000); Seraina Gruenewald, "Financial Crisis Containment and its Implications For Institutional and Legal Reform" (31 December 2009), online: Social Science Research Network papers.ssrn.com/sol3/papers.cfm?abstract_id=1516700.

6 See Kaufman & Scott, *ibid.*

interpretations of the term "systemic risk," ultimately arguing that it refers not simply to the failure of financial institutions but also to events that cause volatility in capital markets more generally. It further argues in favour of a regulatory regime that can indeed be structured to address systemic risk.

At root, the debate over whether Canada should have a national securities regulator stems from questions about the appropriate institutional supervisory structure for Canada's financial system. While a specific question is whether securities regulation should be dispensed provincially or federally, a larger question pertains to the optimal regulatory structure for Canadian financial markets and the institutions required for such regulation. Historically, prudential regulation and securities regulation have been separate beasts. The financial crisis, and particularly the causes of that crisis, highlighted the fact that a complete separation between these two areas of law is no longer tenable.[7] For example, over-the-counter (OTC) derivatives issued or traded by a financial institution give rise to securities law (on the disclosure side) and prudential concerns (on the counterparty exposure side). A legal regime in which regulators in each sphere are not coordinated will likely be unable to respond comprehensively to systemic risk concerns stemming from the trading of OTC derivatives as they arise.

Section B below focuses on definitional issues relating to systemic risk and the liberalization of this term in recent months. It also examines the concept of macroprudential regulation, which, broadly speaking, is policy that seeks to mitigate systemic risk. Section C examines the asset-backed commercial paper (ABCP) crisis and, in so doing, points to aspects of the Canadian economy that can give rise to systemic risk. Section D discusses the appropriate policy response to these issues, culminating in a discussion of the need for more research on systemic risk that may ultimately lead to the establishment of a separate federal regulatory authority. Section E concludes.

---

7   See Anand, above note 5.

B. What Is "Systemic Risk"?

Most commentators agree that there is no universally accepted definition of systemic risk.[8] Thus it comes as no surprise that a primary criticism lodged against proponents of regulating systemic risk is that the term defies precise definition: "If we cannot define it, how can we regulate it?" An examination of the academic literature, as well as writings and speeches of policy makers during and following the financial market crisis, suggests that the term "systemic risk" has itself evolved over time. While originally conceived as describing the failure of one financial institution that in turn causes the domino-style failure of others, "systemic risk" now generally describes a possibility of financial meltdown that affects an entire economic system.

Traditionally, the literature has focused on the concept of systemic risk in the financial sector, referring to a triggering event that causes a chain of negative economic consequences.[9] Crockett explains the domino effect as follows:

> For banks, this effect may occur if Bank A, for whatever reason, defaults on a loan, deposit, or other payment to Bank B, thereby producing a loss greater than B's capital and forcing it to default on payment to Bank C, thereby producing a loss greater than C's capital, and so on down the chain.[10]

Thus, originally, the concept underlying the term "systemic risk" related specifically to financial institution failure brought on by defaults in contractual relationships between and among institutions.[11]

---

8 Taylor states, "The recent crises show how far away we are from defining and agreeing on systemic risk . . . .": Taylor, above note 5 at 47.

9 Some commentators identify the triggering event as a default by a market participant, while others see it as an economic shock, and still others do not define the "event" but leave it general. See George Kaufman, "Bank Failures, Systemic Risk, and Bank Regulation" (1996) 16 The Cato J 17.

10 Andrew Crockett, "Why Is Financial Stability a Goal of Public Policy?" in *Maintaining Financial Stability in a Global Economy* (Kansas City, MO: Federal Reserve Bank of Kansas City, 1997) at 7–36.

11 This formal definition may appear somewhat extreme if one believes that systemic risk can arise even where defaults amount to less than a bank's capital. Systemic risk during the financial crisis likely occurred when doubts about banks' willingness and ability to pay arose.

This definition of systemic risk accords with the use of the term by the Bank for International Settlements, which defines it as

> the risk that the failure of a participant to meet its contractual obligations [specifically, counterparty risk in the case of credit default swaps used primarily in synthetic collateralized debt obligations] may in turn cause other participants to default with a chain reaction leading to broader financial difficulties.[12]

The term may also refer to the potential for substantial volatility in asset prices, corporate liquidity, bankruptcies, and efficiency losses brought on by economic shocks.[13] The risk of a "domino effect" certainly seems central to the concept of systemic risk,[14] as does the risk of some triggering event that occasions the fall of the first domino.[15]

There are of course numerous ambiguities inherent in this conception of "systemic risk," some of which can be articulated in the following questions: At what point must the "risk" crystallize in order to be referred to as "systemic"? Is evaluation of the risk possible only *ex post,* after the financial institution has failed (for example, by declaring bankruptcy)? If only one financial institution fails, and others survive because of government intervention, does systemic risk arise? What type of triggering event can cause systemic risk — only the failure of financial institutions to meet their contractual obligations?

---

12 Bank for International Settlements (BIS), *64th Annual Report* (Basel, Switzerland: BIS, 1994) at 177 [BIS].

13 See Schwarcz, above note 5 at 196–97 citing Paul Kupiec & David Nickerson, "Assessing Systemic Risk Exposure from Banks and GSEs under Alternative Approaches to Capital Regulation" (2004) 48 J Real Estate Fin Econ 123 at 123.

14 US Commodity Futures Trading Commission, *CTFC Glossary*, online: CFTC www.cftc.gov/opa/glossary/opaglossary_s.htm cited in Schwarcz, *ibid* at 197.

15 See Claudio Borio, "Towards a Macroprudential Framework for Financial Supervision and Regulation" (2003) 49 CESifo Econ Stud 181. See also Schwarcz, above note 5, who states that, in defining the risk, it is not clear whether the trigger event must occur or whether it merely has the potential to occur; BIS/Central Banks of the Group of Ten Working Group, *Recent Developments in International Interbank Relations* (Basel, Switzerland: BIS, 1992) at 61, which defines systemic risk as "the risk that a disruption (at a firm, in a market segment, to a settlement system, etc.) causes widespread difficulties at other firms, in other market segments or in the financial system as a whole."

The ambiguity inherent in the term "systemic risk" has led Taylor to develop a more structured definition. He highlights three components of any definition of "systemic risk": the risk of a large triggering event; the risk of financial propagation of such an event through the financial sector; and macroeconomic risk that the entire economy will be affected.[16] The triggering event can arise from the failure of a financial institution, as described above; as Taylor explains, however, it may also arise from an exogenous shock — such as a terrorist attack (9/11) or natural disaster — and the contracting of liquidity in the public sector.[17]

While Taylor's three-part definition of systemic risk leaves room for questions (for example, what is "financial propagation"?),[18] at the very least it suggests that the term can (and should) be interpreted more broadly to include risks that not only occasion the failure of financial institutions but also destabilize an entire economy.[19] Along these lines, Kaufman and Scott explain that the term "refers to the risk or probability of breakdowns in an entire system, as opposed to breakdowns in individual parts or components, and is evidenced by comovements (correlation) among most or all of the parts."[20] Similarly, Dijkman asserts that "systemic risk usually refers to financial shocks that are likely to be serious enough to damage the real economy . . . ."[21] Thus, a link is drawn between the financial markets and the "real economy," that is, the economy concerned with producing and consuming goods and services as opposed to buying and selling financial products.

Policy makers have adopted a more general understanding of systemic risk. The Group of Ten states that "systemic risk" refers to the risk that an event will trigger the loss of economic value or loss of confidence in, and increasing uncertainty about, a substantial portion of the financial system that is serious enough to occasion adverse effects on the real economy, in all probability.[22] Bank of Canada Governor Mark Carney refers to the "probability

---

16 Taylor, above note 5.
17 *Ibid.*
18 See *ibid* at 36.
19 A further example is the ABCP crisis discussed in Section C, below.
20 Kaufman & Scott, above note 5 at 371.
21 Dijkman, above note 5 at 6.
22 Group of Ten, "Report on Consolidation in the Financial Sector" (BIS, 2001), online: Bank for International Settlements www.bis.org/publ/gten05.pdf.

that the financial system is unable to support economic activity."[23] The Chair of the Australian Securities and Investment Commission, Greg Medcraft, "sees systemic risk as the risk of a major disruption to the flow of finance that threatens significant economic damage."[24] According to Sir Mervyn King, Governor of the Bank of England and Vice-Chair of the European Systemic Risk Board, systemic risk is the possibility that "the failure of a bank can have an impact that goes well beyond the importance of that bank alone."[25] Similarly, Federal Reserve Chairman Ben Bernanke writes that the concept of "systemic risk" should be broadly defined[26] to include "developments that threaten the stability of the financial system as a whole and consequently the broader economy, not just that of one or two institutions."[27]

This broad understanding of systemic risk seems to match the view held by the Supreme Court of Canada, which defined the term as "risks that occasion a 'domino effect' whereby the risk of default by one market participant will impact the ability of others to fulfill their legal obligations, setting off a chain of negative economic consequences that pervade an entire financial system."[28] It is this broader interpretation that should form the

23 Mark Carney, cited in Nikil Chande, Nicholas Labelle & Eric Tuer, *Central Counterparties and Systemic Risk* (Bank of Canada, Financial System Review, December 2010) at 1.
24 Greg Medcraft, Chair, Australian Securities and Investments Commission (ASIC), "Systemic Risk: The Role of Securities Regulators" (Speech delivered at *Systemic Risk, Basel III, Financial Stability and Regulation Conference, Institute of Global Finance*, 28 June 2011).
25 Sir Mervyn King to British Bankers Association, London "Banking and the Bank of England" (Speech to British Bankers Association, London, 10 June 2008), online: Bank of England www.bankofengland.co.uk/publications/speeches/2008/speech347.pdf.
26 Including institutions with "unsafe amounts of leveraging by banks, gaps in regulatory oversight and the possibility that the failure of a large interconnected firm could lead to a breakdown in the wider financial system": Corey Boles, "Bernanke Offers Broad Definition of Systemic Risk", *The Wall Street Journal* (18 November 2009), online: The Wall Street Journal blogs.wsj.com/economics/2009/11/18/bernanke-offers-broad-definition-of-systemic-risk/; Edward Green & Katia Kirova, "'Too Big To Fail': Should Breaking Up Large Financial Institutions be an Answer? U.S. and European Approaches" 16 Colum J Eur L 19 (2009), online: The Columbia Journal of European Law www.cjel.net/online/16_1-greene-kirova.
27 Letter from Ben Bernanke to Senator Bob Corker (30 October 2009).
28 *Securities Reference*, above note 2 at para 103. This definition is drawn from the expert evidence of Michael Trebilcock and is consistent with the

basis of regulation on a prospective basis.[29] It is the type of risk to which Jenkins and Thiessen refer as "procyclical risks," a newer concept of system-wide risks that accumulate over time.[30]

Even with a broad understanding of "systemic risk," the question arises of whether the existence of systemic risk is knowable *ex ante* (i.e., before the risk arises) or only *ex post* (i.e., after a breakdown in the financial system has made the risk evident). The development of policy relating to systemic risk mitigation depends on the ability to make and understand the validity of predictions. There were moments before the crisis in the United States when regulators could have responded to systemic risk. For example, the former chair of the Commodity Futures and Trade Commission (CFTC), Brooksley Born, is widely acknowledged to have predicted the crisis in OTC derivatives prior to the 2007 financial market crash. Yet the US Congress moved to enact legislation that prevented the CFTC from taking any preemptive regulatory action.[31]

If we agree that systemic risk may in fact require regulation, then we move into the sphere of "macroprudential regulation," a term that refers to a definite intention by regulators to respond to systemic risk (above and beyond merely identifying it). The Group of 30 has declared that "macroprudential policy is concerned not only with systemic risk but also with developing the appropriate responses to those risks in order to strengthen the financial sys-

---

Bank for International Settlements definition, which is the "risk that the failure of a participant to meet its contractual obligations may in turn cause other participants to default": BIS, above note 12 at 177 cited in Kaufman & Scott, above note 5 at 372.

29 As discussed below, it is interesting that this understanding of systemic risk appears to go beyond that set forth by the Supreme Court of Canada in the Reference. The Court did not analyze the concept of systemic risk in great detail in its judgment.

30 Paul Jenkins & Gordon Thiessen, "Reducing the Potential for Future Financial Crises: A Framework for Macro-Prudential Policy in Canada" (2012) CD Howe Institute Commentary No. 351 at 3 ("'Procyclical risks' . . . are those that cumulate over time and reflect the tendency of the financial system to procyclical behaviour that exacerbates economic booms and busts.")

31 Pat Garofolo, "Former CFTC Chair Who Predicted the Derivatives Crisis Endorses Dodd-Frank Financial Reform Bill", *ThinkProgress* (2 July 2010), online: ThinkProgress thinkprogress.org/economy/2010/07/02/173371/brooksley-born-endorse/?mobile=nc.

tem and avoid similar crises in the future."[32] The focus is on "the interconnectedness of financial institutions and markets, common exposures to economic variables, and procyclical behaviours [that] can create risk."[33] The reforms contemplated below modify this concept by seeking to ensure that any regulatory response to the crisis takes into account not just common institutions and markets but also the fact that historically separate legal spheres also require coordination.

C. Systemic Risk and the Canadian Financial System

Section B analyzed the definition of systemic risk and considered the usefulness of the concept of "macroprudential regulation." In light of the broad understanding of the term "systemic risk," some may have difficulty discussing such risk in the Canadian context, not only because of the definitional issues associated with the concept but also because, looking at Canadian capital markets, which fared relatively well during the recent financial crisis, they may argue that systemic risk is not and has not been an issue for Canadian regulators, especially given that systemic risk has been historically regulated at least in the clearing and settlement process by the Bank of Canada.[34] However, there are aspects of the Canadian economy that can give rise to systemic instability, as this Section suggests in its examination of the ABCP crisis.

---

32 Group of Thirty Report, "Enhancing Financial Stability and Resilience: *Macroprudential Policy, Tools, and Systems for the Future*" (October 2010), online: Group of Thirty www.group30.org/images/PDF/Macropru-dential_Report_Final.pdf [G30 Report].

33 Macroprudential regulation does not seek to remove economic shocks, but it does aim to identify and address a financial system's exposure to such shocks *ex ante*, so that they can be addressed and the market's ability to resist such shocks can be established. *Ibid* at 17.

34 See e.g. Michael D Bordo, Angela Redish & Hugh Rockoff, *Why didn't Canada have a banking crisis in 2008 (or in 1930, or 1907, or . . .)?* (The National Bureau of Economic Research (NBER) Working Paper No 17312, August 2011), online (abstract): NBER www.nber.org/papers/w17312. Regarding the Bank of Canada's role in clearing and settlement see generally the *Payment Clearing and Settlement Act*, SC 1996, c 6, Sch. Canada was one of the first countries to have a statutory definition of systemic risk (since 1996) and it served as a model for years: *Payment Clearing and Settlement Act, ibid.* The argument here is that this model is outdated and in need of amendment.

Many commentators rightly point to the efficacy of Canada's regulatory framework in safeguarding against financial contagion.[35] Nevertheless, a general consensus seems to be emerging regarding certain sources of systemic risk, perhaps applicable in any jurisdiction, that augmented the scale of the financial crisis.[36] These include regulatory capital requirements;[37] credit ratings;[38] derivatives trading; registration exemptions;[39] clearing and settlement systems;[40] lending standards; securitization;[41] and endemic conflicts of interest or other moral hazard problems — particularly those associated with creditors (bank and non-bank), rating agencies, monoline insurance policy providers, and distribution

35 Lev Ratnovski & Rocco Huang, *Why are Canadian Banks More Resilient?* (International Monetary Fund (IMF) Working Paper No 152, 2009), online: Social Science Research Network papers.ssrn.com/sol3/papers. cfm?abstract_id=1442254; Franklin Allen & Douglas Gale, *Comparing Financial Systems* (Cambridge, MA: MIT Press, 2000) (who argue that bank supervision is more effective in a concentrated banking system by comparing the US history marked by greater financial instability to the UK and Canada where the banking sector is dominated by fewer big banks); IMF, *Canada – 2008 Article IV Consultation, Preliminary Conclusions of the IMF Mission* (Article IV Staff Reports, 17 December 2007), online: IMF www.imf.org/external/np/ms/2007/121707.htm. See also Anita Anand, "Canada's Banks: Conservative by Nature", *Financial Post* (31 March 2009), online: Financial Post www.financialpost.com/.

36 See e.g. Expert Panel on Securities Regulation, *Final Report and Recommendations* (Ottawa: Department of Finance Canada, 2009), online: Expert Panel www.expertpanel.ca/eng/documents/Expert_Panel_Final_Report_And_Recommendations.pdf; Financial Stability Board (FSB), *Progress in the Implementation of the G20 Recommendations for Strengthening Financial Stability* (Basel, 10 April 2011), online: FSB www.financialstabilityboard.org/publications/r_110219.pdf; IMF, *Initial Lessons of the Crisis for the Global Architecture and the IMF* (Prepared by the Strategy, Policy, and Review Department, January 2009), online: IMF www.imf.org/external/np/pp/eng/2009/021809.pdf; Ben Bernanke, "Financial Reform to Address Systemic Risk," (Speech delivered at the Council on Foreign Relations, Washington, DC, 10 March 2009); Janis Sarra, "Risk Management, Responsive Regulation, and Oversight of Structured Financial Product Markets" (2011) 44 UBC L Rev 779; Masahiro Kawai & Michael Pomerleano, *Regulating Systemic Risk* (ADBI Working Paper Series No 189, January 2010).

37 See John Chant, *The ABCP Crisis in Canada: The Implications for the Regulation of Financial Markets* (Report for the Expert Panel on Securities Regulation, 2009) at 34 [Chant].

38 *Ibid* at 21.

39 *Ibid* at 22.

40 *Payment Clearing and Settlement Act*, above note 34.

41 Chant, above note 37 at 23.

agents (dealers and investment advisors) — which reveal significant distortions in the compensation and risk-taking incentives governing industry participants.

The importance of some of these factors became evident during Canada's ABCP crisis.[42] The collapse of the ABCP market involved "conduits" — trusts holding pools of assets that issue notes or commercial paper — established and managed by sponsors (corporations, banks, or other third parties,[43] which provided standby liquidity to the conduits),[44] while ratings agencies rated the ABCP and investment dealers marketed and sold it to investors.[45] Experts agree that the US sub-prime mortgage crisis was the catalyst for the near collapse of Canada's ABCP market,[46] which was averted through restructuring pursuant to the *Com-*

42 Although the ABCP market reached its peak in 2007 and has declined significantly since then, the market is beginning to show some signs of a rebound. It ended 2011 at $27.4 billion, still far away from the $117 billion valuation it achieved in 2007: see DBRS, Press Release, "DBRS Releases Monthly Canadian ABCP Report for December 2011" (23 February 2012) online: DBRS www.dbrs.com/research/245560/dbrs-releases-monthly-canadian-abcp-report-for-december-2011.html; Chant, *ibid* at 4.

43 Such as *Coventree Capital Inc.* and *Newshore Financial Services Inc.*: Chant, *ibid* at 7.

44 Standby liquidity arrangements were necessary because of the maturity mismatch between the assets held by the conduit, which generally had a long-term maturity period, and the shorter maturity of the ABCP issued against these assets. These conduits were also highly leveraged, with very little equity to protect them in the event of a run of investor redemptions: *ibid* at 19.

45 *Ibid* at 6.

46 See Bank of Canada, *Financial System Review* (December 2007) at 3; *ATB v Metcalfe & Mansfield Alternative Investments II Corp*, [2008] OJ No 2265, 47 BLR (4th) 74 at paras 17–19 (SCJ), Blair JA (based on the affidavit of Purdy Crawford, QC, sworn 17 March 2008 and filed in the Ontario Superior Court of Justice (Commercial List) cited in this decision), cited in Jeffrey Leon & Shara N Roy, "Pain and Promise: Lessons from the Collapse of the Third-Party ABCP Market in Canada" (2009) 14:3 Corporate Securities and Finance Law Report 41 [Leon & Roy]; Investment Industry Regulatory Organization of Canada (IIROC), "Regulatory Study, Review and Recommendations Concerning the Manufacture and Distribution by IIROC Member Firms of Third-Party Asset-Backed Commercial Paper in Canada" (October, 2008) at 10 [IIROC Report] cited in Leon & Roy, *ibid*; Canadian Securities Administrators (CSA), "Securities Regulatory Proposals Stemming from the 2007-08 Credit Market Turmoil and its Effects on the ABCP Market in Canada" (October 2008) at 5; Scott Hendry, Stéphane Lavoie, & Carolyn Wilkins, *Securitized Products, Disclosure, and the Reduction of Systemic Risk* (Bank of Canada, *Financial System Review*, June 2010), online: Bank of

panies' Creditors Arrangement Act[47] under the guidance of Purdy Crawford.[48] Had the $32 billion ABCP market collapsed, the default would have propagated throughout our financial system. Thus we must ask, what precisely were the aspects of the ABCP crisis that gave rise to a near systemic collapse? Responding to this question may shed light on the value of regulating systemic risk after the crisis, an issue discussed in more detail in Section D below.

ABCP was distributed almost exclusively in the exempt market, with little oversight relative to the level of oversight exercised over issuers of securities (and their disclosure) in the public markets. In particular, ABCP was issued under the short-term debt exemption from the prospectus requirement, which is available if the note or commercial paper "has an approved credit rating from an approved credit rating organization."[49] While ABCP could be issued without prospectus-level disclosure,[50] some information did accompany the distribution of these securities: the distributing entities provided an information memorandum, a legal opinion, and a report by the associated rating agency, which in all cases was the Dominion Bond Rating Service (DBRS).

Canada www.bankofcanada.ca/wp-content/uploads/2011/12/fsr-0610-hendry.pdf [Hendry, Lavoie, & Wilkins]; and Chant, above note 37 at 23.

47 RSC 1985, c C-36.

48 Crawford was appointed chair of the Pan-Canadian Investors Committee for Third Party Structured ABCP (the "Crawford Committee") which was charged with restructuring all existing non-bank sponsored ABCP in August 2007. See also Brendan O'Neill & Mike Dean, "Restructuring of Canada's $32 billion market in Asset-Backed Commercial Paper completed through a *CCAA* Plan of Compromise and Arrangement" INSOL World, Second Quarter (2009), online: Goodmans LLP www.goodmans. ca/files/file/docs/Restructuring%20of%20Canada's%20$32%20Billion%20 Market.pdf; Leon & Roy, above note 46 at 50.

49 See section 2.35 of NI 45-106, which provides, "The prospectus requirement does not apply to a distribution of a negotiable promissory note or commercial paper maturing not more than one year from the date of issue, if the note or commercial paper distributed . . . (b) has an approved credit rating from an approved credit rating organization" [NI 45-106]. According to Chant, this provision meant that, "credit rating agencies provided the rating that exempted ABCP from prospectus requirements and made it an eligible investment for many investors": Chant, above note 37 at 4.

50 In particular, ABCP was issued under either the accredited investor exemption or the short-term debt exemption, which are based on investor sophistication and approval of a credit rating agency respectively: see s. 1.1 ("accredited investor" definition), s. 2.3, and s. 2.35 NI 45-106, *ibid.*

What factors gave rise to the ABCP crisis? First, ABCP issuers were exempt from securities law prospectus requirements, which would have mandated a certain level of disclosure with respect to the notes or commercial paper being issued.[51] As Chant observes, the disclosure that accompanied ABCP failed to communicate the associated risks; for example, information relating to the quality, mix, and weighting of the assets underlying the notes (including highly leveraged exposure to derivatives) or the contingency of liquidity provision agreements that would have been useful information for investors in these securities.[52]

Second, sponsors of ABCP issuers, or their activities in respect of them, were in many cases not subject to regulatory supervision. Banks treated their sponsorship of ABCP conduits as an off-balance-sheet activity, which allowed them to evade regulatory capital and other prudential requirements. Securitization and the ABCP market were attractive to banks for this reason: by transferring assets to conduits, which are legally separate entities, banks insulated themselves from the default risk associated with these assets, and thus were able to eliminate the capital charges that would apply if these assets were held on their balance sheets.[53]

Third, these domestic and foreign banks, as well as nonbank financial institutions, also acted as liquidity providers to the ABCP conduits, providing them with standby lines of credit. Many such liquidity providers were not subject to capital requirements and were otherwise minimally regulated (i.e., if the provider was not a financial institution). Under banking regulations obtaining at the time, Canadian banks faced zero capital charges on conditional liquidity facilities (so-called Canadian-style liquidity provisions) extended to ABCP issuers.[54] Until recently,

---

51 Anand, above note 5 at 954. Chant, above note 37 at 9.
52 Chant, *ibid* at 10-12, 23. See also Hendry, Lavoie, & Wilkins, above note 46.
53 For details, see Chant, above note 37; IIROC Report, above note 46 at 4.
54 Under OSFI Guideline B-5, in contrast to so-called global liquidity arrangements, credit facilities "available in the event of a general market disruption" attracted zero capital charges: see s 4.3.3 OSFI Guideline B-5, *Asset Securitization* (2004). These rules have been changed to eliminate the favourable capital treatment of this type of liquidity arrangement: see OSFI Advisory (October 2008) at 3 (warning that general-market disruption liquidity facilities would, going forward, "receive the same credit conversion factors and capital treatment as global style liquidity facilities."). See also Jean St-Gelais, President & CEO, Autorité des marchés financiers, Letter to Edward Greenspoon, Editor-in-chief of

off-shore and non-bank lenders were free from capital requirements, although they entered into the same type of conditional
credit arrangement with ABCP issuers.[55]

Fourth, the conduct of rating agencies (in this case DBRS)
was unregulated, yet these were the agencies that were approving the securities for distribution.[56] The use of the short-term
debt exemption effectively delegated responsibility for oversight
of the ABCP market from securities regulators to rating agencies.
The rating agencies are not regulators, however, and thus did not
fulfill the monitoring role that seems to have been necessary in
this instance.[57] Furthermore, their ongoing commercial relationship with issuers whose products they were charged with policing
placed them in a conflict of interest position.[58]

Fifth, the risks borne by ABCP were passed on to the public
by investment dealers and salespeople, who are subject to "know
your client" and "suitability" rules administered by the Investment Industry Regulatory Organization of Canada (IIROC) but
not to any explicit fiduciary duty.[59] These salespeople did not
understand the products they were selling,[60] and dense disclosure meant that investors had little hope of understanding the
securities they were purchasing, even if they tried.

The ABCP crisis demonstrates that various aspects of Canada's financial system were poorly regulated. Regulatory authorities failed to act in a coordinated manner, which in turn allowed
the ABCP crisis to evolve more quickly and to reach greater pro-

---

The Globe and Mail (15 January 2009) at 2–3 online: Securities Canada
www.securitiescanada.org/2009_0115_amf_english.pdf [St-Gelais].

55 St-Gelais, *ibid.* Prior to the introduction of Basel II, most countries did
not impose capital charges on banks' liquidity arrangements, conditional
or not: Chant, above note 37 at 13. Non-bank lenders likewise did not
face capital charges: *ibid.*

56 Anand, above note 5.

57 *Ibid.*

58 *Ibid* at 13. The absence of regulation governing the conduct of rating
agencies has since been addressed by the Canadian Securities Administrators, though to a limited extent. See NI 25-101, adopted by the CSA in
January, 2012, which requires credit rating agencies to establish, maintain, and comply with a code of conduct which is substantially consistent
with international standards developed by the International Organization of Securities Commissions (IOSCO) for the regulation of these agencies [NI 25-101].

59 Chant, above note 37 at 15.

60 IIROC Report, above note 46 at 74.

portions than if regulators had worked together to forestall it.[61] Thus, the diffusion of regulatory oversight (i.e., different bodies overseeing different aspects of the same market) reduced the ability of these bodies to appreciate the size and scope of the crisis and to act effectively *ex ante* to contain its effects.[62]

The ABCP crisis also revealed the conspicuous absence of regulation relating to OTC derivatives in Canada. The systemic risks associated with OTC derivatives contracts are well acknowledged: for example, if American International Group (AIG) had been permitted to collapse in September 2008, the domino effect caused by bilateral netting arrangements across the global financial system would have produced an even worse financial crisis than the one we collectively experienced. Under a "cascade of cross defaults" scenario, even prudently managed financial firms and many corporations would have been stressed extensively by the interconnectedness of OTC derivatives. Thus, the two main policy reforms that appear to be important after the crisis relating to OTC derivatives — central clearing and trade repositories — are fundamental. But at present, though there has been much discussion, neither institutional structures nor legislation relating to OTC derivatives has been implemented.[63]

What does the failure of regulators to oversee the ABCP tell us in hindsight? It suggests that there were gaps in securities regulation in theory and practice. But it does not necessarily underline the importance of a national securities regulator; the lack of oversight in that market could have occurred at the federal level just as it did at the provincial level. Arguments in favour of federal regulation of capital markets must acknowledge this

---

61 Chant, above note 37 at 40.

62 Although Chant does not explicitly advocate consolidation of financial regulation in Canada, he notes that "[w]ith consolidation, the regulator would be able to take a broad view and consider the overall effects of the measure and respond appropriately. The case for consolidation would be strengthened if there is evidence that communication between different parts of a single agency proves more effective than communication among agencies": *ibid.*

63 See below note 82. Currently Quebec is the only Canadian province that has enacted legislation regulating OTC derivatives: see *Derivatives Act* (Québec), RSQ c I-14.01; Alix d'Anglejan-Chatillon, "Quebec Derivatives Act Proclaimed in Force" Canadian Securities Law, Stikeman Elliot LLP (21 Janurary 2009), online: Canadian Securities Law www.canadianse-curitieslaw.com/2009/01/articles/securities-distribution-tradin/quebec-derivatives-act-proclaimed-in-force/.

fact. Hindsight perhaps tells us that crises in markets outside of Canadian borders can have vast effects on similar markets inside Canadian borders: the ABCP market and its relation to the US subprime crisis is a key example. It also tells us that coordination among regulatory bodies on an ongoing basis is likely to be beneficial.

D. Regulating Systemic Risk

The traditional focus of "prudential" regulation (i.e., regulation of financial institutions) has been to supervise financial institutions and, in particular, the soundness of their financial condition.[64] By contrast, securities regulation has been concerned with investor protection and market efficiency.[65] Managing systemic risk has not traditionally fallen squarely within the mandates of either of these regulators, though central banks have undertaken this task to some degree.[66] In particular, the Bank of Canada has held statutory responsibility since 1996 for overseeing and controlling systemic risk in the context of clearing and settlement systems.[67]

---

64 OSFI's mandate under the *Office of the Superintendent of Financial Institutions Act*, RSC 1985, c 18 (3d Supp), is:

(a) to supervise financial institutions to determine their sound financial condition and compliance with governing statutory requirements; (b) to promptly advise senior management or the board of directors a financial institution if the institution is not in sound financial condition or is not complying with its governing statutory requirements and in such circumstances to take or require the management or board to take appropriate correction action; (c) to promote management and boards of financial institutions to adopt policies and procedures to control and manage risk; and (d) to monitor and evaluate system-wide or sectoral events or issues which could negatively impact the financial condition of financial institutions: *ibid*, ss 4(2)(a)–(d).

See also Franklin Allen & Richard Herring, "Banking Regulation versus Securities Market Regulation" Wharton School Center for Financial Institutions, University of Pennsylvania (11 July 2001).

65 *Securities Act* (Ontario), RSO 1990, c S.5, s 1(1).

66 The Bank of Canada is responsible for Canada's monetary policy, bank notes, financial system, and funds management: *Bank of Canada Act*, RSC 1985, c B-2. See also Bank of Canada, "What We Do," online: Bank of Canada www.bankofcanada.ca/about/what-we-do. The issue of the appropriate scope of central banking activity is the topic of another research project that I am currently undertaking.

67 The Bank's responsibilities stem not only from the *Bank of Canada Act*, above note 66 but also from the *Payment Clearing and Settlement Act*,

A common thread running through the legal mandates of all of these bodies — securities regulators, monitors of financial institutions, and central banks — is that the same (i.e., consumer-based) populace is ultimately served under each regime.[68] Now, it is likely the case that central banks as well as prudential regulators would not view their mandate as one about consumer protection. Central banks seek to reduce risk in the financial system. Prudential regulators seek to supervise financial institutions, limit their risk-taking, and ensure that they meet capital requirements. But the effect of both central banking and prudential regulation is to ensure that consumers in our society are protected and, in the case of prudential regulators, that their funds are safely maintained. This understanding of the ultimate beneficiaries of central banking and prudential regulation is fundamental to my argument here. Once we accept this point, and in particular that the stability of the financial system and the institutions that comprise this system ultimately seek to serve economic actors (consumers) — the question of who should have comprehensive oversight of systemic risk in financial markets remains open.

A first option is to retain the *status quo*. Under the passport system, originally established in 2003 by the Canadian Securities Administrators (CSA), if an issuer or investment dealer complies with the rules of one jurisdiction, it is deemed also to be in compliance with those of the other participating jurisdictions.[69] The passport system is intended as a system of mutual recognition wherein provinces defer to the decisions and judgments of other provinces. For example, when obtaining a receipt for a prospectus, a firm can choose one jurisdiction as its "principal regulator" to

---

above note 34.

68 Anand, above note 5. Note that the International Organization of Securities Commissions (IOSCO) has had as one of its principles that securities regulators should "have or contribute to a process to monitor, mitigate and manage systemic risk, appropriate to its mandate": see e.g. IOSCO, *Mitigating Systemic Risk: A Role for Securities Regulators* (IOSCO Discussion Paper OR01/11, February 2011), online: IOSCO www.iosco.org/library/pubdocs/pdf/IOSCOPD347.pdf.

69 See Passport System, OSC MI 11-102, (2008) 31 OSCB 1009; Process for Prospectus Reviews in Multiple Jurisdictions, OSC NP 11-202, (2008) 31 OSCB 1009; Process for Exemptive Relief Applications in Multiple Jurisdictions, OSC NP 11- 203, (2008) 31 OSCB009 in Anita Anand & Andrew Green, "Why is this Taking so Long? The Move towards a National Securities Regulator" (2010) 60:2 UTLJ 663 at 679 [Anand & Green].

regulate the offering (review the prospectus, provide comments, etc.); all other jurisdictions then defer to the decision of the principal regulator, which is typically chosen based on the location of the issuer's head office. Issuers continue to pay filing fees to thirteen separate regulatory authorities, however, and enforcement actions are initiated and prosecuted separately, though regulators may cooperate with respect to any particular enforcement matter. Ontario, because it views a national securities regulator as the optimal regulatory structure for Canada, has declined to participate in the passport system.[70]

The main problem with relying on the CSA to manage systemic risk is that because of its non-mandatory nature, no true and timely national response can take place under its purview; at any point, provinces can refuse to participate in an initiative. This may be why even those who object to a national securities regulator argue that the current system requires reform and that a pan-Canadian body is preferable.[71] Even if all provinces delegated authority to a joint non-federal pan-Canadian body, however, problems would persist regarding such body's jurisdiction to regulate securities matters that have interprovincial or international dimensions[72] — that is, those "matters that transcend the local and concern Canada as a whole."[73] Accountability could

---

70 See "OSC rejects passport system of regulation", *CBC News* (28 March 2007), online: CBC News www.cbc.ca/money/story/2007/03/28/oscpassport.html in Anand & Green, *ibid.*

71 See the comment letter of Jeffrey MacIntosh, submission to the Wise Persons' Committee (2003) [MacIntosh], online: Wise Persons' Committee www.wise-averties.ca/submitted_en.asp?file=sub_mac_int. For example, although vocal in his opposition to a central federal securities regulator, MacIntosh argues that "there is a compelling case for reforming the institutional structure of securities laws" in Canada: *ibid.* Such reform could involve the establishment of a "pan-Canadian" securities regulator which would operate nationally based on authority delegated to it by participating provinces. Under this model, the regulator would consist of representatives from each of the participating provinces rather than a central federal regulator; it thereby "side-steps political problems associated with ceding a current area of provincial authority to the federal government" while "achiev[ing] many of the efficiencies associated with a single regulator": *ibid.* See also Jeffrey MacIntosh, "Not Even Close" *Financial Post* (23 December 2011), online: National Post www.nationalpost.com/opinion/even+close/5902435/story.html.

72 The Canadian Bankers Association's Submission to the Wise Persons' Committee (2003) at 34 online: Canadian Bankers Association www.cba.ca/contents/files/misc/msc_wpcsubmission_en.pdf [CBA].

73 *Securities Reference*, above note 2 at para 89.

also be an issue if responsibility for the Financial Markets Regulatory Authority (FMRA) or some similar body is accorded to multiple jurisdictions.[74] Perhaps most critically, a pan-Canadian regulator would not resolve the difficulty of having to rely on provincial cooperation.[75]

A second policy option is for the federal government to pass reforms itself rather than relying on the CSA to do so. Recall that in the *Securities Reference* case, the Supreme Court of Canada explained in *obiter* that "[p]revention of systemic risk may trigger the need for a national regulator empowered to issue orders that are valid throughout Canada and impose common standards, under which provincial governments can work to ensure that their market will not transmit any disturbance across Canada or elsewhere."[76] The Court then focused explicitly on systemic risk and data collection as legitimate avenues for the federal government to pursue in this area.[77]

To follow the Court's lead, there are particular provisions in the proposed *Securities Act* that could form the basis of the legislative regime underpinning the creation of a separate body to regulate risk. The risk regulator, which could be called the FMRA would "contribute, as part of the Canadian financial regulatory framework, to the integrity and stability of the financial system; and would monitor and evaluate issues and developments affecting the integrity or stability of capital markets."[78] In addition, it would "work closely with, and share pertinent information, as appropriate, with other financial authorities such as the Department of Finance, the Bank of Canada, the Office of the Superintendent of Financial Institutions, the Canada Deposit and Insurance Corporation, and the Financial Consumer Agency of Canada."[79]

---

74 CBA, above note 72 at 34.
75 As MacIntosh observes, this institutional structure is therefore unlikely to be very stable, since participating provinces could always threaten to (or actually) withdraw at any time if they oppose any policy or course of action adopted by the regulator. See MacIntosh, above note 71.
76 *Securities Reference*, above note 2 at para 104.
77 *Ibid* at paras 104–5.
78 Proposed Act, above note 3, s 16(2)(d). See also Paul Jenkins et al, "Who Likes Surprises? A Policy Framework for Avoiding Financial Crises" Paper for the CD Howe Institute (May 2012).
79 Proposed Act, *ibid*, s 16(2)(e).

But questions arise: How would systemic risk be monitored? Apart from data sharing, what else is involved in monitoring systemic risk? Once data is collected about transactions and securities that may give rise to "systemic risk," what will be done with it? What are the costs and benefits of implementing a data-sharing regime? Recall that the Financial Transactions Reports Analysis Centre of Canada (FINTRAC) oversees a data-collection regime in the area of anti-terrorism whose correlation to the tracking of terrorists is questionable.[80] Further research on these questions is warranted before any one body is established to monitor risk.

If the FMRA were established, its mandate could include monitoring specific sectors of the market that, following the discussion above in Section C, can give rise to systemic risk. For example, the financial crisis highlighted the problems with OTC derivatives, which gave rise to systemic concerns.[81] As no one regulator has historically gravitated toward regulating OTC derivatives, perhaps that task will fall to the risk regulator, in combination with other organizations — including the Bank of Canada, which has been instrumental in moving Canada toward a regulatory solution to OTC derivatives.[82] The federal government may be

---

80 Anita Anand, "Combatting Terrorist Financing: Is Canada's Legal Regime Effective?" (2011) 61 UTLJ 59.

81 Anand, above note 5.

82 Regulators are moving towards more robust regulation of Canada's OTC derivatives market in accordance with Canada's Group of Twenty commitment that (i) by the end of 2012, "all standardized OTC derivatives contracts be traded on exchanges or electronic trading platforms, where appropriate, and cleared through central clearing counterparties"; (ii) OTC derivatives contracts be reported to trade repositories; and (iii) higher capital requirements be imposed on non-centrally cleared contracts: see the communiqué of Group of Twenty Pittsburgh Summit (24–25 September 2009), online: G20 Information Centre www. g20.utoronto.ca/2009/2009communique0925.html. The Canadian OTC Derivatives Working Group (the OTCDWG) and the CSA have each released consultation papers which address these objectives in more detail: see OTCDWG, *Reform of Over-the-Counter Derivatives in Canada: Discussion Paper from the Canadian OTC Derivatives Working Group* (26 October, 2010), online: Bank of Canada www.bankofcanada.ca/wp-content/uploads/2010/10/reform.pdf; Canadian Securities Administrators Derivatives Committee (CSADC), *Consultation Paper 91-401 on Over-the-Counter Derivatives Regulation in Canada* (2 November 2010) [Consultation Paper 91-401], online: Ontario Securities Commission www.osc.gov. on.ca/documents/en/Securities-Category9/csa_20101102_91-401_cp-on-derivatives.pdf. The CSA has so far released three out of a planned series of eight consultation papers which build on its proposals in Consultation

redundant in this field, however, as the CSA is currently working on proposals for the regulation of derivatives trading, which will conceivably be adopted by each of the participating provinces. Until this occurs, however, one asks whether it would be possible to lift the provisions relating to OTC derivatives from the proposed *Securities Act* and include them in the federal statute that authorizes the creation of the macroprudential regulator.[83]

Another question that arises is why a separate regulator (i.e., the FMRA) is necessary. Why not use existing agencies to monitor and manage systemic risk? This appears to be the option favoured by Nicholas Le Pan, past Superintendent at the Office of the Superintendent of Financial Institutions (OSFI), in a 2009 report.[84] Le Pan contends that "macroprudential regulation is ill-defined and has the potential to conflict with both the regulation and supervision of individual institutions."[85] He argues against assigning responsibility for the stability of the financial system to a single (newly created) agency because "what matters more are processes to promote the realistic consideration of risk . . . to resolve tradeoffs among different policies, and to strengthen the will to act."[86]

On this model, the regulatory structure would change relatively little to accommodate concerns relating to systemic risk. Le Pan cites OSFI's mandate, which includes "monitoring and evaluating system-wide or sectoral events or issues that may have a negative impact on the financial condition of financial institutions"; the implication is that OSFI is the institution best suited for the task. However, it seems that OSFI's mandate to evaluate system-wide conditions relates to microprudential purposes (i.e.,

---

Paper 91-401 and propose specific rules governing the OTC derivatives market in Canada, see CSA Consultation Paper 91-402 – Derivatives: *Trade Repositories* (23 June 2011); CSA Consultation Paper 91-403 – Derivatives: *Surveillance and Enforcement* (25 November 2011); and, CSA Consultation Paper 91-404 – Derivatives: *Segregation and Portability in OTC Derivatives Clearing* (10 February 2012). The remaining papers are expected to be released for public comment by end of May 2012.

83 Proposed Act, above note 3, Section 7, ss 89–92.

84 Nick Le Pan, "Look Before You Leap: A Skeptical View of Proposals to Meld Macro- and Microprudential Regulation" (2009) CD Howe Institute, Commentary No 296.

85 *Ibid* at 2.

86 *Ibid* at i.

assessing the impact on the depositors, policyholders and creditors of financial institutions) rather than macroprudential.[87]

Further, there may be a conflict of interest if OSFI's role is to focus on the monetary system as a whole. OSFI must advise financial institutions of material deficiencies and, if such deficiencies are found, must require management and boards of directors to take necessary corrective measures expeditiously. Thus, OSFI's concern is the health and well-being of individual financial institutions. If OSFI were also in charge of monitoring the system as a whole, it would be evaluating its own success at maintaining the stability of financial institutions.

The FMRA, on the other hand, would be a separate body with a specific mandate to focus on the system as a whole and to ensure information sharing among existing regulators. This body should have legislative authority over securities markets, especially in times of financial crisis. It would be a federal body comprised of provincial representatives (likely from current securities commissions) and would seek counsel from the relevant institutions: the federal Department of Finance, OSFI, the Canada Deposit Insurance Corporation, the Financial Consumer Agency of Canada (FCAC), and the Bank of Canada. The FMRA would be charged with assessing systemic risks on a regular basis and discussing measures to mitigate those risks.

It is clear that those operating the FMRA will need to "inform and be informed by monetary, fiscal, prudential, competition, and other government policies."[88] The Bank of Canada, as the country's central bank, will play a crucial role in macroprudential oversight, especially because of its current role in controlling systemic risk in the clearing and settlement systems as well as its role and expertise in assessing risks in the derivatives markets and the financial system generally. Yet the Bank cannot and should not be the macroprudential regulator itself, given

---

87 Under the *Office of the Superintendent of Financial Institutions Act*, above note 64, s 18, there exists a committee structure that is effective as an information sharing and coordinating body amongst Finance, OSFI, Bank of Canada and CDIC. The current mandate of this committee however is explicitly limited to consultations on matters relating directly to the supervision of financial institutions. Its current mandate and role is thus ill-suited for macro-prudential oversight. There is also the Senior Advisory Committee (SAC), but it is a non-statutory body and therefore has no formal mandate, powers or accountability.

88 G30 Report, above note 32 at 16.

its existing mandate and the possibility that its independence — and, indeed, its effectiveness — in its current areas of jurisdiction could be compromised. As the Group of 30 explain, " . . . the macroprudential supervisor should not be so closely linked to the fiscal authorities that its political independence is, or appears to be, compromised."[89]

Some argue that Canada has too many regulators, and that adding an additional body such as the FMRA would detract from the focus on each regulator's individual mandate. However, this multifaceted institutional landscape is the very reason that Canada needs a separate federal body with a specific mandate to oversee its complex financial markets. Given their individual responsibilities over separate aspects of the financial system, none of the existing bodies can realistically be charged with monitoring the entire system: As thirteen provincial securities regulators, one financial institution regulator, and a central bank, as well as other bodies (e.g., FCAC), pursue their respective mandates, issues of systemic risk may well "get lost." Responding to guidance given by the SCC, the federal government should thus introduce a legislative scheme for systemic risk oversight (i.e. the FMRA), with participation by the relevant federal agencies. The provinces would also be invited to participate but, to the extent that some provinces refused or delayed, the federal government would proceed nonetheless on the basis of the *Securities Reference*.

In creating the FMRA, Canada would not be out of step with other jurisdictions, which are also focusing on macroprudential regulation. The European Systemic Risk Board (ESRB) was established in 2010 with a mandate to manage systemic risks to financial market stability in the European Union;[90] in the United States, the Financial Stability Oversight Council (FSOC), established under the *Dodd-Frank Act*, performs a similar function, with fifteen members representing, among other organizations,

---

89 *Ibid* at 74. The viewpoint is contrary to that of Jenkins et al, above note 78, who argue that a formal committee is the preferred governance arrangement for monitoring systemic risk.

90 See EC, *Regulation (EU) No 1092/2010 of the European Parliament and of the Council of 24 November 2010 on European Union macro-prudential oversight of the financial system and establishing a European Systemic Risk Board*, [2010] OJ, L 331/1; EC, *Council Regulation (EU) No 1096/2010 of 17 November 2010 conferring specific tasks upon the European Central Bank concerning the functioning of the European Systemic Risk Board*, [2010] OJ, L 331/162.

the Federal Reserve, Treasury, FDIC, Consumer Financial Protection Bureau, and SEC. As the main body responsible for macroprudential regulation of the US financial system, the FSOC has the authority to set capital requirements, limit leverage, and restrict risky trading with respect to any "systemically significant firm" and to intervene to break up any firm that poses a "grave threat" to market stability.[91] In Australia, responsibility for systemic risk oversight is shared by the Australian Prudential Regulation Authority (APRA) and the Reserve Bank, which fulfills its financial stability mandate through its influence over monetary policy, by monitoring the health of the financial system by collecting/assessing aggregate financial data, and, by working to ensure the safety and stability of the payments system through its operation of the Payments System Board.[92] The APRA oversees the stability of the financial services industry at the institutional level, regulating deposit-taking institutions such as banks and credit unions as well as insurance dealers, superannuation plans, and so on.[93] Thus, other jurisdictions have taken steps to establish a centralized body or bodies responsible for macroprudential regulation, and it is consistent with international developments for Canada to move in this direction as well.

A critic of the above argument in favour of an FMRA or similar body might argue that creating such an agency is mere window-dressing, a political response to the 2008 credit crisis. The justice of this critique would need to be evaluated over time. Does the FMRA provide meaningful input into policy making regarding systemic risk that other institutions do not currently provide? Can the FMRA coordinate its efforts with provincial securities regulators as well as existing federal regulators (e.g., OSFI) and the Bank of Canada? Do the benefits of establishing the FMRA outweigh the costs? These are questions that will be

---

91 See *Dodd-Frank Wall Street Reform and Consumer Protection Act*, Pub L 111-203, Title 1 (establishing the FSOC), s 112(a)(1) (setting out its objectives).

92 For more details, see the Reserve Bank of Australia's (RBA) website, online: Reserve Bank of Australia www.rba.gov.au/fin-stability/reg-framework/cfr.html; and the RBA's Financial Stability Review (March 2009), online: Reserve Bank of Australia www.rba.gov.au/publications/fsr/2009/mar/html/contents.html).

93 For details, see the FSB "Peer Review of Australia - Review Report" (21 September 2011), online: Financial Stability Board www.financialstabilityboard.org/publications/r_110926b.pdf.

asked long after the creation of a federal systemic risk agency in order to evaluate its long-term efficacy and importance.

E. Conclusion

In this chapter I have called for regulation in the area of systemic risk, an area in which the federal government has constitutional jurisdiction following the *Securities Reference* case. I have also called for coordination among regulatory bodies on issues relating to systemic risk. While the term "systemic risk" contains ambiguities, and has in the past been narrowly construed as pertaining solely to the successive failures of financial institutions in a domino-like fashion, the concept should be broadly interpreted to refer to the possibility of financial meltdown of an entire economic system. Adopting this broad definition seems appropriate when one considers the ABCP crisis in Canada and its effect on Canadian financial markets.

The ABCP crisis highlighted the fact that securities regulation and prudential regulation share certain objectives: ultimately, they both aim to serve consumers' common interest in living in a society with a sound financial system. The idea that systemic risk should be regulated by a newly-created institution is motivated by an understanding of consumers' needs. But determining the appropriate policy response in an economy in which complex securities are bought and sold, and in which systemic risk is an ever-present possibility, is a difficult task. Developing such a policy will require research, institutional coordination, and legal input but is not beyond the reach of the federal government and the provinces acting together, as the Supreme Court of Canada suggested in the *Securities Reference* case.

CHAPTER 12

A National Securities Commission? The Headless Horseman Rides Again

Jeffrey G. MacIntosh

A. Introduction

According to the website of the Canadian Securities Transition Office,

> In June 2009, the Government of Canada launched the initiative to transition from the current system of 13 provincial and territorial regulators to a single Canadian securities regulator. It established the Canadian Securities Transition Office (CSTO or Transition Office) to lead and manage the transition.

I argue here that the prospect of creating a single national regulator, whether federally or provincially constituted, was never more than a chimera. Under the doctrine of paramountcy, the draft federal legislation that was the subject of the *Reference Re Securities Act*[1] would not have displaced provincial legislation. Thus, given the state of Canadian politics, even if the federal government had been successful in arguing that its legislation was constitutional, this would merely have been the prelude to a difficult and drawn-out negotiation in which some but not all of the provinces would have joined the federal scheme.[2] Inevitably, some would have remained outside the fold. It is therefore clear that some kind of passport system lies in Canada's securities regula-

---

1   *Reference Re Securities Act*, 2011 SCC 66 [*Securities Reference*].
2   As I note below, because the three territories hold power delegated from the federal government, they can be forced to join a national commission.

tory future. Only the identities and numbers of participants in the passport system remain in question.

Because of the controlling nature of political factors, the decision of the Supreme Court in the *Securities Reference* is likely to have little impact — either positive or negative — on the likelihood that Canada will get a single securities regulator. Both before and after the *Securities Reference,* cooperative federalism was the only way forward. The decision adds some measure of certainty about what the federal government can and cannot do.[3] However, a federally constituted multijurisdictional regulator was, and remains, an inferior option to a provincially constituted regulator, since (regardless of the result of the *Securities Reference*), the latter is virtually certain to attract more sign-ups.

While some have criticized the *Securities Reference* as a throwback to a prior epoch of constitutional adjudication, or the product of political forces, I argue that it is a well-reasoned decision fully consistent with prior (and recent) Supreme Court jurisprudence. The five presumptive *indicia* for validity set out in *General Motors of Canada Ltd. v City National Leasing*[4] centre on a single theme: sustaining the federal union by maintaining a workable balance of power between the federal and provincial governments. As the Court emphasizes, the draft federal statute was a virtual copy of existing provincial statutes; upholding this legislation under the trade and commerce power, therefore, would potentially have wrought massive change in this delicate balance, ceding to the federal government the power to aggressively enter a wide array of new domains heretofore occupied only or mainly by the provinces. Particularly given the futility of pursuing a single commission under the aegis of the federal government, effecting

---

3   At least two sources of uncertainty remain, however. First, the Court indicated, but only in very general terms, and only in *obiter dictum,* what kinds of federal legislation might meet the test of constitutionality. Second, the decision lacks finality in that it deals only with the general branch of the trade and commerce power. Thus, it is possible to argue that the federal government still has a window to legislate under the international and interprovincial branch of the trade and commerce power, or other heads of power such as criminal law, banking law, etc. See generally Philip Anisman & Peter W Hogg, "Constitutional Aspects of Federal Securities Legislation" in Philip Anisman et al, eds, *Proposals for a Securities Market Law for Canada* (Ottawa: Consumer and Corporate Affairs Canada, 1979).

4   *General Motors of Canada Ltd v City National Leasing,* [1989] 1 SCR 641 [*General Motors*].

such a massive shift of power in favour of the feds would have constituted a defining moment in the annals of Pyrrhic victories.

In addition, it cannot be said that the holding is a departure from either the "double aspects" or the "incidental effects" doctrine. The Court was clearly right in rejecting both on the ground that the proposed federal legislation was a virtual copy of existing provincial legislation.

The *Securities Reference* does, however, highlight some difficulties in interpreting the fourth element of the *General Motors* test. I suggest that it is difficult to ascribe a meaning to the fourth criterion that does not degenerate into a *reductio ad absurdum*.

I also suggest that double aspects, concurrency, separation of powers, cooperative federalism, and paramountcy interact much like elements in a mechanical analog computer: when one of these is changed, corresponding changes must be made in all of the others to preserve the original homeostasis of federal–provincial power.

Finally, I suggest that where the preservation of a federal–provincial homeostasis is a key judicial imperative, division of powers adjudication is inevitably path dependent and subject to first-mover advantages. That is, the level of government that gets there first is likely to have the strongest claim. This seems to have been the case in relation to securities regulation.

B. Path Dependency and First-Mover Advantages in Division of Powers Adjudication

In my view, we cannot make sense of the five presumptive criteria for validity in *General Motors* without understanding the path dependency of constitutional adjudication. I thus start my analysis here.

A pivotal factor in the Court's decision in the *Securities Reference* was the extent to which the provinces had already staked out the territory of securities regulation for themselves. The Court stated, for example, that "[w]hile it is obvious that the securities market is of great importance to modern economic activity, we cannot ignore that the provinces have been deeply engaged in the regulation of this market over the course of many years."[5] Indeed, it was the nearly perfect overlap between the proposed federal

---

5   *Securities Reference*, above note 1 at para 115.

statute and the various provincial enactments that persuaded the Court that a federal statute would intrude too deeply on provincial powers to pass muster under the *General Motors* test.[6]

It is difficult to escape the conclusion that path dependency and first mover advantages may play a role — and in this case *did* play a role — in determining which level of government gets the keys to the car. Path dependency is a close cousin of chaos theory. It describes a situation in which current institutional arrangements owe much to pure happenstance; that is, the polity might have taken a variety of paths and, for no better reason than an adventitious roll of the dice, chose one rather than another.[7] In our case, the provinces have been in the securities regulation game for about a hundred years, and the depth and breadth of provincial penetration into this domain are apparent merely by surveying the thickness of any volume containing the consolidated rules of any given province. This provincial presence, however, was not in any way inevitable; it might well have been the federal government that jumped into the game early on and created its own comprehensive regime of rules. Had it done so, the shoe might well have been on the other foot, with the provinces pleading constitutional validity for comprehensive securities legislation under the "property and civil rights" power — and losing, given the extent to which their proposed legislation would intrude on a recognized precinct of federal power.

In short, there is a "first-mover" advantage in fixing the division of powers. The level of government that gets there first — particularly if it has been there for a long time and achieved deep penetration — wins the constitutional prize.

---

6   For example, the Court stated:

> [T]he fact that the structure and terms of the proposed Act largely replicate the existing provincial schemes belies the suggestion that the securities market has been wholly transformed over the years. On the basis of the record presented to us, we conclude, as discussed below, that the day-to-day regulation of securities within the provinces, which represents the main thrust of the Act, *remains* essentially a matter of property and civil rights within the provinces and therefore subject to provincial power.

> *Ibid* at para 116 [emphasis added].

7   See e.g. Stan Liebowitz & Stephen Margolis "Path Dependence" in Boudewijn Bouckaert & Gerrit De Geest, eds, *Encyclopedia of Law and Economics, Volume I. The History and Methodology of Law and Economics* (Cheltenham: Edward Elgar, 2000) at 985.

Both path dependency and the provinces' first-mover advantage in securities regulation are well illustrated by the courts' interpretation of the scope of the "property and civil rights" head of provincial power, *in the context of provincial securities regulation.* As Hogg and Anisman[8] pointed out many years ago, the courts have been munificent to the point of prodigality in defining the constitutional jurisdiction of the provincial securities regulators. Although the Constitution gives the provinces the right to regulate matters relating to "property and civil rights *in the province,*" the courts have not demurred from allowing provincial regulators to regulate transactions extending across provincial or national borders.[9] Indeed, the public interest powers may be engaged even in cases of transactions occurring entirely outside the province, if there is a material effect on the capital markets of the province.[10] The proximate cause for this generosity (which has stretched the "ancillary effects" doctrine to or beyond its breaking point) has been the absence of federal securities law. Striking down the provincial laws, or restricting them primarily to intraprovincial interactions, would create a serious void in the regulatory oversight of Canada's capital markets. Again, the unseen puppet master is the path-dependent manner in which the securities field is currently occupied.[11]

In part, this turns division of powers adjudication — and the approach adopted in the *Securities Reference* — on its head. Rather than resolving constitutional disputes by the application of pristine abstract principles that flow inevitably (and uniquely) from the words of the Constitution, constitutional adjudication owes much to questions of path dependency and the state of cur-

---

8   Anisman & Hogg, above note 3.

9   The pertinent cases are neatly digested by the Court in the *Securities Reference*, above note 1 at para 45.

10   *Québec (Sa Majesté du Chef) v Ontario Securities Commission* (1992), 10 OR (3d) 577 (CA), leave to appeal to SCC refused, (*sub nom R. du chef du Québec v. Ontario Securities Commission*) [1993] 2 SCR x. In relation to other subject matters, the "property and civil rights" clause has usually been interpreted far more modestly. See e.g. *Interprovincial Co-Operatives Ltd v Dryden Chemicals Ltd,* [1976] 1 SCR 477.

11   The *Securities Reference,* above note 1 at para 83 states:

> It must, to use the phrase in *General Motors,* be something that the provinces, acting either individually or in concert, could not effectively achieve. To put it another way, the situation must be such that if the federal government were not able to legislate, there would be a constitutional gap. Such a gap is constitutional anathema in a federation.

rent institutional arrangements. These iteratively interact with the abstract words of the Constitution to generate legal outcomes that are themselves path dependent.

A further factor of importance is efficacy or functionality, which is dealt with in Sections E and H.

C. The Elusive Meaning of the Fourth Criterion from *General Motors*

The *Securities Reference* summarizes (and adopts) the five presumptive *indicia* for constitutional validity from *General Motors* as follows:

> (1) whether the impugned law is part of a general regulatory scheme; (2) whether the scheme is under the oversight of a regulatory agency; (3) whether the legislation is concerned with trade as a whole rather than with a particular industry; (4) whether it is of such a nature that provinces, acting alone or in concert, would be constitutionally incapable of enacting it; and (5) whether the legislative scheme is such that the failure to include one or more provinces or localities in the scheme would jeopardize its successful operation in other parts of the country.[12]

With respect to the fourth criterion, the provinces argued that there was nothing the federal government could do that they could not also do by mutual agreement among themselves.[13] In rebuttal, the Court stated:

> The difficulty with the provinces' argument, however, is that, as a matter of constitutional principle, neither Parliament nor the legislatures can, by ordinary legislation, fetter themselves against some future legislative action . . . . The point is simply that because provinces could always withdraw from an interprovincial scheme there is no assurance that they could effectively address issues of national systemic risk and competitive national capital markets on a sustained basis . . . . It follows that the fourth *General Motors* question must be answered, at least partially, in the negative. The provinces, acting in concert, lack the constitutional capacity to sustain a viable national

---

12 *Ibid* at para 80.
13 *Ibid* at para 118.

scheme aimed at genuine national goals such as management of systemic risk or Canada-wide data collection.[14]

The Court held that the proposed federal legislation nonetheless failed to satisfy the fourth criterion, as it "reflects an attempt that goes well beyond these matters of undoubted national interest and concern and reaches down into the detailed regulation of all aspects of securities."[15]

The difficulty with the Court's rejection of the provinces' argument with respect to joint action is that it is inconsistent with the wording of the fourth criterion; namely, "whether it is of such a nature that provinces, acting alone *or in concert*, would be constitutionally incapable of enacting it" (emphasis added). The Court has effectively read the words "or in concert" out of the fourth element, because it will *always* be the case that the provinces may resile from a joint scheme of regulation.

This is merely symptomatic of a more deeply rooted problem: whether it is possible to attribute a meaning to the fourth criterion that does not degenerate into triviality or unproductive fictions. Federal legislation will always apply uniformly right across the country — an advantage that no province acting alone can replicate. However, if national uniformity is the gist of the fourth element (as many federal partisans argue), then it is trivially met by the federal government in every case, in which case the fourth element utterly ceases to have any discriminatory power. If, on the other hand, provincial constitutional incapability can be surmounted on the basis that the provinces can combine to reproduce nationally uniform rules, this too erects a hurdle that is trivially surmounted (this time, in favour of the provinces), again robbing the fourth element of any discriminatory power.

The inquiry into constitutional incapability, as an abstraction, thus seems to pull little freight. An alternative criterion is the relative efficacy of federal and provincial legislation, which is specifically rejected by the Court as a factor in applying the *General*

---

14   *Ibid* at paras 119–21.
15   *Ibid* at para 122.

Motors test.[16] My inclination is to agree with Professor Iacobucci[17] that this rejection cannot withstand analysis. It does not seem possible to decide which level of government prevails on either the fourth or the fifth criterion without delving into the relative efficacy of the federal and provincial legislation.

In upholding the federal *Combines Act* in *General Motors,* for example, the Court based its analysis squarely on the question of relative efficacy. The Court's finding that local regulation would be inadequate was based on the view that provincial legislation would inevitably have the wrong degree of granularity; that is, legislation with a purely provincial purview would be superimposed on a market with an inherently national character. This is, at bottom, a measure of relative functionality. Given the exogenous dictates of market composition (i.e., markets habitually cross provincial borders), federal legislation works in a way that provincial legislation cannot.

However, it is noteworthy that the "wrong degree of granularity" argument was the rallying cry of those anxious to see a single federal regulator. Much was made of the trans-border nature of securities markets, a fact that the Supreme Court acknowledged.[18] Should this not have led to a similar result?

The difference in outcomes in the two cases again illustrates the importance of path dependency and first-mover advantages. In the *Securities Reference,* those who opposed the federal legislation were able to marshal abundant evidence that provincially-based cooperative securities regulation operates with a high degree of efficacy,[19] and that any advantage to be secured by federal legislation would be marginal rather than epochal. Let us

---

16 *Ibid* at para 90. See also *ibid* at para 10 ("[w]hile the parties presented evidence and arguments on the relative merits of federal and provincial regulation of securities, the policy question of whether a single national securities scheme is preferable to multiple provincial regimes is not one for the courts to decide"), and para 127 ("arguments in the reports as to whether securities should be regulated federally or provincially as a matter of policy are irrelevant to the constitutional validity of the legislation.").

17 See Chapter 3.

18 *Securities Reference*, above note 1 ("[n]o doubt, much of Canada's capital market is interprovincial and indeed international." at para 15).

19 See e.g. *Securities Reference, ibid* (Factum of the Attorney General of Alberta), online: Supreme Court of Canada www.scc-csc.gc.ca/case-dossier/cms-sgd/fac-mem-eng.aspx?cas=33718. See also Pierre Lortie, "Securities Regulation in Canada: The Case for Effectiveness" IRPP Study, No 19 (October 2011).

then suppose that *General Motors* arose against a similar factual backdrop; that is, that the provinces had long since staked out the territory of competition law and fashioned a complex cooperative regime similar to that which obtains in the area of securities law. Let us further suppose that the federal government sought to introduce a largely overlapping regime of competition law. In that case, the result in *General Motors* might well have been the same as in the *Securities Reference*, with the Court denying constitutionality on the ground that the federal legislation intruded too deeply on an established beachhead of provincial power.

This makes comparative efficacy less an abstraction than a question to be answered within an existing institutional (and path-dependent) context. While the Supreme Court is anxious to deny that the relative efficacy of provincial securities legislation was a factor in the *Securities Reference* decision, it is easy to imagine a different result if cooperative efforts by provincial securities regulators were manifestly inadequate. This again lifts constitutional principle out of the realm of the Platonic ideal and into the demesnes of the workaday world, replete with untidy pragmatics drawn less from the world of ideas than from the prosaic domain of what is.

Indeed, the very idea of relative efficacy as an abstraction seems to degenerate into a *reductio ad absurdum*, much like the other ways of understanding the fourth *General Motors* criterion, because in many cases the only obstacles to an efficacious cooperative regulatory scheme at the provincial level are time and will. These are empirical and not metaphysical data.

As the Court reiterates in the *Securities Reference* (drawing on settled law[20]), we live in a world in which the "dominant tide" of constitutional interpretation is double aspects rather than "watertight compartments." The existence of a number of broad-textured provincial powers, such as "Property and Civil Rights in the Province,"[21] "Local Works and Undertakings,"[22] and "Generally all Matters of a merely local or private Nature in the Province,"[23] means that federal and provincial authorities will

---

20 See *Securities Reference*, above note 1 at paras 57–62.
21 *Constitution Act, 1867* (UK), 30 & 31 Vict, c 3, s 92(13), reprinted in RSC 1985, App II, No 5.
22 *Ibid*, s 92(10).
23 *Ibid*, s 92(16). Other more specific powers are nonetheless quite wide-ranging, including "The Establishment, Maintenance, and Management of Hospitals, Asylums, Charities, and Eleemosynary Institutions in and

frequently cross swords. When this happens, a court has no alternative but to consider the relative functionality of federal and provincial legislation (whether openly or implicitly), within the existing institutional context.

D. Maintaining a Balance of Power: The Pivotal Element Underlying the Five Presumptive Criteria in *General Motors*

Much of the debate about whether the federal government has or should have the authority under the general branch of the trade and commerce power to enter the securities regulatory domain has completely ignored the extent to which a favourable ruling would have broad and potentially far-reaching consequences for the distribution of constitutional authority between the federal and provincial governments. The words "The Regulation of Trade and Commerce" are capable of bearing many meanings, both broad and narrow. Toward the broader end of the spectrum, the power is potentially so imperialistic as to give the federal government a power essentially correlative with the provinces' right over "Property and Civil Rights in the Province." Thus, as Table 1 illustrates, these words could conceivably be extended to embrace part or all of contract law, commercial law, consumer law, trusts, personal property security, insurance, sale of goods, mortgages and real property, the professions (law, medicine, engineering, accountancy, etc.), the trades, insurance brokers, real estate brokers, health care, environmental law, employment contracts, health and safety law, civil actions, and, of course, securities law and the stock exchanges.

---

for the Province" (*ibid*, s 92(7)), and "Municipal Institutions in the Province" (*ibid*, s 92(8)).

Table 1

Commercial Law	*Absconding Debtors Act*
	Bulk Sales Act
	Canadian Public Accountability Reporting Act
	Conveyancing and Law of Property Act
	Construction Lien Act
	Creditors Relief Act
	Factors Act
	Fraudulent Conveyances Act
	Frustrated Contracts Act
	Gas and Oil Leases Act
	Insurance Act
	International Commercial Arbitration Act
	International Sale of Goods Act
	Limited Partnerships Act
	Loan and Trust Corporations Act
	Marine Insurance Act
	Mercantile Law Amendment Act
	Mortgage Brokerages, Lenders and Administrators Act
	Mortgages Act
	Partnerships Act
	Pawnbrokers Act
	Personal Property Security Act
	Repair and Storage Liens Act
	Sale of Goods Act
	Securities Act
	Securities Transfer Act
	Short Forms of Leases Act
	Statute of Frauds
	Ticket Speculation Act
	Toronto Stock Exchange Act
	Travel Industry Act
	Trustee Act
	Unconscionable Transactions Relief Act
	Variation of Trusts Act
	Vendors and Purchasers Act
	Warehouse Receipts Act
	Wine Content and Labelling Act

Professions and Trades	Barristers Act
	Certified General Accountants Act
	Certified Management Accountants Act
	Chartered Accountants Act
	Chiropody Act
	Chiropractic Act
	Dentistry Act
	Dietetics Act
	Drugless Practitioners Act
	Fair Access to Regulated Professions Act
	Homemakers and Nurses Act
	Homeopathy Act
	Kinesiology Act
	Law Society Act
	Lobbyists Registration Act
	Massage Therapy Act
	Midwifery Act
	Naturopathy Act
	Nursing Act
	Notaries Act
	Opticianry Act
	Optometry Act
	Physiotherapy Act
	Powers of Attorney Act
	Private Security and Investigative Services Act
	Professional Engineers Act
	Professional Foresters Act
	Professional Geoscientists Act
	Psychology Act
	Psychotherapy Act
	Real Estate and Business Brokers Act
	Registered Insurance Brokers Act
	Solicitors Act
	Surveyors Act
	Surveys Act
	Trades Qualification and Apprenticeship Act
	Traditional Chinese Medicine Act
	Veterinarians Act
Environment	Environmental Protection Act
	Environmental Bill of Rights
	Environmental Assessment Act
	Green Energy Act
	Greenbelt Act
	Ministry of the Environment Act
	Oak Ridges Moraine Preservation Act
	Oak Ridges Moraine Conservation Act
	Ontario Clean Energy Benefit Act
	Ontario Water Resources Act
	Safe Drinking Water Act
	Toxics Reduction Act

Employment Contracts	*Colleges Collective Bargaining Act* *Crown Employees Collective Bargaining Act* *Employer Health Tax Act* *Employers and Employees Act* *Labour Relations Act* *Ministry of Labour Act* *Ontario Municipal Employees Retirement* *System Act* *Public Sector Dispute Resolution Act* *Rights of Labour Act* *Social Contract Act* *Statute Labour Act* *Wages Act*
Health and Safety	*Employment Standards Act* *Food Safety and Quality Act* *Mental Health Act* *Ministry of Community and Social Services Act* *Occupational Health and Safety Act* *Ontario Mental Health Foundation Act* *Safety and Consumer Statutes Administration Act* *Smoke-Free Ontario Act* *Technical Standards and Safety Act* *Workplace Safety and Insurance Act*
Consumer Protection	*Consumer Protection Act* *Discriminatory Business Practices Act* *Ministry of Consumer and Business Services Act* *Ontario New Home Warranties Plan Act*
Human Rights	*Human Rights Code* *Victims Bill of Rights*
Civil Actions	*Negligence Act* *Occupiers Liability Act* *Trespass to Property Act*

It would be very surprising if this were what the drafters of the Constitution intended. While the Constitution is replete with overlapping authorities, there are few express instances of purely duplicative authority.[24] While the federal and provincial corporate codes are largely duplicative, the federal power to incorporate companies "with federal objects" does not appear in the Constitution; rather, it was interpretively woven into the fabric of the Constitution by the Privy Council under the "residual clause" (the authority "to make Laws for the Peace, Order, and good Govern-

---

24 One area of explicit overlap may be found in *ibid*, s 95, which creates concurrent federal and provincial jurisdiction over agriculture and immigration.

ment of Canada"[25]), essentially as a foil to the provincial authority to legislate in relation to "The Incorporation of Companies
with Provincial Objects."[26] The general aim of the drafters of the
Constitution seems clear: to give both federal and provincial governments dominant or primary spheres of legislative authority,
and the federal government a residual power to deal with matters not specifically allocated to one level or the other. Thus, one
starts with the presumption that the words "trade and commerce"
cannot and should not be given anything like plenary authority.
This sentiment is fully captured by the Supreme Court in the
Securities Reference:

> On its face, the general trade and commerce power (as distin-
> guished from the more specific federal power to regulate inter-
> provincial and international trade and commerce) is broad—so
> broad that it has the potential to permit federal duplication
> (and, in cases of conflict, evisceration) of the provincial powers
> over large aspects of property and civil rights and local mat-
> ters. This would upset the constitutional balance envisaged by
> ss. 91 and 92 and undermine the federalism principle. To avoid
> this result, the trade and commerce power has been confined to
> matters that are genuinely national in scope and qualitatively
> distinct from those falling under provincial heads of power re-
> lating to local matters and property and civil rights. The es-
> sence of the general trade and commerce power is its national
> focus . . . . As a consequence, a federal head of power cannot be
> given a scope that would eviscerate a provincial legislative com-
> petence . . . . The jurisprudence on the general trade and com-
> merce power reflects this fundamental principle. . . . Thus, the
> starting point is that the general trade and commerce power
> under s. 91(2) does not encompass all trade and commerce; the
> power is necessarily circumscribed.[27]

The need to preserve a balance of power between the two levels
of government, however, is more than merely a motivation for restricting the trade and commerce power. It is also the primary
factor used to determine where the pivot point between federal
and provincial authority resides. This sentiment is at the very
core of both *General Motors* and the *Securities Reference*. In the
former, Dickson CJ stated,

---

25 *Ibid*, preamble to s 91.
26 *Ibid*, s 92(11) [emphasis added].
27 *Securities Reference*, above note 1 at para 70.

In examining cases that have considered s. 91(2), it is evident that courts have been sensitive to the need to reconcile the general trade and commerce power of the federal government with the provincial power over property and civil rights . . . . The true balance between property and civil rights and the regulation of trade and commerce must lie somewhere between an all pervasive interpretation of s. 91(2) and an interpretation that renders the general trade and commerce power to all intents vapid and meaningless.[28]

Dickson J also made it clear that each of the five presumptive elements of the test for constitutional validity was formulated with a view to preserving this balance. With respect to the first three criteria (initially formulated by Laskin CJ in *MacDonald v Vapor Canada Ltd*[29]), Dickson J stated,

Each of these requirements is evidence of a concern that federal authority under the second branch of the trade and commerce power does not encroach on provincial jurisdiction. By limiting the means which federal legislators may employ to that of a regulatory scheme overseen by a regulatory agency, and by limiting the object of federal legislation to trade as a whole, these requirements attempt to maintain a delicate balance between federal and provincial power.[30]

With respect to the last two presumptive elements (emanating from the judgment of Laskin CJ in *AG (Can) v Can Nat Transportation, Ltd*[31]), Dickson CJ stated that "These [last] two requirements, like Laskin [CJ]'s three criteria, serve to ensure that federal legislation does not upset the balance of power between federal and provincial governments"[32] — in short, "The five factors articulated in *Canadian National Transportation* merely represent a principled way to begin the difficult task of distinguishing between matters relating to trade and commerce and those of a more local nature."[33] In each case, the extent of the federal encroachment on provincial power is a pivotal element: "As the seriousness of the encroachment on provincial powers varies, so does the test required to ensure that an appropriate constitu-

28 *General Motors*, above note 4 at paras 28 and 30.
29 [1977] 2 SCR 134.
30 *General Motors*, above note 4 at para 32.
31 [1983] 2 SCR 206.
32 *General Motors,* above note 4 at para 34. See also paras 30, 32, 45–46, 67, and 78.
33 *Ibid* at para 34.

tional balance is maintained."[34] Thus, in examining a particular provision whose constitutionality is challenged,

> The first step should be to consider whether and to what extent the impugned provision can be characterized as intruding into provincial powers . . . . In most cases like the present, however, it will be concluded that the impugned provision can be characterized, prima facie, as intruding to some extent on provincial powers: the question is to what extent.[35]

Similarly, in the *Securities Reference*, a unanimous Court stated:

> It is a fundamental principle of federalism that both federal and provincial powers must be respected, and one power may not be used in a manner that effectively eviscerates another. Rather, federalism demands that a balance be struck, a balance that allows both the federal Parliament and the provincial legislatures to act effectively in their respective spheres. Accepting Canada's interpretation of the general trade and commerce power would disrupt rather than maintain that balance. Parliament cannot regulate the whole of the securities system simply because aspects of it have a national dimension.[36]

This balancing of federal and provincial power is absolutely central to an understanding of both *General Motors* and the *Securities Reference*.

E. Incidental and Ancillary Effects, Efficacy, and Substantial Overlap

In *General Motors*, the Court adopts Hogg's description of the incidental and ancillary effects doctrine:

> The pith and substance doctrine enables a law that is classified as "in relation to" a matter within the competence of the enacting body to have incidental or ancillary effects on matters outside the competence of the enacting body.[37]

---

34 *Ibid* at para 46.
35 *Ibid* at para 41.
36 *Securities Reference*, above note 1 at para 7.
37 *General Motors,* above note 4 at para 45. Paragraphs 45–47 discuss the doctrine and prior case law.

Thus, "[b]oth provincial and federal governments have equal ability to legislate in ways that may incidentally affect the other government's sphere of power."[38]

In *General Motors,* even though the extent of the encroachment was more than merely incidental and ancillary, the federal enactment was found to be constitutional. In the words of the Court,

> not only is the Act meant to cover intraprovincial trade, but . . .
> it must do so if it is to be effective . . . . [C]ompetition cannot be
> successfully regulated by federal legislation which is restricted
> to interprovincial trade.[39]

General Motors thus effectively enunciates a second category of permissible encroachment, which might be styled the "efficacy" doctrine, insofar as a greater intrusion is warranted where the efficacy of the legislation requires it. Initially, this would seem more likely to add dimension to federal than provincial powers, since federal legislation, which is inherently national in scope, may in some cases be more efficacious than provincial legislation. It is important to recognize, however, that cases may arise where provincial legislation is more efficacious — even where the phenomenon being regulated is "national" in scope (such as securities markets). I discuss this further in Section H.

The degree of intrusion on provincial powers in the *Securities Reference* exceeded that which can be justified on either the incidental and ancillary effects doctrine or the efficacy doctrine. In the words of the Court,

> This is not a case of a valid federal scheme that incidentally intrudes on provincial powers. It is not the incidental effects of the scheme that are constitutionally suspect; it is rather the main thrust of the legislation that goes beyond the federal power.[40]

Figure 1 is a Venn diagram illustrating the different relationships that may arise. The first set of overlapping circles illustrates the operation of the incidental and ancillary or incidental effects doctrine. Under this doctrine, legislation that encroaches to a relatively modest extent upon the domain of the other level of government will be permitted, so long as the "pith and substance" of the legislation fits within a head of constitutional power.

---

38 *Ibid.*
39 *Ibid* at para 63.
40 *Securities Reference*, above note 1 at para 129.

The second set of overlapping circles is illustrative of a case like *General Motors*; the federal power overlaps the provincial power in a manner that cannot be justified under the incidental and ancillary doctrine, but the federal legislation is nonetheless constitutionally valid because all of the elements of the *General Motors* test are met. There is a compelling "national interest" that "is engaged in a manner that is qualitatively different from provincial concerns."[41]

The third set of overlapping circles illustrates a case like the *Securities Reference*. The federal legislation greatly overlaps the provincial legislation, but *without a compelling national interest* (or, more properly, a compelling national functionality). The overlap is well beyond that which can be justified under the incidental and ancillary doctrine, and the federal legislation fails.

---

41 *Ibid* at para 46. The overlap between the federal and provincial legislation need not be partial; it could be complete. Michael Trebilcock, see Chapter 2, and Iacobucci, above note 17 both argue that, in *General Motors,* the Court was wrong in concluding that efficacious competition law demanded a federal presence. I am not in a position to gainsay this view. Nonetheless, I note that in *General Motors* the Court had before it an evidentiary record that provided ample ammunition for its contrary finding of fact. In particular, the Court drew upon argument presented by two distinguished law professors (Peter W. Hogg & Warren Grover, "The Constitutionality of the Competition Bill" (1976) 1 Can Bus LJ 197) and an equally distinguished professor of economics (Albert E Safarian, "Canadian Federalism and Economic Integration" (Ottawa: Privy Council Office, 1974)) that the very existence of the economic union — one of the underlying *desiderata* of confederation — is critically dependent upon treating Canada as a single market for competition law purposes. Drawing upon the work of these scholars, the Court held that "[i]t is evident from this discussion that competition cannot be effectively regulated unless it is regulated nationally," and "not only is the Act meant to cover intraprovincial trade, but . . . it must do so if it is to be effective." *General Motors,* above note 4 at para 63. See also *ibid* at para 65. It was further held that "competition cannot be successfully regulated by federal legislation which is restricted to interprovincial trade." *Ibid* at para 63. If the Court was in error in so holding, it nonetheless cannot be said that it was naïve (as Professor Iacobucci suggests) or lacking a sufficient empirical or evidentiary foundation for its ruling.

Figure 1

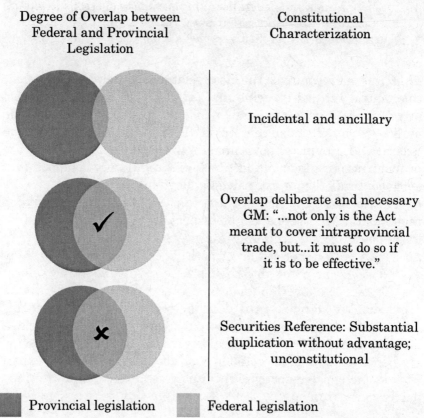

Degree of Overlap between Federal and Provincial Legislation	Constitutional Characterization
	Incidental and ancillary
✔	Overlap deliberate and necessary GM: "...not only is the Act meant to cover intraprovincial trade, but...it must do so if it is to be effective."
✘	Securities Reference: Substantial duplication without advantage; unconstitutional

■ Provincial legislation   ▨ Federal legislation

F. Preserving the Balance of Power: The Relationships between Double Aspects, Concurrency, Separation of Powers, Cooperative Federalism, and Paramountcy

The Supreme Court has made it clear that double aspects has gained ascendency over watertight compartments. In *Multiple Access Ltd v McCutcheon,* for example, the Court endorsed as "apposite" the following quote from WR Lederman's article:

> As Dr. [JA] Corry has pointed out, our country is increasingly moving away from the older classical federalism of "watertight compartments" with provincial legislatures and federal parliament carefully keeping clear of one another. We seem to be moving towards a co-operative federalism. "The co-ordinate governments no longer work in splendid isolation from one another but are increasingly engaged in cooperative ventures in

which each relies heavily on the other". See JA Corry, "Constitutional Trends and Federalism," in the volume of essays *Evolving Canadian Federalism* (Durham, N.C., U.S.A., 1958), p. 96. The multiplication of concurrent fields is one of the facets of this trend. [42]

This passage recognizes the close relationship between an expansive double aspects doctrine and the need for cooperative federalism. Since a generous double aspects doctrine results in "the multiplication of concurrent fields," it puts an increased onus on federal and provincial governments to cooperate for the purpose of constructing sensible and functional regulatory schemes that avoid contradiction or excessive duplication.

Paramountcy is another important component of this analog relationship. In essence, double aspects theory is a "live and let live" theory of constitutional interpretation. That is, it points to an expansive interpretation of both federal and provincial powers. However, as noted in *Multiple Access*, this inevitably enhances the degree of overlap (or "concurrency") between federal and provincial legislation. If the doctrine of paramountcy is broadly construed, then, by the simple expedient of playing its paramountcy trump card, the federal government may claim much of the benefit of double aspects for itself. For this reason, an expansive double aspects doctrine inevitably requires a circumscribed doctrine of paramountcy.

---

42 William R. Lederman, "The Concurrent Operation of Federal and Provincial Laws in Canada" (1962–1963) 9 McGill LJ 185 at 199 n39, cited in *Multiple Access Ltd. v McCutcheon*, [1982] 2 SCR 161 at para 48 [*Multiple Access*]. See also *General Motors,* above note 4 at 45 in which Dickson CJ stated:

> I reiterate what I said on this general theme (although in a slightly different context) in *OPSEU v Ontario (Attorney General)*, [1987] 2 S.C.R. 2, at p. 18:
>
>> The history of Canadian constitutional law has been to allow for a fair amount of interplay and indeed overlap between federal and provincial powers. It is true that doctrines like interjurisdictional and Crown immunity and concepts like "watertight compartments" qualify the extent of that interplay. But it must be recognized that these doctrines and concepts have not been the dominant tide of constitutional doctrines: rather they have been an undertow against the strong pull of pith and substance, the aspect doctrine and, in recent years, a very restrained approach to concurrency and paramountcy issues.

Yet another participant in the constitutional dance is the "separation of powers," or the extent to which federal and provincial powers occupy distinct fields. If the double aspects doctrine is interpreted so broadly that both levels of government can legislate in relation to virtually anything, there is little point in having constitutionally allocated powers. Moreover, in the presence of a restrained doctrine of paramountcy, habitual concurrent jurisdiction creates both awkwardness and inefficiency. In exposing citizens to a heightened danger of excessive and possibly inconsistent regulation, it leans *excessively* on cooperative federalism as a mechanism for sorting out problems of overlap. It creates unproductive tension between federal and provincial governments, and requires an excessive devotion of governmental resources to keeping the legislative accountancy straight.

This is well recognized in the *Securities Reference*. After noting that in *OPSEU v Ontario (Attorney General)*[43] Dickson CJ "summarized the situation aptly" in observing that the modern approach is to exercise "a very restrained approach to concurrency and paramountcy issues," the Court stated,

> While flexibility and cooperation are important to federalism, they cannot override or modify the separation of powers. The *Secession Reference* affirmed federalism as an underlying constitutional principle that demands respect for the constitutional division of powers and the maintenance of a constitutional balance between federal and provincial powers . . . . The "dominant tide" of flexible federalism, however strong its pull may be, cannot sweep designated powers out to sea, nor erode the constitutional balance inherent in the Canadian federal state.[44]

Table 2 illustrates the relationships between double aspects, concurrency, separation of powers, paramountcy, and the need for cooperative federalism. The assumption that drives Table 2 is that we wish to maintain a more or less homeostatic distribution of power between the federal and provincial governments. In the left-hand column, I take each of the above five variables in turn as the "independent variable." The idea is that if we decide (for whatever reason) that we wish to change that variable, we can see how we need to change the other variables in order to maintain a homeostatic distribution of power.

---

43 [1987] 2 SCR 2.
44 *Securities Reference*, above note 1 at paras 61–62.

Table 2: Maintaining the Federal/Provincial Balance

Independent Variable	Dependent Variables			
Double Aspects ↑	Concurrency ↑	Separation of Powers ↓	Need for Cooperative Federalism ↑	Permissible Scope of Paramountcy Doctrine ↓
Concurrency ↑	Double Aspects ↑	Separation of Powers ↓	Need for Cooperative Federalism ↑	Permissible Scope of Paramountcy Doctrine ↓
Scope of Paramountcy Doctrine ↑	Double Aspects ↓	Concurrency ↓	Separation of Powers ↑	Need for Cooperative Federalism ↓
Desired Extent of Cooperative Federalism ↑	Double Aspects ↑	Concurrency ↑	Separation of Powers ↓	Permissible Scope of Paramountcy Doctrine ↓

In the first column, for example, if we exogenously decide we would like to have a broader double aspects doctrine, then the degree of concurrency (legislative overlap) goes up, the extent to which we achieve a separation of powers goes down, the need for cooperative federalism is increased, and the doctrine of paramountcy needs to be more carefully circumscribed (so that the benefits of enhanced double aspects do not flow uniquely to the federal government).

Table 2 can also be used to illustrate the dangers inherent in taking any of the independent variables to an extreme. If, for example, we take the double aspects doctrine to an extreme, then we also end up with extreme concurrency, virtually no separation of powers, a pandemic requirement for cooperative federalism, and a virtually non-existent doctrine of paramountcy. Clearly, solutions in the middle ground are preferable to what an economist would call "corner solutions."

Table 2 is congruent with Dickson CJ's statement (above) in *OPSEU* that the courts must observe "a very restrained approach to concurrency and paramountcy issues." This is not to say that the Court should *simultaneously* observe restraint in the two doctrines, for, as Table 2 illustrates, preservation of a homeostatic power relationship means that these two variables are inversely related. Rather, Justice Dickson meant to suggest that the courts

should avoid *extremes* in the extent of either concurrency or paramountcy.

Viewed through this portal, the *Securities Reference* is not a
denial of double aspects, nor does it resemble "an early-twentieth-
century judgment of the Privy Council."[45] Rather, it flows both
logically and comfortably out of prior (and recent) Supreme Court
jurisprudence. It recognizes the fact that extreme overlap in
legislative competency threatens a fundamental re-casting of the
power relationships that underlie our federal union. As is repeatedly recognized and articulated in prior holdings in the Supreme
Court, the general branch of the trade and commerce power is a
potentially imperialistic colonizer of provincial power. More particularly, the draft federal securities statute was virtually a car-
bon copy of existing provincial legislation, both in purpose and
in functional detail. To allow the federal government to trench
so deeply on existing provincial competencies would truly be to
admit the camel's nose into the tent — with the assurance that
the rest of the camel would soon follow.

G. The Silent Actor: The Doctrine of Paramountcy

1) Paramountcy and Federal Securities Regulation

The federal government's reference to the Supreme Court of
Canada framed the constitutional question purely in respect of
legislative authority; that is, whether the federal government's
proposed *Securities Act* fell within the legislative dominion of the
Parliament of Canada. It did not ask the Supreme Court to opine
on the issue of whether, and to what extent, federal legislation
might displace provincial securities legislation under the doctrine of paramountcy. This left the only constitutional actor that
really matters offstage.

If, as I argue below, federal legislation cannot displace provincial legislation under the doctrine of paramountcy, then the
question of whether there will ever be a national (or even quasi-
national) regulator is purely a question of politics. In a world in
which the federal government cannot force any province to cede
jurisdiction, each province must decide on its own whether it

---

45 See Chapter 4.

wishes to be part of a multijurisdictional regulator. The passage of a federal statute can never be more than an invitation to treat.

Quite coincidentally, the leading case on the doctrine of paramountcy — *Multiple Access Ltd v McCutcheon*[46] — is a corporate/securities law case. In *Multiple Access*, the defendants were alleged to have engaged in insider trading. At the behest of two shareholders, a court ordered the Ontario Securities Commission to commence a civil proceeding, under the *Securities Act*, in the name and on behalf of the corporation. The defendants, however, argued that the pertinent provisions of Ontario's *Securities Act* substantially duplicated insider trading provisions found in the *Canada Corporations Act*, pursuant to which *Multiple Access* was incorporated. On this basis, they invited the Court to find that the Ontario provisions were "suspended and inoperative due to the doctrine of paramountcy."[47]

Identifying the "matter" of the federal insider trading provisions as "company law," the Court followed prior authority[48] in holding that the federal legislation was constitutionally sound. Characterizing the provincial insider trading provisions as "securities regulation," the Court (again, following established authority[49]) held that the provincial legislation was also constitutionally valid. The stage was thus set for a consideration of whether paramountcy applied.

Justice Dickson, for the majority, held that the doctrine is engaged only if there is an "actual conflict or contradiction" between the federal and provincial statutes:

> With Mr. Justice Henry I would say that duplication is, to borrow Professor Lederman's phrase, "the ultimate in harmony". The resulting "untidiness" or "diseconomy" of duplication is the price we pay for a federal system in which economy "often has to be subordinated to . . . provincial autonomy" (Hogg, at p. 110). Mere duplication without actual conflict or contradiction is not sufficient to invoke the doctrine of paramountcy and render otherwise valid provincial legislation inoperative . . . .[50]

---

46 Above note 42.

47 *Ibid* at 8.

48 *John Deere Plow Co v Wharton*, [1915] AC 330 (PC) (upholding federal corporate law under the "peace, order and good government" clause).

49 *Lymburn v Mayland*, [1932] AC 318 (upholding provincial securities legislation under the "property and civil rights in the province" clause). See *Multiple Access*, above note 42 at para 35.

50 *Multiple Access, ibid* at para 47.

In principle, there would seem to be no good reason to speak of paramountcy and preclusion except where there is actual conflict in operation as where one enactment says "yes" and the other says "no"; "the same citizens are being told to do inconsistent things"; compliance with one is defiance of the other . . . .[51]

When are statutes duplicative of one another? "Duplication" does not mean that the federal and provincial legislation are exact or even near copies; rather, the Supreme Court held that it is sufficient if there is "an identity of purpose, conduct and remedy." There is no question that the draft federal legislation — and, indeed, any comprehensive federal scheme of securities legislation — will be duplicative of provincial legislation within the sense articulated by the Supreme Court. It will share the foundational purposes of investor protection and of fostering fair and efficient capital markets and confidence in capital markets.[52] It will embrace essentially the same subject matters, including primary and secondary market disclosure, registration of market professionals, insider trading, takeover bids, and corporate governance. It will address essentially the same types of wrongdoing, and will specify some combination of criminal, administrative, and civil actions to address the various instances of misbehaviour. In short, it will be duplicative of the provincial legislation in precisely the same way that the federal insider trading provisions in *Multiple Access* were duplicative of the provincial provisions. Thus, the doctrine of paramountcy will no more operate to suspend provincial securities legislation than it did in *Multiple Access*. More importantly, as I discuss below, the principle enunciated in *Multiple Access* can be extended to a *non-comprehensive* scheme of securities regulation that also sports "an identity of purpose, conduct, and remedy" to the provincial legislation.

It is now apparent, however, that there are two branches to the paramountcy doctrine, of which *Multiple Access* represents only the first. The second branch invokes paramountcy if Parliament's *purpose* or *intention* is frustrated by provincial legislation.

---

51 *Ibid* at para 48.
52 Section 1.1 of the Ontario *Securities Act*, RSO 1990, c S.5 [OSA] states:

   The purposes of this Act are,

   (a) to provide protection to investors from unfair, improper or fraudulent practices; and
   (b) to foster fair and efficient capital markets and confidence in capital markets.

The first of these cases is *Bank of Montreal v Hall*.[53] In *Hall*, federal banking legislation[54] allowed a bank to realize on its security over real property, in the event of a default, without notice to the debtor. The Saskatchewan *Limitation of Civil Rights Act*,[55] however, required that the bank file a "Notice of an Intention to Seize," failing which the debtor would be released from all liability. In addition, once the notice was filed, the provincial legislation allowed a judge to decide on what terms and conditions the creditor might repossess its collateral. The Court stated,

> The contrast with the comprehensive regime provided for in ss. 178 and 179 of the *Bank Act* could not be more striking. The essence of that regime, it hardly needs repeating, is to assign to the bank, on the taking out of the security, right and title to the goods in question, and to confer, on default of the debtor, an immediate right to seize and sell those goods, subject only to the conditions and requirements set out in the *Bank Act*.[56]

Thus, the provincial legislation substantially eviscerated the scheme created by Parliament in the *Bank Act*. In deciding whether the doctrine of paramountcy applied, however, the Supreme Court had at its disposal only the "operational conflict" test supplied by *Multiple Access*. The Court recognized that, strictly speaking, it could not be said that "'the same citizens are being told to do inconsistent things'; compliance with one is defiance of the other," since the bank might satisfy both pieces of legislation by complying with the most stringent.

Nonetheless, the Court held that the provincial legislation frustrated the purpose of the federal legislation, and was thus suspended by the doctrine of paramountcy. In delivering the judgment of the Court, La Forest J drew upon a passage in *Multiple Access* in which Dickson J stated,

> *there is no true repugnancy in the case of merely duplicative provisions since it does not matter which statute is applied; the legislative purpose of Parliament will be fulfilled regardless of which statute is invoked by a remedy-seeker; application of the provincial law does not displace the legislative purpose of Parliament.*[57]

---

53 [1990] 1 SCR 121 [*Hall*].
54 *Bank Act*, RSC 1985, c B-1, ss 178–79.
55 RSS 1978, c L-16, ss 19–36.
56 *Hall*, above note 53 at 152 [emphasis in the original].
57 *Ibid* at 151 [emphasis added by the Court in *Hall*].

Fastening on Dickson J's invocation of "the legislative purpose of Parliament," La Forest J stated:

> On the basis of these principles, the question before me is thus reducible to asking whether there is an "actual conflict in operation" between the *Bank Act* and *The Limitation of Civil Rights Act* in the sense that the legislative purpose of Parliament stands to be displaced in the event that the appellant bank is required to defer to the provincial legislation in order to realize on its security.[58]

In answering this question in the affirmative, La Forest J could perhaps be forgiven for engaging in some creative interpretation of the "operational conflict" test. In *Quebec (AG) v Lacombe*,[59] however, the artificiality of shoehorning a conflict of legislative purpose into the "conflict in operation" test was recognized. While preserving the substantive expansion of the law of paramountcy effected by *Hall* and its ilk, *Lacombe* divides the paramountcy landscape into two branches. The first is the "operational conflict" test from *Multiple Access*, in which "'the same citizens are being told to do inconsistent things'; compliance with one [statute] is defiance of the other . . . ."[60] The second is the *Hall* expansion, which the Court describes as a "conflict of legislative purposes."[61]

---

58 *Ibid* at 151–52. Similarly, La Forest J stated:

> A showing that conflict can be avoided if a provincial Act is followed to the exclusion of a federal Act can hardly be determinative of the question whether the provincial and federal acts are in conflict, and, hence, repugnant. That conclusion, in my view, would simply beg the question. The focus of the inquiry, rather, must be on the broader question whether operation of the provincial Act is compatible with the federal legislative purpose. Absent this compatibility, dual compliance is impossible.

Ibid at 155.

59 [2010] 2 SCR 453 [*Lacombe*].

60 *Ibid* at para 120.

61 *Ibid*. Another of the "purpose" or "intentions" cases is *Law Society of British Columbia v Mangat*, [2001] 3 SCR 113. In *Mangat*, the federal *Immigration Act* (RSC 1985, c I-2, ss 30 and 69(1)) permitted a person who was not a lawyer to represent another person, for a fee, at an immigration hearing. The BC *Legal Profession Act* (SBC 1987, c 25, s 26), however, permitted only lawyers to do so. As in *Hall*, the Court held that there was "an operational conflict," even though "a person who seeks to comply with both enactments can succeed either by becoming a member in good standing of the Law Society of British Columbia or by not charging a fee." *Ibid* at para 120. *Mangat* must now also be understood as a "conflict of legislative purposes" case.

It is noteworthy, however, that in *Lacombe* the Court gave the second branch of the paramountcy doctrine a very restrictive reading. Paramountcy is said to arise in this respect only when *two* preconditions are met. The first is the "loss of a right" expressly conferred by the other level of government:

> With the concept of a conflict of legislative purposes comes the danger of an "impressionistic" interpretation of the conflict. To avoid this, the initial enquiry must be limited to situations in which compliance with the rule of a government at one level results in the loss not of a simple freedom that exists in the absence of an express prohibition, but of a right positively created in the rule of a government at the other level.[62]

The superadded element is described as follows:

> There is a second requirement, namely that the provincial prohibition in question be, if not identical, at least similar in nature, to the prohibition to which the federal positive right can only form an exception.[63]

This second element thus seeks to determine the degree of functional overlap between the provincial and federal law. The two laws in question may deal with related but only loosely overlapping subject matters, in which case the doctrine of paramountcy does not arise.

The Supreme Court illustrated the strict limits of both branches of the test by reference to *114957 Canada Ltée (Spraytech, Société d'arrosage) v Hudson (Town)*.[64] In *Spraytech,* the federal *Pest Control Products Act*[65] authorized the "import, export, sale, manufacture, registration, packaging and labelling"[66] of pesticides in Canada. The Supreme Court held that a municipal by-law prohibiting the use of pesticides for purely aesthetic purposes (but not for business or agricultural use) was not suspended by the doctrine of paramountcy. In the words of the Court,

> This [federal] legislation is permissive, rather than exhaustive, and there is no operational conflict with By-law 270. No one is placed in an impossible situation by the legal imperative of complying with both regulatory regimes. Analogies to motor

---

62 *Lacombe*, above note 59 at para. 121.
63 *Ibid* at para 24.
64 2001 SCC 40, [2001] 2 SCR 241 [*Spraytech*].
65 RSC 1985, c P-9.
66 *Spraytech*, above note 64 at para 35.

vehicles or cigarettes that have been approved federally, but the use of which can nevertheless be restricted municipally, well illustrate this conclusion. There is, moreover, no concern in this case that application of By-law 270 displaces or frustrates "the legislative purpose of Parliament."[67]

Lacombe further notes that "an authorization to import, manufacture, sell, and distribute pesticides was not frustrated by the prohibition on spreading pesticides for purely aesthetic purposes."[68] Thus, while there was some degree of overlap between the federal and provincial statutes, it was more incidental than foundational. The provincial legislation did not deprive any citizen of a core right conferred by the federal legislation; it merely conditioned that right.

The Court's expansion of the doctrine of paramountcy in *Lacombe* makes eminent good sense. Even though in *Hall* citizens were not commanded to do inconsistent things, the provincial legislation in *Hall* sterilized a fundamental element of the federal scheme. In this regard, La Forest J was able to draw upon ample primary and secondary sources suggesting that a foundational purpose underlying the adoption of section 178 of the *Bank Act* was to allow banks to lend money nationwide, free of the variegated and often arcane provincial rules regarding realization on security, and with the intention of lowering the cost of bank borrowing. He was also able to draw upon ample evidence that the *Bank Act* had achieved this purpose, and had played a vital role in extending capital to many growing Canadian businesses on terms that would not otherwise have been available.[69]

---

67 It is a nice question whether, if these municipal directives were universally adopted, the Court might have reached a different result. As it was, the Court was not troubled by the fact that some 37 Quebec municipalities had by-laws restricting pesticide use. See *ibid* at para 4. This is just over a third of the approximately 108 Quebec municipalities: see "List of regional county municipalities and equivalent territories in Quebec", online: Wikipedia en.wikipedia.org/wiki/List_of_regional_county_municipalities_and_equivalent_territories_in_Quebec. Arguably, however, even if all of these municipalities were to adopt similar restrictions, the interference with federal legislation would be insufficient to trigger the application of paramountcy, given that pesticides could still be used for business and agricultural purposes.

68 *Lacombe*, above note 59 at para 125.

69 Justice La Forest states: "It is generally agreed that this provision of Canadian banking legislation has, in large part, met its objective of providing natural resource and manufacturing industries nationwide with a readily

The restrictions on the second branch of the doctrine also make good sense. The question of whether provincial legislation interferes with rights conferred by federal legislation cannot be represented by a simple binary variable (either a "yes" or a "no"). Rather, there are varying degrees of interference, arrayed along a continuum from merely incidental or tangential obstruction (e.g., *Spraytech*) to outright sterilization (e.g., *Hall* and *Mangat*). Limiting the second branch to cases on or near the latter end of the spectrum is consistent with the Court's enunciation of the trade-off between double aspects and separation of powers, discussed earlier in relation to constitutional validity. Paramountcy is an integral part of the same constitutional ecosystem, and must be guided by the same overarching principles.

Importantly, there is no indication in any of the Supreme Court holdings discussed above that the Court would have decided *Multiple Access* any differently. That is, provincial legislation that is essentially duplicative of federal legislation will not trigger the paramountcy doctrine. This supplies a guide for interpreting the second branch's requirement that the provincial legislation must interfere with a positive right created by the federal government; mere duplication in pursuit of the same or similar regulatory objective does *not* fulfill this requirement.

Suppose, for example, that federal corporate legislation required a takeover bidder seeking to acquire a CBCA corporation to leave its bid open for thirty-five days, while overlapping Ontario securities legislation required sixty days. A proponent of a broad reading of the paramountcy doctrine would no doubt argue that the thirty-five-day period in the federal legislation could be construed as a "positive right" ceded to takeover bidders, and that "the provincial prohibition in question [is], if not identical, at least similar in nature, to the prohibition to which the federal positive right can only form an exception." Adding to the case, this proponent might argue that the provincial legislation is of the same nature as that found in *Hall*. That is, while it is possible to comply with both statutes by complying with the most stringent, take-over bidders are nonetheless denied the ability to take advantage of the lesser federal requirement, and thus that right is effectively sterilized.

---

available stimulus of capital that would otherwise not have been available, or available only at a much higher cost." *Hall*, above note 53 at 138.

As persuasive as this might seem, the lesson from *Multiple Access* is that differences in detail arising out of a common regulatory objective will *not* cause paramountcy to be invoked. There is no sterilization, but merely a relatively trivial difference in regulatory design in pursuit of a common end. By contrast, in *Hall*, the underlying purposes of the federal and provincial legislation were fundamentally at odds. To allow the provincial legislation to operate would have completely negated a fundamental right that was central to the operation of the federal scheme (and to its avowed purpose of lowering the cost of capital for bank borrowers).

The likelihood of the result I have suggested is reinforced by the frequent comments in the Supreme Court jurisprudence that courts must adopt a "restrained approach" to the doctrine of paramountcy, the Court's restrictive reading of the second branch of the doctrine of paramountcy in *Lacombe*, and its pointed comment that "[t]he purposes of legislators are not as easily frustrated as one might be tempted to think."[70]

This puts the Court's ruling in the *Securities Reference* in perspective. Had the draft federal Act been found to be constitutional, this would in no way have automatically reduced the number of securities regulators to one, since neither branch of the doctrine of paramountcy would have come into play.

2) The Effect of a Paramountcy Clause

A further question arises, however: Would an expressed parliamentary intention to suspend provincial legislation and create a single national regulatory scheme (a "paramountcy clause") make the invocation of the doctrine of paramountcy more likely? Two of three expert legal opinions secured by the so-called Wise Persons' Committee answered this question in the affirmative. I would answer it in the negative. If the federal government could enhance the likelihood that paramountcy will be invoked simply by writing an "intentions" clause into its legislation, this would cede to the federal government a powerful tool to unilaterally tip the scales in its own favour, altering the balance of power that the Court has so valiantly striven to maintain.

The view that a paramountcy clause matters might appear to be supported by the Court's comment that "[i]ntrinsic evidence,

---

70 *Lacombe*, above note 59 at para 126.

such as purpose clauses and the general structure of the statute, may reveal the *purpose* of a law."[71] What this quote establishes, however, is that a purpose clause may serve as a useful aid in characterizing the "pith and substance" or subject matter of a law. A paramountcy clause aimed at limiting provincial jurisdiction, however, is a horse of a different colour. Rather than classifying a statute's subject matter, it evinces an intention to pre-empt overlapping provincial legislation. The latter question, however, is entirely for the courts to determine through the application of paramountcy doctrine, as derived from the legal strictures emanating from the Supreme Court. It simply is not possible for the federal government to bootstrap itself into a paramount position through aspirational statements standing totally aside from the pivotal test of relative functionality. The only federal intention that is relevant is that which relates to the Hohfeldian matrix[72] of rights, duties, obligations, and so on that Parliament intended to create. The rest is for the courts.

3) The Effect of a Purpose Clause

A related question is the extent to which a purpose clause embodied in the statute (much like that in the Ontario *Securities Act*[73]) would strengthen the federal government's case. A purpose clause of this nature would fall squarely within the principle enunciated in the *Securities Reference*, above, since it would go to the characterization of the "matter" or "pith and substance" of the legislation. I wish in particular to address Lee's argument that the federal government might succeed in promulgating a comprehensive scheme of securities regulation under the general branch of the trade and commerce power by re-characterizing the foundation of the legislation as allocative efficiency, or "the efficient

---

71 *Securities Reference*, above note 1 at para 64 [emphasis in the original].
72 See Wesley Hohfeld, "Some Fundamental Legal Conceptions as Applied in Judicial Reasoning" (1913) 23 Yale LJ 16; Wesley Newcomb Hohfeld, "Fundamental Legal Conceptions as Applied in Judicial Reasoning" (1917) 26 Yale LJ 710.
73 OSA, above note 52, s 1.1 states: The purposes of this Act are,

>   (a) to provide protection to investors from unfair, improper or fraudulent practices; and
>   (b) to foster fair and efficient capital markets and confidence in capital markets.

allocation of financial resources to productive ventures across the economy, regardless of industry sector." [74]

In my view, this would not succeed, nor should it. For one thing, a purpose clause is only one of the factors the Court will consider in assigning a subject matter to legislation. The Court should decline to give a purpose clause any weight at all if it is inspired by a colourable motive — namely, to validate by stealth that which the Court has already declared to be unconstitutional. Suppose, however, that Parliament genuinely subscribes to this re-characterization. In my view, a court would be entitled to say that the re-characterization amounts to a distinction without a difference. The Ontario *Securities Act*, for example, states that one of its fundamental purposes is "to foster . . . efficient capital markets and confidence in capital markets."[75] To an economist, the word "efficient" means, in the first instance, allocative efficiency — the *desideratum* that Lee would have the federal government pursue. Moreover, while allocative efficiency has economy-wide implications, securities regulation in pursuit of allocative efficiency is no more macroeconomic in character than existing securities regulation. The *Merriam-Webster* dictionary, for example, defines macroeconomics as a "study of economics in terms of whole systems especially with reference to general levels of output and income and to the interrelations among sectors of the economy."[76] Thus, in my view, the attempted re-characterization of the legislative foundation of securities regulation fails to bear fruit.

To the extent that allocative efficiency is indeed something different from investor protection, enshrining it as the solitary goal of securities regulation could lead to results uncongenial to both investors and (of more importance to politicians) voters. In pursuit of efficiency, economists are more or less agnostic about investor compensation. As long as an instance of abuse results in a prospective change in the rules sufficient to deal with the inefficiency, and as long as future potential miscreants are adequately deterred (e.g., by criminal sanctions), compensation is essentially irrelevant. While in many or even most cases requiring compensation is an effective tool for conditioning incentives, it

---

74 Lee, above note 45.
75 *Ibid.*
76 See also Olivier Jean Blanchard & Stanley Fischer, *Lectures on Macroeconomics* (Cambridge, MA: MIT Press: 1989).

is by no means indispensable. Thus, for example, miscreants that have received criminal sanctions for their behaviour might argue in a civil court that they should not be forced to compensate investors for their wrongdoing because there are already sufficient deterrents in place to discourage others from following in their footsteps. If allocative efficiency were the sole goal of securities regulation, it would be hard for a court to disagree.[77]

4) Paramountcy and Federal Securities Legislation Addressing Information Gathering and/or Systemic Risk

Suppose that the federal government proceeds to adopt securities legislation for the purpose of gathering data and controlling systemic risk. How would this relate to provincial regulation?

By virtue of the restricted nature of the paramountcy doctrine, it seems highly doubtful that the federal rules would suspend the operation of overlapping provincial regulation. Suppose, for example, that the federal government adopted rules regulating the trading of derivatives (one of the matters suggested by the Court as potentially falling within federal competence). As discussed further below, the provinces already have rules regulating derivatives. Even if the federal legislation is based on "genuinely national concerns" and the federal government has some unique capacity to see the big picture (and/or to enforce its rules, and/or to negotiate with other countries' regulators, etc.), federal and provincial legislation would differ only in the details — not in their fundamental purpose or general attributes. Thus, neither the first branch of paramountcy, articulated in *Multiple Access*, nor the second branch, articulated in *Lacombe*, would come into play. The federal government would simply be adding an additional layer of legislation to the existing infrastructure. This is at odds with the number one *desideratum* of many proponents of a national commission: a single regulator and a simplified regulatory structure.

---

77 I note that Professor Lee takes an agnostic stance on whether legislation founded on this single goal would be good from a policy perspective. If we can answer that question in the negative, however, there does not seem to be much reason to pursue this option.

H. National Importance Versus National Efficacy

In the *Securities Reference*, the Court held that, in order to pass muster under the *General Motors* criteria, federal legislation must exhibit a compelling "national interest" that "is engaged in a manner that is qualitatively different from provincial concerns."[78] Many partisans of federal securities legislation (including Trebilcock, Iacobucci, Ford and Gill, and Anand, in this volume) have argued that because Canadian securities markets are national in scope, the "national interest" test is easily met. There are, however, a number of situations where a subject matter of national interest might nonetheless be better handled by the provinces. These include the following non-exhaustive list.

1) Matching Local Preferences to Legislative Outcomes

One important datum to be considered in determining the efficacy of legislation is the degree of variation in local citizen preferences. Where there is little variation in preferences across the country, efficacy may lean toward federal legislation. Where, however, there is substantial variation, decentralizing decision making is likely to enhance the degree of match between citizen preferences and policy outcomes. This, in turn, is likely to enhance overall welfare. In a country as diverse as Canada, with large francophone and ethnic minorities and widely differing political preferences (as evidenced by the heterogeneous distribution of dominant political parties), differences in local preferences are likely to be common.

Variations in local preferences may also spring from differences in local institutional and market structures. Canada's financial markets provide an example. British Columbia and Alberta's markets have a plenitude of small resource companies, while Ontario is home to many of Canada's largest public companies. It is no secret that this has led to material differences in regulatory philosophies. Indeed, western anxiety about being forced to submit to policy choices made in Ontario has been one of the chief stumbling blocks in creating a national regulatory agency.

---

78   *General Motors*, above note 4 at para 46.

2) Variations in Local Resource Endowments and Wealth

As the existence of substantial interprovincial transfer payments makes clear, there are material variations in provincial economies. A robust local economy and a healthy tax base create budgetary options that do not exist in a depressed economy with a marginal tax base. Moreover, it is well known that as personal income increases or decreases, substitution and income effects can result in an alteration of an individual's basket of consumption and production goods. The same is true at the level of the state. Variations in wealth can alter the optimal mix of public goods and services provided by the government.[79] The degree of welfare enhancement achieved by the decentralization of governmental authority is correlative to the degree of variation in wealth. In a country like Canada, with relatively pronounced regional and provincial variations in economic bases, we might well expect a strong addition to overall welfare by decentralizing governmental authority.

3) Innovation and Experimentation: Competitive Federalism and Data Gathering

Another reason why we might prefer to leave a subject matter of national importance to the provinces is to encourage productive experimentation and innovation, leading to superior policy outcomes. Ceding policy-making to local units, for example, can generate a "competitive federalism" dynamic that results in enhanced efficiency. This has been observed to be the case, for example, in relation to US corporate law[80]— a domain that is closely allied with the subject matter at hand.

---

79 See e.g. David N Hyman, *Public Finance: A Contemporary Application of Theory to Policy*, 9th ed (Mason, OH: Thomson South-Western, 2008). The Ontario and federal budgets delivered contemporaneously with the writing of this paper are a good illustration of income and substitution effects at work. Both levels of government, under considerable economic duress, have announced significant changes to the basket of public goods and services that they intend to deliver to the public. While this illustrates that longitudinal changes in policy may result from changes in wealth, the same principles are at work in relation to cross-sectional variations in wealth.

80 See e.g. Roberta Romano, *The Genius of American Corporate Law* (Washington DC: American Enterprise Institute, 1993). Professor Romano has argued that the same paradigm should be operative in relation to securi-

Decentralized policy-making, however, need not be "competitive" to be productive of superior policy outcomes. Law is at the apex of the social science pyramid. At least from a normative perspective (and increasingly from a descriptive perspective) law takes as competing inputs virtually all of the other social sciences at every step of policy formation, encompassing the identification both of the ends that the law should pursue and the means whereby those ends can and should be achieved. Because of the enormous uncertainty that legislators face in relation to both (not to mention constitutionality, particularly in light of the Charter), the formulation of legislation is necessarily a process of Baysian updating. That is, a vector of hypotheses is formulated regarding desired ends and means. Then, legislation — the functional cipher linking hypotheses to societal outcomes — is unleashed on the world. Finally, data flows back to legislators regarding the correctness of its vector of hypotheses, and (at least if they are acting as responsible legislators) suitable changes are made. Because of the complexity and uncertainty involved in defining both means and ends,[81] making good legislation is essentially a never-ending iterative process. Any experimental process of this nature, however, requires data — the more the better. A monopoly regulator generates a limited number of data points. By subjecting alternative legal regimes to the process of Baysian updating, decentralized decision making furnishes many more. In fields (such as securities law) where the subject matter of the regulation experiences rapid and essentially continuous evolution, Baysian updating is particularly important. This creates an inherent bias in favour of decentralized legislative competence.

---

ties regulation. See Roberta Romano, *The Advantage of Competitive Federalism for American Securities Regulation* (Washington, DC: American Enterprise Institute, 2002).

81 In addition, society is not static: electoral preferences as to ends and means often change over time. Added to this, the particular forces acting upon the legislature at any one time are virtually certain to be path-dependent, giving rise to some instability in the identification of ends and means.

I. "It's the Politics, Stupid"[82]

1) The Inevitability of Cooperative Federalism and a Passport System

The nature of our doctrine of paramountcy indicates what would have happened had the federal government received a decision in its favour in the *Securities Reference*. Had the federal government enacted a comprehensive scheme of securities regulation, it would not have displaced the provincial legislation; thus, the goal of a single regulator would not have been achieved unless *all* of the provinces signed up. Since the likelihood of this occurring is essentially indistinguishable from zero, the only way to simplify the existing system, and to effect the business community's much-sought-after goal of providing each market actor with a single regulator, is via a comprehensive passport system.[83]

This is unlikely to change in the near, or even the not-so-near, future. The *Securities Reference* outlines in brief the history of the many attempts to create a single regulatory commission in Canada, going back to 1935.[84] These attempts have all foundered on the shoals of Canadian politics, inspired by cultural differences; regional mistrust and antipathies; differences in the size, industrial structure, and composition of local capital markets; and correlative differences in perspectives on how capital markets should be regulated.[85]

---

82 With apologies to Bill Clinton ("It's the economy, stupid.")

83 At present, all provinces and territories other than Ontario are members of the passport system. See Passport System, OSC MI 11-102, (2008), 31 OSCB 1009; Process for Prospectus Reviews in Multiple Jurisdictions, OSC NP 11-202, (2008), 31 OSCB 1009; and Process for Exemptive Relief Applications in Multiple Jurisdictions, OSC NP 11- 203, (2008), 31 OSCB 1009. The passport system is not entirely comprehensive, however, covering only some areas of the *corpus* of securities regulation.

84 *Securities Reference*, above note 1 at paras 11–28.

85 I can claim some consistency on this issue: see Jeffrey MacIntosh, "Who Needs a Monopoly?" *National Post* (25 July 2007) FP19; Jeffrey MacIntosh, "Let 'Passport' Work" *National Post* (29 June 2006) FP23; Jeffrey MacIntosh, "Passport Power" *National Post* (29 January 2004) FP15; Jeffrey MacIntosh, "Canada's Passport to Regulatory Competition: Backers of a National Securities Regulator Have it All Wrong" *National Post* (18 March 2004) FP15; Jeffrey MacIntosh, "Not a 'Wise' Idea" *National Post* (18 Dececmber 2003) FP15; Jeffrey MacIntosh, "A Better Way to Tame our Markets' Hydra: Instead of Setting Up a National Regulator for Capital Markets, Why Not Reform the System to Make Provincial Regulators Mutually Reliant?" *National Post* (6 June 2002) FP15.

Quebec, which prizes its "national" sovereignty above all, has always and will always oppose a single regulator, however constituted. The western provinces have always suspected that a national commission would be run with an eastern Canadian (or, worse, Torontonian) perspective, unsympathetic to what they characterize as their "venture capital" market — that is, a capital market dominated by relatively small private and public firms concentrated in oil and gas and mining. Doing little to dispel Western fears, Ontario, the centre of Canada's capital market activity, has always expected to play a key role in any national agency, in addition to hosting the head office. The existence of these antipathetic interests has not been a recipe for success in creating a national commission, whether constituted federally or provincially.

In connection with the *Securities Reference*, Quebec, Alberta, Manitoba, and New Brunswick all unconditionally opposed a federal statute based on the general trade and commerce power. British Columbia and Saskatchewan also opposed the Act, although

> neither province opposes the idea of a national securities regulator, so long as it is achieved in a manner that respects the division of powers. However, these provinces contend that Parliament's participation in securities regulation is best achieved through an exercise in federal-provincial cooperation, similar to the cooperation existing in the agricultural products marketing context.[86]

Table 3 indicates just how ineffective — or even counterproductive — a federal win would have been in accomplishing the aims of single-regulator proponents. The three options examined are the *status quo*, a federally constituted multijurisdictional regulator (MJC), and a provincially constituted MJC. I assume that had the federal government won, the three territories[87] and

---

86 *Securities Reference*, above note 1 at para 34.
87 A somewhat overlooked factor in the debate is that the *Constitution Act, 1871* (UK), 34 & 35 Vict, c 28, s 4, gives the federal government the power to enact laws (spanning the entire spectrum of federal and provincial powers) for the territories. The federal government has delegated the full array of provincial powers, including "property and civil rights," to the territories. See *Northwest Territories Act*, RSC 1985, c N-27, s 16(h); *Yukon Act*, SC 2002, c 7, s 18(j); *Nunavut Act*, SC 1993, c 28, s 23(l). Thus, all the federal government need do to guarantee territorial participation is to create a legislative carve-out from "property and civil rights" in the area of securities regulation.

four of the provinces[88] would have joined the federal regulatory
scheme, while Quebec, BC, Alberta, Manitoba, Saskatchewan,
and New Brunswick would have remained outside the fold; on
the other hand, as many as eight provinces (Quebec and Alberta
being the exceptions) might sign up to a provincially constituted
MJC.

Table 3: Comparison of Options

Regime	How Many Voices at International Table?	Enforcement Jurisdictions	Passport Jurisdictions	CSA Members	Major Regulatory Cost Generators
Status quo	4 (Ontario, Quebec, Alberta, BC)	13*	13*	13*	4†
Federal MJC	4 (MJC, Quebec, BC, Alberta)	7‡	7‡	7‡	4 (MJC, Quebec, BC, Alberta)
Provincial MJC	3 (MJC, Quebec, Alberta)	3§	3§	3§	3§

* All provinces, territories.
† Ontario, Quebec, BC, Alberta
‡ Federal Commission, BC, Alberta, Saskatchewan, Manitoba, Quebec, New Brunswick.
§ MJC, Alberta, Quebec

One of the points stressed by federal proponents is the need
for a single voice in international negotiations over securities law.
Currently, four provinces (BC, Alberta, Ontario, and Quebec)
typically participate.[89] If the Reference had confirmed the federal
government's constitutional authority to establish an MJC, there
would still have been four voices at the table (the MJC, Quebec,
Alberta, and BC);[90] under a provincially constituted MJC, however, there would likely be only three voices at the table (the MJC,
Quebec, and Alberta).

---

88 Ontario, Newfoundland and Labrador, Nova Scotia, and Prince Edward
    Island.
89 All, for example, are members of the International Organization of Secu-
    rities Commissions.
90 I assume that, as now, smaller provinces would show no inclination to get
    involved.

Another sore point for federal apologists is the difficulty of enforcement, given the high number of enforcement jurisdictions. Again, however, a provincially constituted MJC wins the contest of the three options, as it does in respect of the number of members of the passport system and of the Canadian Securities Administrators (CSA). A further criticism of the current system is that the duplication of functions at the different regulators results in excessive overall costs. Once more, a provincially constituted MJC beats the other two options, with only three major regulatory cost generators, as opposed to four under either the *status quo* or a federal MJC.

What this illustrates is that the *Securities Reference* is in many ways irrelevant. All that ever mattered was politics. The prospect of a single national regulator was never more than a quixotic fantasy. Moreover, the closest that we can get to the goals envisioned by the federalists is (via cooperative federalism) a *provincially constituted* MJC, perhaps with a federal sidecar having information-gathering responsibilities and some role in addressing systemic risk.

2) The Likelihood of a Provincially Constituted MJC

Above, I assumed that as many as eight provinces would join a provincially constituted MJC. This may be overly optimistic. While a major issue for many of the provinces is whether the MJC is federally or provincially constituted, there are many other issues, some of the most difficult of which are digested in Table 4. Table 4 highlights both intraprovincial conflicts and federal–provincial conflicts that are likely to arise in any attempt to put together a provincially or a federally constituted MJC.[91] I have also attempted to assess the magnitude of each conflict on a scale from 1 to 3.

---

91 C.f. Anita I Anand and Andrew J Green, "Side-Payments, Opt-Ins and Power: Creating a National Securities Regulator in Canada" (2011) 51 Can Bus LJ 1 (2011).

Table 4: The Devil Is in the Details

	P vs P	F vs P
Head office	YYY[a]	Y[b]
Governance structure	YY[c]	YY[d]
Policy making	YY[e]	YY[f]
Operations	N[g]	Y[h]
Carve-outs	Y[i]	YYY[j]
Compensation	Y[k]	YYY[l]
Hiring	YYY[m]	Y[n]
Official Languages Act	Y[o]	YYY[p]

a Strong conflict between west and Ontario; little appetite to create a nationalized version of the OSC.

b Federal interest is to have the head office in Ottawa; that is unacceptable to Ontario.

c Should Ontario have weighted representation because of the concentration of capital markets in Ontario? Ontario will think so, other provinces not. Should small provinces have the same representation as big provinces?

d Feds will want to centralize governance as much as possible; the provinces will want to participate.

e BC and Alberta in particular demand participation in policy making re mining, oil and gas, small companies. Other provinces likely to resist this (e.g. Ontario, by dollar value, has more mining companies than BC).

f The federal government will want to centralize policy making as much as possible, provinces not.

g The provinces have a common interest in de-centralizing decision-making and giving provincial or regional offices significant powers.

h The federal government will want to centralize operations as much as possible.

i The provinces may have a common interest in creating carve-outs. However, some provinces, such as Ontario, might oppose carve-outs if they think that this will subtract from the power of the common regulator.

j The feds have already demonstrated in their draft legislation that they want opting-in provinces to completely leave the field.

k The extent to which provinces earn net revenue from the business of securities regulation varies from province to province. Provinces will jockey to earn federal pay-out cash.

l The feds would prefer not to have to pay compensation.

m There will be strong jockeying between the provinces to have their people hired.

n There will be provincial pressure on the federal government to overhire, in order to accommodate as many current provincial employees as possible. The federal government would obviously prefer to avoid doing this.

o Some provinces with significant French-speaking minorities, such as New Brunswick and Ontario, may favour application of the *Official Languages Act*. Others, like Alberta and BC, may not.

p The federal government will not wish to give any dispensations from the *Official Languages Act*.

With respect to the first issue — the location of the head office — the federal government would likely prefer the national capital, Ottawa. Ontario has made it quite clear that it will not tolerate any location other than Toronto. The western provinces have made it equally clear that, wherever the head office is located, it must *not* be Toronto. This is not fertile ground for agreement, with respect to either a federal MJC or a provincial MJC.

Governance structure, policy-making, and operations are equally problematic. At stake is the extent of provincial involvement at each level of the organization, including political (i.e., to whom is the organization ultimately answerable?); high-level operations and policy-making (e.g., who sits on the board of directors or similar body?); whether there is an opportunity for input from provincial ministers and/or bureaucrats; whether particular provinces are given responsibility for policy-making in particular areas; and issues associated with day-to-day operations (e.g., are there regional offices? do they have a material degree of autonomy?). Again, given varying regional and provincial regulatory agendas and styles, coupled with historical animosities and mistrust, resolving these issues is a challenging task. In fact, these issues may be more difficult to resolve in connection with a provincial MJC, since this model creates no natural focal point for political responsibility.

The issue of carve-outs — the extent to which provinces retain jurisdiction over securities regulation — is also fraught with difficulty. This is illustrated by the death of the 1996 "agreement" between First Ministers to create a national commission. One of the key issues on which the agreement ultimately foundered was the extent to which the provinces would retain authority over exempt-market transactions and purely local issuances of securities.

An equally vexing issue in 1996 was that of compensation — the next item in Table 4. Securities regulation has been a profit centre for many of the provinces, which therefore insisted on substantial compensation in return for yielding up this source of revenue to the federal government. Because the extent of the revenue generation has been quite different in the different provinces, however, the issue of compensation pits province against province as well as the provinces against the federal government. This issue is not elided in a provincial MJC — some agreement on parcelling out the revenue is still required.

The question of hiring — which employees from which provincial commissions will be taken on by a national commission —

pits every province against every other province. It is reasonable to start with the presumption that there are economies of scale in moving to a national commission.[92] The greater the economies of scale, the greater the number of provincial employees receiving pink slips. Given the multiparty nature of this negotiation and the stakes involved, one would hardly expect negotiations to be easy going.

Finally, an issue that has largely flown under the radar in connection with a federal MJC is the effect of the *Official Languages Act*[93] (OLA), which applies to all federally constituted agencies (a category that would include a national securities regulator[94]). The proximate effect of the OLA is to require virtually all personnel in geographic areas designated by regulation to be bilingual.[95] Ottawa is so designated.[96] In addition, however, a head office, irrespective of location, would be required to "ensure that any member of the public can communicate with and obtain available services from its head or central office in either official language."[97] Even in non-designated areas, if there is "significant demand for communications with and services from that office or facility in that language," *all* offices in that area must offer bilingual services. This might well include an office in Toronto.[98]

---

92 See e.g. Charles Rivers Associates, "Securities Enforcement in Canada: The Effect of Multiple Regulators" in Doug Harris, ed, *Wise Persons' Committee Research Studies* (Ottawa: Department of Finance Canada, 2003); Anita I Anand and Peter Charles Klein, "Inefficiency and Path Dependency in Canada's Securities Regulatory System: Towards a Reform Agenda" (2005) 42 Can Bus LJ 41.

93 RSC 1985, c 31 [OLA].

94 *Ibid*, ss 3(1)(e)–(h).

95 *Ibid*, s 36.

96 See "Regions of Canada prescribed under subsection 35(2) of the *Official Languages Act*," online: Treasury Board of Canada Secretariat www.tbs-sct.gc.ca/pubs_pol/hrpubs/offlang/chap5_101-eng.asp.

97 OLA, above note 93, s 23(1). See also *ibid*, s 22(b).

98 The rules for determining whether there is "significant demand" are complex, but could well include a Toronto office. See *Official Languages (Communications with and Services to the Public) Regulations*, SOR/92-48, ss 3–5, as well as Treasury Board of Canada Secretariat, "Minority Populations by First Official Language Spoken (2001 Census Data)," online: Treasury Board of Canada Secretariat www.tbs-sct.gc.ca/res/mppm200101-eng.asp.

Wherever the head office is located, all rules and other documents would have to be made available in both English and French.[99] As comments on proposed rules and policy statements would be received from bilingual areas of the country,[100] the MJC would have to have bilingual personnel to read, access, and respond in both English and French. Thus, even if the full rigour of the bilingualism requirement did not apply, there might be a practical imperative to become substantially bilingual.[101]

These rules have obvious implications for the question of who will be hired and from which provincial regulators. Indeed, as Quebec will not join a federal MJC, one could be forgiven for wondering whether there are enough bilingual regulators in Canada to competently staff a federal regulator. More importantly, the application of the OLA would constitute a material disincentive for provinces to join a federally constituted regulator, if it meant that few of the employees currently employed by that province's regulator would be hired on to a federal commission.

3) A Modest Proposal[102]

While a provincial MJC might not be right around the corner, it seems the only realistic alternative to the *status quo*. The federal government could guarantee the participation of the territories, in the manner indicated earlier,[103] and could employ its so-called spending power to help grease the wheels — for example, by making compensatory payments to those provinces that would lose revenue by forsaking securities regulation.

Despite the existence of multiple regulators, every market actor can be assured of having but a single regulator (one of the main goals of single regulator proponents) by the simple expedient of extending the existing passport system to include all subject matters covered by securities regulation. In order to encourage innovation and responsiveness, all actors should be given a choice of regulator. While some fear that this might lead to a

---

99 OLA, above note 93, s 12.

100 For example, New Brunswick or parts of Ontario.

101 In addition, the Governor in Council (i.e. the Cabinet) could make regulations requiring that the regulator be fully bilingual.

102 With apologies to Jonathan Swift. The employment of this title is not meant to suggest any satirical content in the idea of a provincial MJC.

103 See above note 87.

"race to the bottom," the experience with Delaware corporate law suggests otherwise.[104]

Under a passport system, there would be no need for national instruments and policy statements, which would render the policy-making function more nimble and responsive than it currently is.[105] The CSA should assume the role of research institution and policy facilitator where the various regulators could continue to meet to discuss policy matters. It could continue to produce consensus — but non-binding — instruments and policy statements designed to embody "best practices," to be adopted or modified as each regulator sees fit.[106]

J. What Is the Scope for Federal Legislation After the *Securities Reference*?

The *Securities Reference* does not rule out the possibility that the general branch of the trade and commerce power could support

---

104 This argument is more fully elaborated in Jeffrey MacIntosh, "Who Needs a Monopoly?" *National Post* (25 July 2007) FP19; Jeffrey MacIntosh, "Canada's Passport to Regulatory Competition: Backers of a National Securities Regulator Have it All Wrong" *National Post* (18 March 2004) FP15; Jeff MacIntosh, "A Better Way to Tame our Markets' Hydra: Instead of Setting Up a National Regulator for Capital Markets, Why Not Reform the System to Make Provincial Regulators Mutually Reliant?" *National Post* (6 June 2002) FP15. The success of Delaware corporate law in improving investor welfare extends from a number of factors. See Roberta Romano, "Law as a Product: Some Pieces of the Incorporation Puzzle" (1985) 1 JL Econ & Org 225; Roberta Romano, *The Genius of American Corporate Law*, above note 80. The federal government could help to create a truly competitive market for corporate and securities law by delegating to the provinces control over judicial appointments, so that provinces could compete on the basis of relative judicial competence. The provinces could also do much to enhance the quality and competitiveness of their securities law, not only by appointing to the bench corporate practitioners with a deep understanding of corporate and securities law, but also by creating courts analogous to Delaware's Chancery Court, which hears only corporate law cases.

105 As Anita Anand pointed out to me, "this would only be the case under a passport system in which provinces could not opt out; i.e. where the body had the ability to implement laws in all member jurisdictions without the need to have each jurisdiction implement the instrument at the provincial level."

106 This argument is made at somewhat greater length in Jeffrey MacIntosh, "Let Provinces Run it; The Court Says Ottawa Can't Impose a Single Securities Regulator. But There Is a Solution that Would Work Well" *National Post* (27 Jan 2012) FP11.

federal securities legislation motivated by "genuinely national concerns."[107] However, the decision is short on guidance as to what might potentially address genuinely national concerns. The two categories flagged as potentially falling within this bailiwick (as argued by the federal government) are provisions that address systemic risk[108] and those that address nationwide data collection.[109] In the words of the Court,

> Without attempting an exhaustive enumeration, the following provisions of the proposed Act would appear to address or authorize the adoption of regulations directed at systemic risk: ss. 89 and 90 relating to derivatives, s. 126(1) on short-selling, s. 73 on credit rating, s. 228(4)(c) relating to urgent regulations and ss. 109 and 224 on data collection and sharing.[110]

Federal securities legislation nationalizing data collection, while potentially useful, would do little more than reduce the federal presence in securities regulation to an abbreviated footnote. And, as Table 5 makes clear, each and every provision on the Supreme Court's list already has an analogue in provincial legislation.[111] While federal apologists might argue that only the federal

---

107 *Securities Reference*, above note 1 at para 130.
108 See *ibid* at paras 104–5 and 114.
109 The Court stated:

> The emphasis in the proposed Act on nationwide data collection may similarly be seen as aimed at anticipating and identifying risks that may transcend the boundaries of a specific province. By analogy with Statistics Canada, it might be argued that broad national data-collecting powers may serve the national interest in a way that finds no counterpart on the provincial plane.

Ibid at para 105.
110 *Ibid* at para 103.
111 The Court was aware of this, stating (in *ibid* at para 120) "[i]ndeed, some provincial securities schemes contain provisions analogous to the ones aimed at systemic risk found in the proposed Act." The first item on the Court's list is the designation of credit rating agencies. As of 20 April 2012, National Policy 11-205 ("Process for Designation of Credit Rating Organizations in Multiple Jurisdictions") will govern the process for applying for recognition as a credit rating agency in more than one jurisdiction. Under the policy, an applicant may apply for recognition across the country by making two applications: one to a "principal regulator" under the passport system, and a second to the Ontario Securities Commission (since Ontario is not a member of the passport system). Also as of 12 April 2012, National Instrument 25-101 will implement national standards for the recognition of a credit rating agency. Federalization of this regime would economize on paper work (and result in the

government is positioned to make the "systemic risk" provisions work, it is not at all clear what advantage would be achieved by federalization. Between 80 and 90 percent of Canadian capital market activity takes place in Ontario, and any market actor wishing to do business on a national basis must deal with the Ontario Securities Commission, which has long been recognized as a *de facto* national regulator.

---

payment of a single fee, rather than two), but would not likely result in a substantive regime of rules that is materially different from NI 25-101, nor broader national coverage.

The second and third provisions cited by the Court deal with derivatives. Section 89 of the draft federal statute provides that only recognized exchanges may trade in exchange-traded derivatives, and s 90 requires a disclosure document for designated derivatives. Each of these provisions has an analogue in the Ontario *Securities Act* (in s 64.1), although these provisions have not yet been proclaimed.

In respect of the duty to keep records, and the ability of the regulator to share information with other persons or agencies, all of the provincial enactments have similar provisions. It is true that a national regulator could collect information in a single format and have it collated in one place. However, there is little reason to believe that a similar outcome could not be achieved via a cooperative arrangement between the provinces and the federal government — or indeed between the provinces themselves.

It is not entirely clear why the Court fastened upon the remaining two provisions as demonstrative of factors ostensibly connected with systemic risk and in respect of which the federal government would have a putative enforcement advantage. Short sales not only fall within the bailiwick of provincial regulation, but IIROC as well, which is responsible for the "Universal Market Integrity Rules ("UMIR") that apply right across the country, and the stock exchanges and other trading fora. See "About IIROC," online: IIROC www.iiroc.ca/about/Pages/default.aspx, and "UMIR Marketplace Rules," online, IIROC www.iiroc.ca/industry/rulebook/Pages/UMIR-Marketplace-Rules.aspx.

The reference to the "urgent regulations" provision is presumably made to suggest that a single national regulator would move more nimbly and responsively in response to securities market developments. However, this provision also appears in provincial enactments, including that of Canada's *de facto* national regulator, the Ontario Securities Commission.

Table 5: Systemic Risk Provisions Mentioned by the
Supreme Court Of Canada, and Their Provincial
Analogues

Nature	Draft Federal Statute	Ontario Securities Act
Designating a credit rating agency	73	22
Only recognized exchanges may trade in exchange-traded derivatives	89	64.1(5) (not yet declared)
Disclosure document for designated derivatives	90	64.1(1) (not yet declared)
Duty to keep records	109	19
Declaration by short-seller to broker	126(1)	48
Sharing of information with other persons and agencies	224	153
Urgent regulations without usual notice	228(4)(c)	143.2(5)(d)

In addition, the CSA, an informal group representing all
of the securities regulators in Canada, has adopted a plethora
of "national instruments" and "national policy statements" that
apply right across the country.[112] Much of what is important in
each of the areas covered by securities regulation — primary
market disclosure, secondary market disclosure, takeover bids,
insider trading, registration, and corporate governance — is embodied in these common standards.[113]

---

112 Formally, each national instrument is adopted by each province as a rule,
regulation, or legislative amendment.
113 While some of these instruments either have carve-outs for particular
provinces, or are "multilateral" rather than national, most are truly
national in scope.

This is to say nothing of the self-regulatory organizations that promulgate rules that apply country-wide. The Investment Industry Regulatory Organization of Canada (IIROC) nationally regulates investment dealers, brokers, and all trading on equity and debt marketplaces in Canada (including the stock exchanges, quotation and trade reporting systems, and alternative trading systems). Its website states that "IIROC sets high quality regulatory and investment industry standards, protects investors and strengthens market integrity while maintaining efficient and competitive capital markets."[114] Similarly, the Mutual Fund Dealers Association of Canada regulates mutual funds on a national basis. In addition, the Toronto Stock Exchange (including its junior arm, the Venture Exchange) and other trading fora promulgate rules for the regulation of trading.[115]

It is not entirely clear whether the Supreme Court appreciated the extent to which national standards already exist in Canadian securities regulation via a combination of interprovincial cooperation, the *de facto* national regulatory role played by the Ontario Securities Commission, and the various self-regulatory organizations referred to above.[116]

K. A Federal "Clearinghouse" Regulator?

Ford and Gill argue that the *Securities Reference* authorizes the federal government to create a "data collection and systemic risk clearinghouse."[117] The hallmark of this clearinghouse is that it would have the power to force provincial regulators not only to collect and remit information to the federal government, but also to meet minimum regulatory standards for the purpose of containing systemic risks. In the words of Ford and Gill,

> the clearinghouse articulates broad goals and sets minimum standards around systemic risk (including systemic risk with international origins or implications), and data collection . . . . [T]he federal government must have the ability to mandate extensive disclosure requirements from provincial and territorial

---

114 See "About IIROC," online: IIROC www.iiroc.ca/English/About/Pages/default.aspx.
115 See e.g. "Trading Rules & Regulations," online: TMX www.tmx.com/en/trading/rules_regulations/index.html.
116 Although see *Securities Reference*, above note 1 at para 42.
117 See Chapter 9.

securities regulators. It must require that provinces and territories push fine-grained, high-quality information upward, in forms capable of being aggregated, on all matters that concern systemic risk . . . . The federal systemic risk regulator may also want to consider mandating particular operational processes for provinces and territories, if those processes are likely to produce better quality data.[118]

In addition,

the federal systemic risk regulator could decide that provinces should establish consumer or investor panels, like Ontario's or the FSA's, to ensure the explicit incorporation of a fuller range of stakeholder voices into the data-generating architecture at the provincial and territorial level. The clearinghouse regulator monitors the provinces' and territories' comparative successes and challenges in meeting federally-defined broad goals on matters bearing on systemic risk . . . .

It may decide to establish any number of positive and negative incentives for provincial and territorial regulators . . . .

The clearinghouse would be able to require provinces to coordinate and to meet performance standards set by other provinces, in the interest of managing systemic risk.[119]

The ostensible authority for these activities is the following passages from the *Securities Reference:*

Prevention of systemic risk may trigger the need for a national regulator empowered to issue orders that are valid throughout Canada and *impose common standards*, under which provincial governments can work to ensure that their market will not transmit any disturbance across Canada or elsewhere.[120]

* * * * *

Legislation aimed at *imposing minimum standards* applicable throughout the country and preserving the stability and integrity of Canada's financial markets might well relate to trade as a whole.[121]

---

118 *Ibid.*
119 *Ibid.*
120 *Securities Reference*, above note 1 at para 104 [emphasis added].
121 *Ibid* at para 114 [emphasis added]. The second statement does not go so far as to state that all five *indicia* in the *General Motors* test are met — only the third element. Nonetheless, the first passage suggests that "prevention of systemic risk" might pass muster under all five presump-

It should be pointed out, however, that these statements are merely *obiter dicta*, and thus form a singularly shaky foundation upon which to build a bold new regime of federal law. This is particularly so given that the postulated federal legislation incorporates a command and control regime, with provincially constituted agencies acting upon instruction as federal factors. This is both utterly unprecedented in Canadian constitutional law and unsupported by any other case authority — *dicta* or otherwise.

If provincial agencies are to become federal agents, they will very likely be "federal institutions" within the meaning of the *Official Languages Act*.[122] Many will be staffed by employees who do not meet the bilingualism requirements of the Act. This would produce considerable disruption and quite possibly result in the loss of many employees at both operations and management levels.

In addition, it is very likely that any attempt by the federal government to institute a regime of this nature would be met by the same vigorous provincial opposition that led to the *Securities Reference*. It is not clear that the federal government has the appetite to burn any further political capital in seeking to establish a comprehensive regime of securities law.

Perhaps more importantly, the purport of the *Securities Reference* and its kin is that the scope and extent of the general trade and commerce power is conditioned by a keen interest in preserving the federal–provincial balance of power. Particularly given that Ford and Gill view essentially every corner of securities regulation as implicated in systemic risk issues, allowing the federal government to establish minimum regulatory standards would facilitate a less-than-subtle end run around the *Securities Reference*, and would almost certainly precipitate a massive alter-

---

tive tests. The Court also states that measures that "transcend intraprovincial regulation of property and civil rights . . . would fall within the circumscribed scope of the general trade and commerce power." *Ibid* at para 125. Arguably, this statement is trivially true: the real question is what transcends intraprovincial regulation of property and civil rights. The following passage addressing the question of whether the fifth criterion would be satisfied is more definite: with respect to "national data collection and prevention of and response to systemic risks, the answer must be yes — much for the reasons discussed under the fourth question. On these matters a federal regime would be qualitatively different from a voluntary interprovincial scheme." *Ibid* at para 123. See also *ibid* at para 128.

122 OLA, above note 93, s 3(1) (definition of "federal institution," particularly s 3(1)(h)).

ation in the distribution of powers. One could well imagine, for example, that the federal government would not be content to limit its mandated minimum standards to securities regulation. Might it not also legislate on this basis in relation to the closely allied fields of corporate law, contract law, and commercial law? All of these could also be said to have international dimensions (or at least implicate "genuinely national concerns"), and so play a role in determining systemic risk. Or perhaps the federal government could mandate minimum standards in relation to health care (other than through the so-called spending power, which is nothing but the power of the purse), the professions, or the environment, all of which might also be said to involve "genuinely national concerns."[123]

But in any case, I would suggest that Ford and Gill have misconstrued the purport of the above-quoted passages from the *Securities Reference*. In my view, the only acceptable interpretation is that federal legislation imposes "common" or "minimum" standards simply by virtue of the fact that it applies uniformly across the entire country, just as the *Criminal Code* establishes common or minimum standards by virtue of its national application. I believe that this is clear from the Court's repeated references to cooperative federalism as the way to break the current logjam.[124] Cooperative federalism is hardly cooperative when it involves the federal government imposing minimum standards on the provinces, or requiring provincial agencies to become its information-collecting operatives. The Court's dual emphasis on

---

123 *Securities Reference*, above note 1 at para 130.
124 For example:

> While the proposed Act must be found *ultra vires* Parliament's general trade and commerce power, a cooperative approach that permits a scheme that recognizes the essentially provincial nature of securities regulation while allowing Parliament to deal with genuinely national concerns remains available.

Ibid at para 130.

In addition, the Court makes a point of reviewing cooperative arrangements in other countries and states:

> The common ground that emerges is that each level of government has jurisdiction over some aspects of the regulation of securities and each can work in collaboration with the other to carry out its responsibilities.

Ibid at para 131.
See also *ibid* at paras 9, 58, 62, 130, and 132.

cooperative federalism and preserving the federal–provincial balance of power sets the stage against which the above passages from the *Securities Reference* must be read. The federal and provincial governments are free to act within their own constitutional spheres of power, but neither is free to tell the other what to do, either by adopting particular legislative provisions or by exercising powers in any particular way.[125]

L. Systemic Risk, Investor Protection, and a National Regulator

In her contribution to this volume, Anand cogently argues that various deficiencies in provincial securities regulation played a role in the credit crisis of 2008.[126] Nonetheless, it is not at all clear that these failures are in any way connected to the absence of a federal regulator.[127] Provincial regulatory failure does not *ipso facto* make a case for a federal regulator. One might just as well argue that federal regulatory failures — of which there has been no shortage — make out a case for transferring various aspects of federal regulation to provincial jurisdiction. In fact, all levels of government slip up from time to time. These slip-ups may, but need not, be evidence that regulatory authority is better managed at a different level of government.

In my view, to the extent that there is a link between securities regulators and systemic risk, it is adequately addressed when regulators are attentive to their historic mandates: protecting investors, ensuring the fairness and efficiency of Canadian capital markets, and promoting public confidence in our capital markets. The regulatory failures associated with the credit crisis were not a result of faithfully following those mandates and missing the forest for the trees but, rather, a result of failing to adequately address the mandates. Indeed, the irony is that while the federal government leaned heavily on the credit crisis in making its case for a federal regulator, Canada, which lacked a national regulator, fared better through the credit crisis than virtually any other

---

125 This is something quite different from the delegation of authority from one level to another, which is permitted.

126 See Chapter 11, notes 31–56 and accompanying text. Accord Chapter 9.

127 I make this argument at greater length in Jeffrey G MacIntosh, "Systemic Fallacy; A National Regulator Wouldn't Have Prevented the Credit Crisis" *Financial Post* (24 November 2010) 15.

country in the world, including the United States, almost all of which had a federal regulator.

M. Conclusion

The *Securities Reference* closely followed prior Supreme Court jurisprudence and reached the right decision. Had the draft federal securities legislation been given the Court's constitutional imprimatur, a profound shift in the balance of federal–provincial power would have resulted. Nonetheless, the decision is likely to have little impact on the likelihood or achievability of a single national regulator, since the controlling factor was never constitutional validity, but politics. The decision, however, leaves some unanswered questions about the nature of the fourth prong of the *General Motors* test for constitutional validity under the general branch of the trade and commerce power.

While the Court gives some guidance on what kind of federal legislation might pass muster under the trade and commerce power, this guidance is far from precise. The provisions that the Court suggests might be suitable in a federal statute addressing systemic risk and information collection all have provincial analogues. Even if it were true that the federal government has a special advantage in collecting information or addressing systemic risk, federal provisions addressing these subject matters would not, under the doctrine of paramountcy, suspend the operation of the parallel provincial provisions. Nor is there constitutional warrant for believing that the federal government could instruct provincial regulators to act as its factors in this regard. Thus, federal legislation would simply add another layer of regulation.

Canada is unlikely to have a single regulator at any time in the near future. There is some prospect for a multijurisdictional regulator constituted by the provinces. There are so many difficult political issues to be overcome, however, that even this may be unlikely for the foreseeable future.

CHAPTER 13

The Provinces' Competence over Securities Regulation in Canada: Taking Stock of the Supreme Court's Opinion

Stéphane Rousseau

A. Introduction

On 22 December 2011, the Supreme Court of Canada rendered a landmark opinion in the *Reference Re Securities Act*.[1] On the question of whether the proposed Canadian *Securities Act* was within the legislative authority of the Parliament of Canada, the Supreme Court answered with a strong and unanimous "no."

The opinion is a milestone in the debate on the possibility (and desirability) of creating a national regulatory framework for securities markets. The Court's opinion arguably blocks the federal government's project of creating a single scheme governing the trading of securities throughout Canada.[2] Nonetheless, commentators quickly observed that "it's not over yet"; they believe that the decision still leaves open the possibility of establishing a national regulator.[3] More recently, in the 2012 Budget, the Minister of Finance stated, "Government is consulting with provinces and territories, a number of which have reaffirmed their interest

---

1   2011 SCC 66 [*Securities Reference*].
2   At the provincial levels, the Alberta and Quebec Courts of Appeal have also ruled that the federal project was unconstitutional. See *Québec (Procureure générale) c Canada (Procureure générale)*, 2011 QCCA 591; *Reference Re Securities Act (Canada)*, 2011 ABCA 77.
3   See e.g. Phillip Anisman, "It's Not Over Yet" *National Post* (29 December 2011).

in working on a cooperative basis toward a common securities regulator."[4]

My contribution to this volume challenges the idea that there is room for a national securities regulator. First, I emphasize the clarity of the Court's decision with respect to the provinces' jurisdiction over the securities sector. Second, I argue that systemic risk cannot form the basis of a full-fledged federal regulatory regime pertaining to securities.

B. The Provinces' Authority over the Securities Sector

1) Historical Perspectives

In its reasons, the Supreme Court explicitly recognized the provinces' jurisdiction over securities by reviewing prior rulings. Referring to the Privy Council decision in *Lymburn v Mayland*,[5] the Court stated that the provinces "have jurisdiction to regulate securities within their boundaries (intraprovincial jurisdiction) as a matter of property and civil rights."[6] Further, the Court emphasized that provincial jurisdiction is not confined to intraprovincial effects but "extends to impacts on market intermediaries or investors outside a particular province".[7] Thus, the provinces also have jurisdiction wherever their respective capital markets are engaged.

But why is securities regulation a matter of property and civil rights? The trite answer is that because the *Constitution Act, 1867,* is silent on this matter, it follows — from a purely legal perspective — that, given the nature of securities and of the trading of securities, securities regulation concerns property and civil rights. That is, of course, unless it is possible to justify federal jurisdiction over securities through section 91.

But what is more interesting, although not developed in the Court's opinion, is that the Fathers of Confederation did not explicitly list securities in section 91 or 92. Yet it should be stressed, from a historical perspective, that a securities market already

---

4   Canada, Minister of Finance, *Jobs Growth and Long-Term Prosperity,* Economic Action Plan 2012 (March 2012) at 128.

5   [1932] AC 318.

6   *Securities Reference*, above note 1 at para 43.

7   *Ibid* at para 45.

existed in Canada at the time of Confederation,[8] supported by a legal infrastructure stemming from the legislation governing public bodies and private companies, which allowed them to raise funds by issuing shares or debt instruments.[9] Further, the Canadian securities market already had an international dimension in the nineteenth century, as the New York and London stock exchanges provided competitive financing sources for government and railway companies, for instance.[10]

The point of this historical sketch is that securities were not unknown to lawmakers before Confederation.[11] Further, and most importantly, having served as legislators, the Fathers of Confederation had participated in passing a number of statutes relating to companies and securities. Thus, it can be argued that regulation of securities was knowingly left to the general property and civil rights heading, rather than being specifically attributed to Parliament, as were other heads of power such as banking.

From Confederation on, the provinces have elaborated legislative schemes to regulate securities.[12] Indeed, we find provisions dealing with securities in the *Civil Code of Lower Canada*, enacted in 1866. Starting in the early twentieth century, provincial legislation laid the foundation for securities regulation. The initial goal of such legislation was to protect investors. To achieve this goal, the laws drew on various techniques during the first few decades of the century, experimenting with the Blue Sky Model and the fraud prevention model. In the 1940s and 1950s, legislation pertaining to securities adopted the disclosure-based

8   See Christopher Armstrong, *Blue Skies and Boiler Rooms: Buying and Selling Securities in Canada, 1870–1940* (Toronto: University of Toronto Press, 1997) at 9–10.

9   FE Labrie & EE Palmer, "The Pre-Confederation History of Corporations in Canada" in Jacob S Ziegel, ed, *Studies in Canadian Company Law/ Études sur le droit canadien des compagnies* (Toronto: Butterworths, 1967) at 33; Luc Le Blanc, *Les valeurs mobilières dans les lois préconfédératives canadiennes et leur portée extraterritoriale* (2003) [unpublished, archived at Université de Sherbrooke, Groupe de recherche sur l'histoire des institutions financières]; Richard CB Risk, "The Nineteenth-Century Foundations of the Business Corporation in Ontario" (1973) 23 UTLJ 270.

10   Ranald C Michie, "The Canadian Securities Market 1850–1914" (1988) 62 Business History Review 35 at 49.

11   N-M Dawson, *La finance : un monde connu des pères de la confédération*, study commissioned by Quebec Ministry of Finance, Sherbrooke, 2002.

12   See *Securities Reference*, above note 1 (Reference Record, AG of Quebec Materials, Vol 6, Stéphane Rousseau, *Securities Regulation in Quebec and the Debate about a Single Securities Commission*).

model set forth in the *Securities Act of 1933* and in the *Securities and Exchange Act of 1934* in the United States. Since then, the provincial regulatory framework has been continually updated to respond to challenges, changes, and criticism.

A look at the evolution of the provincial regulatory framework from the 1950s highlights the provinces' responsiveness in the face of events that tested the regulatory framework's regulation's ability to protect investors while promoting efficiency. The constant and progressive updating of the regulatory framework has allowed it to remain abreast of contemporary issues. Updated in a decentralized model, it has been enriched through diversity and experimentation in an environment characterized by a combination of competition and collaboration among regulators. After taking stock of these developments, the Court summarized by stating that "[w]hile it is obvious that the securities market is of great importance to modern economic activity, we cannot ignore that the provinces have been deeply engaged in the regulation of this market over the course of many years."[13]

2) The Draft Federal Legislation: Fundamental Flaws

In its reasons, the Supreme Court recognized that the Constitution also grants powers to Parliament to adopt laws that relate to aspects of securities and, more broadly, to promote the integrity and stability of the Canadian financial system. Of those powers, the general trade and commerce power appears to offer the most potential.[14] Nevertheless, in the Court's opinion, the federal government could not rely on the general trade and commerce power to justify the constitutional validity of the proposed scheme. Doing otherwise, the Court held, would go against the

---

13 *Securities Reference*, above note 1 at para 155. See generally AD Harris, *A Symposium on Canadian Securities Regulation: Harmonization or Nationalization?* (Toronto: University of Toronto Capital Markets Institute and Canadian Foundation for Investor Education, 2002).

14 For a thorough analysis of the constitutional question, see e.g. Noura Karazivan & Jean F Gaudreault-Desbiens, "On Polyphony and Paradoxes in the Regulation of Securities within the Canadian Federation" (2010) 49 Can Bus LJ 1; Jean Leclair, "Please, Draw Me a Field of Jurisdiction: Regulating Securities, Securing Federalism" (2010) 51 Sup Ct L Rev (2d) 555; Ian Lee, "Balancing and its Alternatives: Jurisprudential Choice, Federal Securities Regulation and the Trade and Commerce Power" (2011) 50 Can Bus LJ 72.

grain of Canadian federalism, which requires striking a constitutional balance between the federal and provincial powers:

> It is a fundamental principle of federalism that both federal and provincial powers must be respected, and one power may not be used in a manner that effectively eviscerates another. Rather, federalism demands that a balance be struck, a balance that allows both the federal Parliament and the provincial legislatures to act effectively in their respective spheres. Accepting Canada's interpretation of the general trade and commerce power would disrupt rather than maintain that balance. Parliament cannot regulate the whole of the securities system simply because aspects of it have a national dimension.[15]

Fundamentally, the draft federal legislation purported to replicate the existing provincial securities laws, with very similar goals and mostly identical regimes to the provincial statutes. Thus, had the federal legislation been adopted, its opt-in mechanism would eventually have subsumed the existing provincial securities regimes under the federal regulation scheme.

Indeed, the Court aptly remarked that "[a] long-standing exercise of power does not confer constitutional authority to legislate, nor does the historic presence of the provinces in securities regulation preclude a federal claim to regulatory jurisdiction,"[16] in this case, the federal government was unable to make its case for the securities industry's having transformed to the point of relating to trade as a whole.[17] In particular, the Court rejected the argument that the globalization of securities markets justified federal intervention. In doing so, the Court's decision underlines the local dimensions of capital markets, as well as the important role of the provinces in regulating those markets.

3) Investor Protection and Market Efficiency

According to the Court, investor protection has historically been a provincial responsibility under section 92(13). This is certainly correct, as underlined above. However, the Court appears to suggest that the goals of ensuring fair, efficient and competitive capital markets are of national concern, and thus justify the recognition of federal competence in this respect.

---

15 *Securities Reference*, above note 1 at para 7.
16 *Ibid* at para 116.
17 *Ibid* at para 33.

The Court's comments should be put in perspective. Starting with the *Kimber Report* in 1965, market efficiency has been identified as a complementary legislative goal of provincial securities regulation;[18] the *Kimber Report* stated that the regulatory system as a whole should promote the efficient allocation of capital. Integrated in provincial securities legislation, the promotion of efficiency has been recognized by the Supreme Court in the *Cartaway Resources*[19] and *Kerr v Danier Leather Inc.*[20] cases. Further, as the *Kimber Report* stressed, the goals of investor protection and market efficiency are closely linked. More recently, this point has been supported by theoretical and empirical studies showing that the extent to which investors' rights are protected influences the development of capital markets.[21]

It is also worth emphasizing that provinces are not incapable of ensuring the efficiency of securities markets. Assessments performed by international bodies such as the Organization for Economic Co-operation and Development (OECD) and the World Bank have ranked Canada's securities regulation framework as among the best in the world.[22] More recently, a study conducted by Lortie has reinforced these findings:

> From an economic and business point of view, available data clearly show that the current securities regulatory architecture serves Canada very well. It is respected internationally, costs are low, compliance is high and it is highly responsive to regional economic conditions and needs.[23]

---

18 *Report of the Attorney General's Committee on Securities Legislation in Ontario* (Toronto: Queen's Printer, 1965) [*Kimber Report*].

19 *Cartaway Resources Corp (Re)*, 2004 SCC 26 at para 58.

20 *Kerr v Danier Leather Inc*, 2007 SCC 44 at para 32 [*Danier Leather*].

21 Rafael La Porta et al, "Law and Finance" (1998) 106 Journal of Political Economy 1113; Rafael La Porta et al, "Investor Protection and Corporate Governance" (2000) 58 Journal of Financial Economics 3.

22 See Council of Ministers of Securities Regulation, *Provincial-Territorial Council of Ministers of Securities Regulation Remains Committed to Ongoing Reform (Founded on Passport)*, 8 February, Communiqué. For a thorough discussion, see Eric Spink, "Federalism and Securities Regulation in Canada" in Nadia Verrelli, ed, *Canada: State of the Federation, 2011* McGill Queen's University Press [forthcoming, on file with author].

23 Pierre Lortie, *Securities Regulation in Canada: The Case for Effectiveness*, IRPP Study No. 19 (Montreal: Institute for Research on Public Policy, 2011) at 24. For a critical view, see Anita Anand, "Another Take on the Lortie Report" *Investment Executive* (December 2010).

Ultimately, the results of these studies reflect the fact that the existing regulatory framework allows for innovation, experimentation, and diversity within a highly harmonized set of rules.[24]

It is doubtful, in other words, that the goal of promoting market efficiency and capital formation could justify national securities legislation that would enact regimes governing the securities sector similar to those that exist under provincial law. Or, to put it more bluntly, Parliament cannot invoke national concerns relating to market efficiency as an excuse to regulate matters pertaining to securities, such as initial public offerings, continuous disclosure, or insider trading.

C. Regulation of Systemic Risk

1) General Observations

According to the Supreme Court, the general trade and commerce power could support legislation that seeks to ensure the preservation of capital markets and the maintenance of Canada's financial stability: "Legislation aimed at imposing minimum standards applicable throughout the country and preserving the stability and integrity of Canada's financial markets might well relate to trade as a whole."[25] More precisely, the Court identified the management of systemic risk as a national concern over which Parliament could claim competence, because, even acting in concert, the provinces "lack the constitutional capacity to sustain a viable national scheme aimed at genuine national goals such as management of systemic risk."[26] Relying on those observations, some commentators argue that this goal would justify the crafting of new federal legislation encompassing subject matters currently dealt with by provincial securities regulation.[27]

---

24 Rousseau, above note 12.
25 *Securities Reference*, above note 1 at para 114.
26 *Ibid* at para 121.
27 See e.g. Anita Anand & Grant Bishop, "Don't Throw in the Towel: Systemic Risk in Securities Markets Must be Federally Regulated" (17 February 2012), online: University of Toronto Faculty of Law Blog utorontolaw.typepad.com/faculty_blog/2012/02/dont-throw-in-the-towel-systemic-risk-in-securities-markets-must-be-federally-regulated.html; Anisman, above note 3.

Is systemic risk the Trojan horse that Parliament will use to support a full-fledged national securities scheme? The short answer is no: Although it can elaborate schemes to improve the management of systemic risk, Parliament cannot legally, in my opinion, use this goal to displace provincial securities legislation. In fact, the Supreme Court was quite clear about this limit:

> The need to prevent and respond to systemic risk may support federal legislation pertaining to the national problem raised by this phenomenon, but it does not alter the basic nature of securities regulation which, as shown, remains primarily focused on local concerns of protecting investors and ensuring the fairness of the markets through regulation of participants.[28]

2) Systemic Risk Management: The Concurrent Competence of Federal and Provincial Legislators

The real issue, then, is to ascertain the potential for a federal scheme for managing systemic risk without regulating securities. It is certainly too early to provide a detailed answer to this question. Still, two points are noteworthy in thinking about this issue.

First, systemic risk is not an all-encompassing notion. Work needs to be done to foster our understanding of the perimeter of systemic risk, as well as its main sources. At a general level, the term *systemic risk* refers to "risks that occasion a 'domino effect' whereby the risk of default by one market participant will impact the ability of others to fulfill their legal obligations, setting off a chain of negative economic consequences that pervade an entire financial system."[29] We do know that systemic risk is a form of negative externality, like pollution; that is, it results from excessive risk taking by parties who do not fully internalize the costs of such risks. However, there is still confusion as to what types of risk are truly systemic and what types of systemic risk must be regulated.[30] Defining systemic risk adequately will

---

28 *Securities Reference*, above note 1 at para 128.
29 *Securities Reference*, *ibid* (Record of the AG of Canada, Vol 1, Expert Report, Michael J Trebilcock, "National Securities Regulator Report" at para 26), cited in *Securities Reference*, *ibid* at para 103.
30 Steven L Schwarcz, "Systemic Risk" (2008) 97 Geo LJ 193 at 196. See also Dimitrios Bisias et al, *A Survey of Systemic Risk Analytics*, US, Department of the Treasury, Office of Financial Research Working Paper 0001 (5 January 2012) ("We are still in the earliest days of understanding the elusive and multi-faceted concept of systemic risk" at 15).

guard against the political manipulation of the concept: Systemic risk "should not be used uncritically as an ex post political label for any large financial failure or downturn."[31] At any rate, whatever else it may mean, systemic risk does not extend into every area of the securities sector.

Second, there is a need to better understand the regulation of systemic risk. This means defining the goals and scope of such regulation, as well as identifying the proper tools for dealing with the regulation of systemic risk. According to Professor Schwarcz, systemic risk regulation should pursue two main goals: a microprudential goal (maximizing market efficiency) that involves correcting market failures, and a macroprudential goal (protecting the financial system) that involves preventing the trigger of systemic risks, as well as its transmission.[32] Relatedly, regulation of systemic risk should stabilize the financial system where it is affected by systemic risk. Clarifying these issues is crucial for thinking about how to allocate responsibilities for regulating systemic risk in keeping with the principles of Canadian federalism.

At any rate, given its breadth, such regulation should not be confined to the federal level.[33] Recall that from the outset, provincial securities regulation has dealt with systemic risk through disclosure regimes and oversight of business conduct.[34] The fact that the proposed federal Act essentially reproduced the existing provincial securities regimes underscores the provinces' role in regulating systemic risk.[35]

Systemic risk is also regulated through federal schemes that are under the purview of the Office of the Superintendent of Financial Institutions (OSFI) and the Bank of Canada. For instance, OSFI has the prudential regulatory power to oversee the securities-related activities of Canadian banks. Likewise,

---

31 Schwarcz, *ibid* at 204.
32 See generally Schwarcz, *ibid*.
33 Eric Spink, "Reacting to the Status Quo in Securities Regulation" (2012) 52 Can Bus LJ 182 at 184–85.
34 International Organization of Securities Commission, *Mitigating Systemic Risk – A Role for Securities Regulators*, Discussion Paper (February 2011) at 51. See Spink, above note 22. For a different view see Anita I Anand, "Is Systemic Risk Relevant to Securities Regulation?" (2010) 60 UTLJ 941.
35 Jeffrey G MacIntosh, "Not Even Close" *Financial Post* (22 December 2011) FP 11, online: Financial Post opinion.financialpost.com/2011/12/22/not-even-close/.

pursuant to the *Payment Clearing and Settlement Act*,[36] the Bank of Canada has the authority to designate securities clearing and settlement systems as subject to the requirements of the Act. As a consequence of these systems' being designated as subject to the Act, the Bank of Canada exercises oversight through a power to issue directives.[37]

Finally, it is worth emphasizing that both levels of regulators also collaborate in the Head of Agencies Committee, both to exchange information and views and to coordinate action on issues of mutual concern. The experience of regulatory collaboration in this area should calm the fears expressed by the Supreme Court that management of systemic risk is always under threat of a province's withdrawing from an interprovincial scheme.

Thus, from this perspective, the real question is whether there are gaps in the current setting and, if so, whether those gaps call for a whole new regulatory framework to deal with systemic risk.[38] In light of Canada's performance in the last financial crisis, and given the current regulatory and policy framework, we should be cautious about concluding that regulatory gaps are sufficiently important to justify a general federal scheme addressing systemic risk that would encroach on the securities sector. It is rather through cooperation between federal and provincial governments and regulators that systemic risk will best be monitored and managed.

D. Conclusion

I have argued above, first, that the Supreme Court's opinion definitely recognizes that the provinces have competence over securities regulation. Most importantly, the Court stated that Parliament does not have the constitutional power to enact a statutory framework that would replicate the existing provincial schemes. Thus, the Court's opinion blocks the federal government's project of creating a single scheme governing the trading of securities throughout Canada. Second, I have argued that

---

36 SC 1996, c 6.
37 For a critical view on the distinction between macro and microprudential regulation, see Nick Le Pan, "Look Before You Leap: A Skeptical View of Proposals to Meld Macro and Microprudential Regulation" (2009) CD Howe Institute Commentary No. 296.
38 See Lortie, above note 23 at 22.

while the Supreme Court recognized that Parliament has competence over the management of systemic risk, Parliament cannot use this goal as an excuse to displace provincial securities legislation. Further, the provinces also have competence over systemic risk, which means that managing and monitoring systemic risk requires cooperation between federal and provincial governments.

CHAPTER 14

The *Securities Reference:*
A Comment

Christopher C Nicholls

It is old news now: the Supreme Court of Canada has ruled that the proposed Canadian *Securities Act* is not within the legislative authority of Parliament, at least not under the so-called general branch of the federal trade and commerce power in section 91(2) of the *Constitution Act, 1867*.[1] Yes, the Court acknowledged, "*aspects* of the securities market are national in scope and affect the country as a whole."[2] But the reach of the proposed Act was not

---

1   *Reference Re Securities Act*, 2011 SCC 66 [*Securities Reference*]. The notion that the s 91(2) trade and commerce power comprised two "branches" was first articulated by the Judicial Committee of the Privy Council in the 1881 decision, *Citizens Insurance Co of Canada v Parsons* (1881), 7 AC 96.

2   *Securities Reference, ibid* at para 6 [emphasis added]. As the Court put it, "Parliament cannot regulate the whole of the securities system simply because aspects of it have a national dimension": *ibid* at para 7. In particular, the Court seemed to object to the attempt by the federal government to regulate the "day-to-day" operations of securities issuers and sellers. The phrase "day-to-day" appears six times in the judgment. The Court offered, as specific examples of the national aspects of the proposed legislation, provisions "aimed at management of systemic risk and at national data collection": *ibid* at para 117. "A federal scheme aimed at such matters," the Court later suggests, "might well be qualitatively different from what the provinces, acting alone or in concert, could achieve": *ibid* at para 121. See also *ibid* at paras 123, 125, and 128. The Court characterized the federal government's argument in this way: the securities markets have evolved. They are now national markets, and so must be regulated by a national regulator. The Court seemed to accept that *some* aspects of securities markets were truly national in nature. But that was not enough.

confined to these limited aspects of national importance,[3] and so, in the Court's view, it could not be supported by the "general branch." Whether the Act might or might not have been upheld on some other constitutional basis — for example, the interprovincial and international branch of the trade and commerce power — we do not know. The Court was not asked to look beyond the "general branch" of section 91(2). No matter (at least for now). The hoped-for comprehensive rationalization and consolidation of securities regulatory authority could, in all likelihood, have been fully achieved only if the Court had accepted the "general branch" argument.[4]

The Court's decision did not sit well with those business and legal professionals and other market watchers who favoured a national securities regulator. The ink on the judgment was barely dry before the sniping began. A few critics quietly raised the delicate issue of institutional expertise. Did a legal education and judicial experience provide the optimal background for those called upon to assess the systemic implications of credit default swaps, CDO-squareds[5] and those other quant-spawned wonders of modern financial innovation? No matter how wise and able its members, they asked, is any generalist court necessarily the best forum in which to argue complex securities regulatory issues? Have we not, after all, long entrusted the regulation of our capital markets to expert securities commissions, rather than "jack-of-all-trades" jurists?[6]

---

3   *Ibid* (federal legislation can be upheld under the "general branch" of the trade and commerce power "where the national interest is engaged in a manner that is qualitatively different from provincial concerns" at para 46).

4   *Ibid* at para 23. As the Supreme Court's brief historical canvass indicates, many previous proposals for a national securities regulator had been premised on a "dual structure," which would have allowed provincial regulators to continue to regulate wholly intra-provincial securities matters. The most recent studies of the issue, however, had come to reject that approach as inefficient and undesirable in light of the nature of Canada's modern securities market.

5   For a brief explanation of these concepts, see Christopher C Nicholls, *Financial Institutions: The Regulatory Framework* (Toronto: LexisNexis, 2008) at 187.

6   As a general matter, the relationship between the growing importance of regulatory bodies and the traditional function of the courts is a fascinating one. Harvard economist Andrei Shleifer has recently argued that the increasing importance of regulation is the result of the courts' failure to perform their role efficiently. See Andrei Shleifer, "Efficient Regulation" in Daniel P Kessler, ed, *Regulation vs. Litigation: Perspectives from Economics and Law* (Chicago: University of Chicago Press, 2011) at 27.

This general institutional critique does not seem entirely apt in this case, however. The *Securities Reference*, after all, involved matters that fell squarely within the Court's jurisprudential wheelhouse. This was a good "old-fashioned" constitutional division of powers dispute. Vintage constitutional law. The only sort of constitutional law that existed when lawyers of my generation began their law school careers, back in the antediluvian days when legal dinosaurs ruled the Earth and the *Canadian Charter of Rights and Freedoms* was just a glimmer in the eye of Prime Minister Trudeau. If corporate and securities law experts occasionally raise eyebrows over the Supreme Court's pronouncements in the corporate and commercial law arena, surely, those same corporate mavens must fairly acknowledge that in this particular instance the critical *constitutional* issue was before the genuine experts. It doesn't take a PhD in finance or deal-carrying experience at Goldman Sachs to interpret the musty language of a 144-year-old statute. It is doubtless, of course, that a differently-formed perspective on the nature and scope of modern Canadian securities markets could have implied a different constitutional conclusion. (If Canadian capital markets in 1867 had resembled today's modern network of complex interprovincial and international transactions, institutions and relationships, it seems inconceivable that legislative authority over those markets would not have been allocated to the federal government.) Yet, the Court went to some pains to emphasize that their decision did not — could not — speak to the issue of what is the "best" way of regulating our capital markets.[7] Their job was to interpret a constitutional text. They would not presume to rewrite the document. No, not even if the greatest securities experts in the world all unanimously agreed on just how it *should* have been written. (And, of course, they didn't.)

---

7   See e.g. *Securities Reference*, above note 1 at para 10: "At this juncture, it is important to stress that this advisory opinion does not address the question of what constitutes the optimal model for regulating the securities market . . . [T]he policy question of whether a single national securities scheme is preferable to multiple regimes is not one for the courts to decide." Later, at para 90, the Court notes that "in applying the *General Motors* test, one should not confuse what is optimum as a matter of policy and what is constitutionally permissible . . . The courts do not have the power to declare legislation constitutional simply because they conclude that it may be the best option from the point of view of policy."

To be clear, I am not neutral about the outcome of the decision. I was disappointed by it. I supported the federal government's position, both as a matter of law and economic policy. I still do. I strongly favour a national securities regulator, and I believe there are sound and compelling reasons for doing so. But in addition to the many legitimate reasons, as fair-minded people must acknowledge, a few exaggerated or specious arguments have also been tossed into the mix. Some of the boldest claims surely go too far. It seems improbable, for example, that a national securities regime will cure all regulatory ills, resolve all enforcement gaps, forever insulate Canada from the shadow of systemic risk, dramatically lower the cost of capital for all Canadian issuers, spur regulatory nimbleness and innovation,[8] make Canada the preferred market for the most prestigious international issuers, and instantly catapult Canada to the apex of the world's capital market pyramid.

But some of the more ardent boosters of the provincial side have also been a little disingenuous. Surely one of the silliest knocks against the federal position was the sometimes-heard observation that "securities regulation" was not expressly assigned to the federal government by the *Constitution Act, 1867*. That is true, of course. References to the Internet, nuclear power, space travel, and cell phones are also conspicuously absent, and for much the same reason: any mention of "securities regulation" in a nineteenth-century statute would have been a baffling anachronism, since the phrase "securities regulation" was not coined until the mid-twentieth century. Professor Louis Loss, the legendary Harvard law professor who literally wrote the book on securities regulation, invented the term as the title for his influential 1951 treatise.[9]

---

8   A recent article in *The Globe and Mail* suggested that the lack of a national regulator has impeded Canadian acceptance of "crowdfunding," an innovative financing technique expressly permitted in certain cases by amendments to the US federal *Securities Act of 1933* introduced by the *Jumpstart Our Business Startups Act*, Pub L 112-106, signed by President Obama on 5 April 2012. See Kevin Carmichael, "Crowdfunding: Why Canada is Far Behind the U.S." *The Globe and Mail* (2 May 2012), online: The Globe and Mail www.theglobeandmail.com/report-on-business/economy/economy-lab/daily-mix/crowdfunding-why-canada-is-far-behind-the-us/article2420066/.

9   "Although the two words, 'Securities Regulation,' now appear almost routinely in the titles of books and other publications in the field, as well as in general conversation, I am quite certain that it had never been publicly

Some of the claims for the benefits of decentralized provincial securities regulation are also unconvincing. The suggestion that sub-national regulation will lead to better regulatory outcomes than centralized national regulation has been advanced by a few leading American scholars, chief among them Roberta Romano of the Yale Law School. Professor Romano's insightful views always deserve careful attention. But it is important to remember that her argument is not simply an endorsement of sub-national securities regulation: she advocates a wholly new legal regime in which sub-national securities regulatory *competition* would be possible.[10] If the regime she supports existed, we might well expect to see the very beneficial regulatory competition she favours. The argument, to rather grossly oversimplify, is that competition between suppliers invariably benefits consumers. Monopolies — especially artificial,[11] government-created monopolies — distort prices, stifle innovation, limit supply, and generally make consumers worse off. What is true in the market for goods and services is also true in the market for law. Support for this position may be found in the apparent success of competitive federalism

---

used before, at least to my knowledge." From Louis Loss, *Anecdotes of a Securities Lawyer* (Boston: Little, Brown and Company, 1995) at 51. In fact, Loss really defined "securities regulation" as an independent field of study, creating the first law school course in the subject following the creation of the US Securities and Exchange Commission in the 1930s.

10 As she acknowledges in her book, *The Advantage of Competitive Federalism for Securities Regulation*, to implement a system of competitive federalism in securities regulation requires not only abandoning a federal regulator but also a "second major policy form — adapting the [existing] choice-of-law rule governing securities transactions (site by site) to one compatible with competition (issuer domicile)." This change, she rightly recognizes, "could be more complicated to accomplish" than the preliminary step of making US federal securities law optional. Roberta Romano, *The Advantage of Competitive Federalism for Securities Regulation* (Washington: The AEI Press, 2002) at 113.

11 Some economists have suggested that some monopolies might be "natural," in the limited sense that in some industries, where there are significant economies of scale, a single producer or supplier can supply the market at lower cost than multiple suppliers or producers. In such markets, it is argued, multiple suppliers would actually be inefficient; competition would be destructive, not only to producers but to consumers. The theory of natural monopolies has been used to justify government-regulated monopolies, chiefly relating to public utilities. The theory of natural monopoly is controversial because, among other things, it can be used by businesses to justify government regulation that will prevent them from having to compete. See generally Richard A Posner, "Natural Monopoly and Its Regulation" (1969) 21 Stan L Rev 548.

in US corporate law[12] — that particular application of the famous Tiebout doctrine[13] that led first New Jersey and then, more recently and more famously, the tiny state of Delaware[14] to become the preferred jurisdiction of incorporation for more than half of America's largest corporations.[15] Investors can decide for themselves which corporate law they prefer and can reveal their preferences by choosing to invest in (or, equivalently, by willingly paying higher prices for) the shares of corporations governed by the laws of their favoured jurisdictions.[16] Without this sort of effective market discipline, legislators, acting on their own, can at best only hope to generate "wouldn't you think" solutions that may or may not actually reflect investor preferences. Worse still, monopoly legislators and regulators may be subject to industry capture. The interests of the concentrated, well-organized, well-funded, and highly incentivized regulated businesses themselves could, over time, come to define the contours of the legislative or regulatory landscape.[17] The more diffuse interests of consum-

---

12　Professor Romano is also one of the leading champions of US corporate charter competition. As she has put it, "The genius of American corporate law is in its federalist organization." Roberta Romano, *The Genius of American Corporate Law* (Washington: The AEI Press, 1993) at 1.

13　See Charles Tiebout, "A Pure Theory of Local Expenditures" (1956) 64 Journal of Political Economy 416.

14　See William E Kirk III, "A Case Study in Legislative Opportunism: How Delaware Used the Federal-State System to Attain Corporate Pre-eminence" (1984) 10 J Corp L 233.

15　See State of Delaware, Department of State, Division of Corporations, online: State of Delaware corp.delaware.gov/aboutagency.shtml.

16　The literature on the Delaware phenomenon is immense. The terms of the modern corporate competitive federalism debate were established in a pair of important articles published in the 1970s: William L Cary, "Federalism and Corporate Law: Reflections upon Delaware" (1974) 83 Yale LJ 663; Ralph K Winter, "State Law, Shareholder Protection, and the Theory of the Corporation" (1977) 6 J Legal Stud 251. In a widely cited 2001 article, Robert Daines offered empirical evidence in support of the proposition that Delaware incorporation improves firm value. See Robert Daines, "Does Delaware Law Improve Firm Value?" (2001) 62 Journal of Financial Economics 525.

17　The "capture theory" of regulation is associated, in particular, with the work of George Stigler. See George J Stigler, "The Theory of Economic Regulation" (1971) 2 Bell J of Economics 3. Stigler's capture theory may be seen as a special case of Buchanan and Tullock's public choice theory. See James M Buchanan & Gordon Tullock, *The Calculus of Consent: Logical Foundations of Constitutional Democracy* (Ann Arbor: University of Michigan Press, 1962). One notes that the term "public choice theory" was not coined by Buchanan and Tullock and, indeed, it has been suggested that Buchanan actually "never cared for this name." See Robert

ers and investors will be shunted aside. The logic is simple and powerful: allowing people to choose freely for themselves is surely the best way to ensure that their preferences are accommodated. No legislator, no regulator, no central planner, and no judge can ever hope to do as well.

For various reasons that do not concern us here, corporate charter competition has never really occurred in Canada.[18] But there is, in any event, a fundamental problem with the model in the securities regulation context: However compelling some may find the theoretical case for competitive federalism in securities law, it breaks down at the stage of practical implementation. At the moment, there is nothing in the securities regulation regime in Canada, the United States, the United Kingdom, or likely any other major industrial nation that parallels the corporate law "internal affairs" doctrine: the idea that a corporation carries its home corporate law around with it wherever it travels in the world. Securities laws work differently. They originated primarily not to enable corporations but to protect the investors who live in the jurisdictions where they are enacted.[19] And it is that difference that makes the hoped-for benefits of securities regulatory competition illusory at the present time. Theoretically, Ontario investors might indirectly express their confidence in specific foreign exchanges or markets by choosing, for example, to seek out and purchase securities in those markets, exclusively in offshore transactions. But when it is the issuers that actively seek to court Ontario residents via Ontario markets, the situation is very different. Then, most Ontario investors cannot, as a practical matter, vote with their pocketbooks by choosing to invest only in those securities publicly-offered to investors in Ontario by firms regulated by the world's "best" securities regimes because

---

L Formiani, "James M. Buchanan: The Creation of Public Choice Theory" (2003) 8 Economic Insight 1 at 2.

18   See Ronald J Daniels, "Should Provinces Compete? The Case for a Competitive Corporate Law Market" (1991) 36 McGill LJ 130; Douglas Cumming & Jeffrey G MacIntosh, "The Role of Interjurisdictional Competition in Shaping Canadian Corporate Law" (2000) 20 Int'l Rev L & Econ 141; Christopher C Nicholls, *Corporate Law* (Toronto: Emond-Montgomery, 2005) at 34–35.

19   It is trite to observe that modern securities laws also have additional purposes, including the fostering of fair and efficient capital markets and confidence in those markets. But no one familiar with the history and actual operation of securities regulation could seriously deny the enduring importance of investor protection as a securities regulatory goal.

any issuer offering securities to the public in Ontario, with very limited exceptions, will be subject to Ontario securities laws. So securities regulation would have to be changed — rather dramatically — before the benefits of regulatory competition could be realized. Ontario could choose to forgo the right to protect its citizens from securities offences committed by issuers who elect to be regulated abroad while actively tapping the Ontario capital markets. But such a choice to stand down would surely not be popular. Indeed, the political reality would make such a policy unthinkable. Moreover, even if such a formal policy of regulatory forbearance (or abdication) could somehow be implemented in the first place, one suspects that at the first sign of trouble, it would quickly be reversed.

Let us suppose a corporation from, say, Brazil were to offer its shares publicly in Canada to Canadian investors. If the investment proved successful, the champagne would flow and thorny questions about enforcement jurisdiction would never arise. If the investment turned sour, however, I suggest that aggrieved Canadian share buyers would be shocked if told that their share purchases were to be governed entirely by Brazilian investor protection laws, and that investigation and enforcement of those laws would be entirely in the hands of Brazilian regulatory and legal authorities. Brazil's laws might well be similar to Canada's; for that matter, they might well be superior. But rest assured that if investor complaints emerged, Canadian regulators and legislators would take a very public drubbing if they were to insist that there was simply nothing they could do.[20]

It is for this reason that to argue for decentralized securities regulation in the current regime, as though that were an end in itself, falls very wide of the mark. It is not simply a question of putting the cart before the horse; it is more like abandoning both cart and horse before any other mode of transportation has even been invented.

In his excellent paper elsewhere in this volume, Jeffrey MacIntosh has suggested that the benefits of decentralized securities regulation could be realized in Canada through a fairly modest change — by extending the existing passport system "to include all matters covered by securities regulation."[21] Though such a

---

20 This example is not entirely fanciful. See, for example, the facts underlying the recent decision of the Ontario Court of Appeal in *Abdula v Canadian Solar Inc*, 2012 ONCA 211.

21 See Chapter 12.

change is theoretically possible, there is arguably a considerable difference between deferring to another provincial regulator in the case of essentially administrative document, exemption, or registration application review and the very different issue of standing down in all matters relating to substantive disclosure and investor protection requirements as well as, presumably, the investigation and enforcement of what, in your own jurisdiction, would have constituted securities law breaches affecting your own citizens' rights and economic interests. If one doubts how difficult it would be for regulators and governments to acquiesce when their own investors' interests are threatened, consider the provincial securities commissions' forays into such quintessential corporate law matters as proxy solicitation[22] and corporate governance standards;[23] the controversy surrounding the US Supreme Court's decision in *Morrison v National Australia Bank,*[24] the consequent *Dodd-Frank* amendments to US federal securities laws,[25] and the SEC's recent report to Congress, pursuant to section 929Y of *Dodd-Frank,*[26] in light of that decision; or, closer to home, the Ontario Court of Appeal's recent judgment in *Abdula v Canadian Solar Inc.,*[27] the British Columbia Court of Appeal's judgment in *Torudag v British Columbia (Securities Commission),*[28] and the recent OSC Staff Notice 51-719 concerning "Emerging Markets Issuer Review."[29]

Then, too, there are some who oppose the very idea of regulatory competition in securities laws, even if the conditions needed to make such competition effective could ever exist. Rejecting the "race to the top" logic endorsed by Romano, these intellectual heirs to William Cary[30] fear, instead, that such competition could lead to a dysfunctional "race to the bottom." The gloomiest

---

22 National Instrument 51-102, Part 9.

23 National Instrument 58-101; National Policy 58-201.

24 130 S Ct 2869 (2010).

25 *Dodd-Frank Wall Street Reform and Consumer Protection Act,* s 929P(b) (2), Pub L 111-203 [*Dodd-Frank*].

26 SEC, *Study on the Cross-Border Scope of the Private Right of Action Under Section 10(b) of the Securities Exchange Act of 1934* (April 2012), online: Securities and Exchange Commission www.sec.gov/news/studies/2012/929y-study-cross-border-private-rights.pdf .

27 Above note 20.

28 (2011), 343 DLR (4th) 743.

29 (2012), 35 OSCB 3004.

30 Above note 16.

fears of inevitable regulatory dystopia I do not share.[31] In fact, if effective and constructive regulatory competition really were possible, perhaps it could well be desirable. The problem, however, is not simply that the changes needed to make salutary competitive federalism in the securities regulatory area possible have not yet been implemented but that it is highly unlikely that they ever will be. In the meantime, all the disadvantages, inefficiencies, waste, and costs of the decentralized Canadian securities regulatory system persist.

Yet it has been argued that decentralized regulation, even within our current system, might well support regulatory diversity and perhaps sensitivity to unique local concerns. The Supreme Court has elsewhere alluded to these presumed benefits. In *Canadian Western Bank v Alberta*,[32] for example, the Court referred to the "diversity of regional experimentation," in a passage cited in the *Securities Reference*.[33] The Court also adverted to provincial diversity when explaining why the courts had chosen to draw careful boundaries around what would otherwise appear to be a very broad federal trade and commerce power, recognizing, they said, "the diversity and autonomy of provincial governments in developing their societies within their respective spheres of jurisdiction."[34] The idea that individual provinces might usefully function as laboratories for limited regulatory experimentation has long been a much-trumpeted justification for our current fragmented securities system. In the past, the Capital Pool Companies program and the SHAIF system[35] were offered as representative examples of how such experimentation can succeed. However, it is not entirely clear whether these two examples illustrate a larger beneficial trend or whether they constitute vir-

---

31 To be sure, there have also been a number of measured, carefully-reasoned economic critiques of the "issuer choice" position. See, for example, Merritt B. Fox, "The Issuer Choice Debate" (2001) 2 Theoretical Inquiries in Law 563 in which Professor Fox argues that an issuer choice regime in US securities law would lead issuers to choose those state securities regulatory regimes mandating a sub-optimal level of issuer disclosure.

32 [2007] 2 SCR 3.

33 *Securities Reference*, above note 1 at para 60.

34 *Ibid* at para 73.

35 The SHAIF system refers to a system of shorter hold periods applicable to resales of certain securities originally acquired in exempt distributions. The SHAIF system, first introduced in British Columbia and Alberta, was eventually widely adopted across Canada.

tually the entire universe of significant provincial experiments eventually adopted nationally. This is not to say that there are no other capital-raising innovations unique to specific provinces; there are.[36] But few of these have migrated outside their provincial boundaries, and they are often essentially regional economic development initiatives frequently linked in one way or another to specific provincial tax programs.

The Supreme Court did recognize that our securities regulatory system could be improved. But improvement, they suggested, must be achieved through cooperative federalism, not through top-down federal legislative initiatives. The Court seemed to envision securities markets that could be readily deconstructed into tidy compartments variously regulated by the provinces and the federal government: systemic components and national data gathering would be subject to federal authority, while the "day-to-day operations" of securities dealers and perhaps traditional consumer protection would remain within the provincial sphere. Near the end of the judgment, the Court says,

> To summarize, we accept that the economic importance and pervasive character of the securities market may, in principle, support federal intervention that is qualitatively different from what the provinces can do. However, as important as the preservation of capital markets and the maintenance of Canada's financial stability are, they do not justify a *wholesale takeover* of the regulation of the securities industry which is the ultimate consequence of the proposed federal legislation.[37]

The term "takeover" is very telling. We often condemn our politicians for lacking the "political will" and courage to take definitive action to do what is right, even if unpopular. Ours, after all, is a Parliamentary, not a "*poll*-a-mentary" democracy. (Such "courage," of course, is invariably applauded only where we personally support the politically unpopular but "necessary" action. In other matters, where our personal views conveniently align with the popular opinion of the masses, we much prefer to remind our politicians that democratic governments must yield to the will of the majority.) The cause of a national securities regulator

---

36 See e.g. CSA Staff Notice 45-304, "Notice of Local Exemptions Related to National Instrument 45-106 Prospectus and Registration Exemptions and National Instrument 31-103 Registration Requirements and Exemptions" (2009), 32 OSCB 9781.

37 *Securities Reference*, above note 1 at para 128 [emphasis added].

had enjoyed varying levels of support from previous governments. But when the current Minister of Finance decided to act and act decisively, the Court evidently was not persuaded that the federal government should be seen as a benign catalyst for enhancing value, but characterized it, instead, as a kind of constitutionally overreaching hostile takeover bidder.

The federal ship, the Court suggested, was sailing against the Court's conception of the "dominant tide" of modern federalism, a tide that has turned toward a "more flexible view of federalism that accommodates overlapping jurisdiction and encourages intergovernmental cooperation."[38] Accordingly, they note that "it is open to the federal government and the provinces to exercise their respective powers over securities harmoniously, in the spirit of cooperative federalism."[39] "Cooperation," the Court tells us, "is the animating force."[40]

It would be wrong, misleading, and unfair to reduce the Supreme Court's homiletic pleas for cooperation to a saccharine invocation to gather together, hand in hand, for a rousing federal/provincial chorus of "Kumbaya." At the same time, it is surely not unfair to point out that reasonable people of good faith and integrity sometimes simply cannot come to agreement on difficult issues. (Even Supreme Court of Canada judgments occasionally include dissents.) Good faith and a cooperative spirit are not always enough. The Court itself noted that a number of proposals for a national regulator stretching back to 1935 — all of which "generally envisaged cooperation between the provinces and the federal government"[41] — have failed. After more than seventy-five years of failure to achieve by cooperation what the federal government proposed, it surely betrays no hopeless defeatism to suggest that, regrettably, this approach doesn't appear to be working.

Is the Supreme Court's judicial reminder that a cooperative approach remains "available" likely to change that? To borrow a phrase from Dr. Johnson (originally coined in a very different context), I may well be allowing hope to triumph over experience,[42] yet I will nevertheless conclude with the sanguine observation

---

38 *Ibid* at para 57.
39 *Ibid* at para 9.
40 *Ibid* at para 133.
41 *Ibid* at para 11.
42 See James Boswell, *Life of Johnson* (Oxford: Oxford University Press, 1970) at 444.

that the story is not yet complete. In March, the federal government extended the mandate of the Canadian Securities Transition Office until 12 July 2013.[43] That is an encouraging step, and perhaps, over the next year, a new cooperative solution can emerge after all. We can at least hope so. Still, with the spectre of unilateral federal action now largely removed from the constitutional equation, there will be challenges ahead in identifying other compelling incentives for the provinces and territories to achieve the workable and worthwhile securities accord with the federal government that has stubbornly eluded us for so many decades.

---

43   Order in Council, Department of Finance, Canadian Securities Regulation Regime Transition Office Act, PC 2012-341 (27 March 2012); Canada Gazette, Part 1, vol 146, no 14 (7 April 2012).

AFTERWORD

Public Policy and Judicial Discourse: Observations on Dialogue with the Court through the *Securities Reference* Decision (2011)

Lawrence E. Ritchie[1]

Since the inception of securities regulation in Canada, the subject matter has been regulated as a matter of "property and civil rights" by the provinces and territories, pursuant to section 92 of the *Constitution Act, 1867*.[2] Nevertheless, for more than seventy-five years many Canadians have been trying to come to grips with the national dimensions of securities regulation within this historical context. Beginning with the 1935 Royal Commission on Price Spreads, more than a dozen major proposals have been made for a Canadian securities regulator.[3] Calls for a national

---

1   With the valuable contribution of Lorne Kotler. Adapted from comments made at "What Next for Canada?: A Roundtable on Securities Regulation in Canada," held on 30 January 2012, and jointly hosted by the University of Toronto Faculty of Law and Torys LLP. The views of the author do not necessarily reflect the views of the Transition Office or of the federal government.

2   (UK), 30 & 31 Vict, c 3, reprinted in RSC 1985, App II, No 5; *Reference Re Securities Act*, 2011 SCC 66 [*Securities Reference*].

3   See e.g. *Report of the Royal Commission on Price Spreads* (Ottawa: King's Printer, 1935); Royal Commission on Banking and Finance, *Report of the Royal Commission on Banking and Finance* (Ottawa: Queen's Printer, 1964); *Report of the Attorney General's Committee on Securities Legislation in Ontario* (Toronto: Queen's Printer, 1965); Ontario Securities Commission, "CANSEC: Legal and Administrative Concepts" (November 1967), OSCB 61; Philip Anisman, "The Proposals for a Securities Market Law For Canada: Purpose and Process" (1981) 19 Osgoode Hall LJ 329 [1979 Proposals]; *Report of the Royal Commission on the*

securities regulator have intensified over the past decade (nearly half of these proposals have been issued since 2001), corresponding with recognition that the securities market, while regulated by provincial commissions, has increasingly become interconnected with and influenced by factors well beyond provincial, and even national borders.[4] While these reports emphasized the *merits* of a single common Canadian securities regulator,[5] their proposals were always sensitive in recognizing the role historically played by the provinces in this area and the unique struc-

Economic Union and Development Prospects for Canada, vol 3 (Ottawa: Minister of Supply of Services Canada, 1985); *Memorandum of Understanding Regarding the Regulation of Securities in Canada*, OSC Notice (1994), 17 OSCB 4401; Keynote Address by David Brown, Dialogue with the OSC (20 November 2001) in (2002) 5:1 Ontario Securities Commission Perspectives 10 at 11; Wise Persons' Committee, *It's Time* (Ottawa: Department of Finance Canada, 2003), online: Wise Persons' Committee www.wiseaverties.ca/reports/WPC%20Final.pdf [Wise Persons' Committee]; Ontario, Management Board Secretariat, *Modernizing Securities Regulation in Canada* (Discussion Draft) (7 June 2004), online: www. ontla.on.ca/library/repository/mon/8000/244722.pdf; Task Force to Modernize Securities Legislation in Canada, *Canada Steps Up: Final Report* (Toronto: Task Force to Modernize Securities Legislation in Canada, 2006), online: Task Force to Modernize Securities Legislation in Canada www.tfmsl.ca/docs/Volume1_en.pdf; Crawford Panel on a Single Canadian Securities Regulator, *Blueprint for a Canadian Securities Commission – Final Paper* (7 June 2006), online: Canadian Bankers Association www.cba.ca/contents/files/misc/msc_crawfordreport_en.pdf; Expert Panel on Securities Regulation, *Creating an Advantage in Global Capital Markets – Final Report and Recommendations* (Ottawa: Department of Finance Canada, 2009) online: Expert Panel on Securities Regulation www.expertpanel.ca/eng/documents/Expert_Panel_Final_Report_And_ Recommendations.pdf.

4   See e.g. Wise Persons' Committee, above note 3 at ch 1.
5   The Canadian Securities Transition Office publicly listed the following, representing the distilled wisdom of past proposals, as advantages of a single regulator:

   • Strong leadership and accountability
   • Better protection for investors across Canada
   • Improved regulatory and criminal enforcement
   • New tools to bolster the stability and integrity of Canada's financial system
   • Faster policy responses to emerging capital market trends
   • Simpler processes for businesses, resulting in lower costs for Canadians
   • Better international representation and influence for Canada

   "About the New Regulator," online: The Canadian Securities Transition Office csto-btcvm.ca/Home.aspx.

ture of Canadian federalism. Such models, therefore, were not proposed in a legal vacuum; most if not all recognized, explicitly or otherwise, that the judiciary would eventually wade into the national conversation about securities regulation.[6]

Governments have historically sought input from courts on public policy matters to provide direction in terms of both how (or how not) to implement government policies, programs, and legislation as a matter of law and certainty that those initiatives are legally sound. In responding, courts have fostered a dialogue among the judiciary, governments, and the public at large on certain aspects of the policy at issue. In the *Securities Reference*, the Supreme Court of Canada was asked to review proposed government policy in the context of the constitutional division of powers (as opposed to the *Canadian Charter of Rights and Freedoms*).[7] "Division of powers" decisions have legal and often policy implications distinct from those with reference to the *Charter*. The impact and meaning of the Court's decision ought to be considered within that context as well.

A. The Involvement of Canadian Courts in Public Policy Dialogue

Canadian courts, particularly the Supreme Court, have historically played and will continue to play an important role in debates over public policy in this country. While ever so careful not to overstep into the sphere of explicit "policy making" (a domain reserved for our elected politicians), Canada's highest court has had a voice in many high-profile public policy debates. Nonetheless, the manner in which courts participate in the public policy debates of the day has changed over time. Perhaps the most significant shift, both in the Court's actual role in public policy debate and in public perceptions of that role, came with the enactment of the *Canadian Charter of Rights and Freedoms*. Before the *Charter*, judicial scrutiny of contentious policy tended to be focused on whether the impugned legislation was consistent with, and appropriate in light of, Canada's constitutional division of powers. In

---

6   See especially 1979 Proposals, above note 3 at vol. 2, "Constitutional Aspects of Federal Securities Legislation."

7   Part I of the *Constitution Act, 1982*, being Schedule B to the *Canada Act 1982* (UK), 1982, c 11.

contrast to *Charter* cases, division of powers cases do not directly concern the rights of individuals but, rather, address the powers of one level of government in relation to another.[8] In deciding these matters, the Supreme Court often emphasizes that it is not commenting on the desirability of a certain government policy or action placed before it; the Court rightly recognizes that its role is limited to saying, "What you want to do can be done by *this* level of government, but not *that* level of government."

The *Charter* can be seen as having changed the rules of the game. In *Charter* litigation, the Supreme Court, rather than being a referee between different levels of government, has become an enforcer of individual protections against the state as a whole.[9] Where division of powers cases have tended to focus upon more mundane subjects, such as which level of government may regulate the marketing of chicken, milk, and eggs,[10] *Charter* cases often engage the basic and universal issue of the relationship between the state (i.e., all levels of Canadian government) and its

8 See discussion in *Beauregard v Canada*, [1986] 2 SCR 56 at paras 27–28 [emphasis added]:

Indeed, two of the sources of, or reasons for, judicial independence in Canada do not exist in the United Kingdom. First, Canada is a federal country with a constitutional distribution of powers between federal and provincial governments. As in other federal countries, there is a need for an impartial umpire to resolve disputes between two levels of government as well as between governments and private individuals who rely on the distribution of powers. In most federal countries the courts play this umpiring role. In Canada, since Confederation, it has been assumed and agreed that the courts would play an important constitutional role as umpire of the federal system . . . . That role, still fundamental today, requires that the umpire be autonomous and completely independent of the parties involved in federal-provincial disputes.

Secondly, *the enactment of the Canadian Charter of Rights and Freedoms* (although admittedly not relevant to this case because of its date of origin) *conferred on the courts another truly crucial role: the defence of basic individual liberties and human rights against intrusions by all levels and branches of government*. Once again, in order to play this deeply constitutional role, judicial independence is essential.

9 See discussion in Katrina Miriam Wyman, "The Independence of Administrative Tribunals in an Era of Ever Expansive Judicial Independence" (2000) 14 Can J Admin L & Prac 61 at 114–15, which cites the proposition in *Beauregard*, above note 8.

10 See for example *Carnation Co Ltd v Quebec Agricultural Marketing Board*, [1968] SCR 238; *AG Manitoba v Manitoba Egg and Poultry Association*, [1971] SCR 689; *Reference Re Agricultural Products Marketing Act*, [1978] 2 SCR 1198.

citizens.[11] Whereas division of powers cases often address which level of government may legally do this or that, *Charter* cases ask whether a policy or action intended by the state may be carried out at all, by any level of government, given its impact on the individual.

The *Charter* not only changed the way the courts approached certain matters but changed the way Canadians viewed the role of the courts, and of the Supreme Court in particular. Since the *Charter* was enacted thirty years ago, more than a generation of Canadians has seen courts tell a government that it cannot do something it wished to do because an impugned action or law infringed upon rights and protections guaranteed under the *Charter*. Over the same period, division of powers cases have tended to recede from the spotlight.[12] Canadians have increasingly become accustomed to thinking in terms of how courts protect *their* rights, as individuals, rather than protecting the powers of a particular level of government.

Courts, especially the Supreme Court, themselves recognized their enhanced role following the enactment of the *Charter*.[13] And over the course of this period, through the Court's language and analysis within that public policy discourse, the Court more clearly articulated these changes. In "public policy" litigation, courts are concerned not only with adjudicating the very specific matters at issue but with helping to frame the debate over ques-

---

11   Peter Hogg, *Constitutional Law of Canada*, 5th ed supplement, loose-leaf (consulted on 23 May 2012), (Toronto: Thomson Carswell, 2007) ch 5 at 25 and ch 36 at 5, which discuss the expansion of the scope of judicial review under the *Charter*.

12   Christopher P Manfredi, "Forum: Judicial Activism and Judicial Deference: Judicial Power and the *Charter*: Reflections on the Activism Debate" (2004) 53 UNBLJ 185 at 188–89:

From 1982 to 2002, the Court decided 436 *Charter* cases (about 21 per year). In 152 of those cases (about 35 percent), the Court upheld the *Charter* claim. As a result, the Court nullified 75 federal and provincial statutes, for a rate of 3.6 nullifications per year . . . . From 1950 to 1984, it decided 177 division of powers cases (about five per year), and it nullified 65 federal and provincial statutes (less than two per year). More recent federalism data are consistent with this trend: from 2000 to 2002 the Court decided eleven division of powers cases (less than four per year) and nullified only one statute on federalism grounds.

13   See especially The Honourable BM McLachlin (as she then was), "The Role of the Court in the Post-*Charter* Era: Policy Maker or Adjudicator" (1990) 39 UNBLJ 43.

tions of public policy. And while no doubt this aspect of judicial decision-making existed before the *Charter, Charter* litigation has empowered courts to take a more visibly activist and higher-profile role in that policy-making discussion. Courts address the issues and parties before them, but they also throw the issues back to policy makers, who are more directly accountable to Canadians, to try again. Constitutional litigation, *Charter* and non-*Charter* alike, sets up a dialogue between the Court and the state through which public policy can be refined. The Court, however, while having the final say on how the law should be interpreted, does not truly have the final say on the substance of the policy matters at issue; how governments respond to the Court's decision is at least as important as what the Court has said about a certain constitutional matter.[14]

B. The Unique Nature and Opportunities of a "Reference"

Perhaps nowhere is the Court's role in the public policy dialogue more apparent than in the context of a Reference.[15] By definition, a Reference is a request from a government to provide clarity about the legality of a particular matter of policy. Unlike most cases heard by the Supreme Court, a Reference does not necessarily involve a dispute, an actual fact situation, or any particular parties

---

14 The relationship between the Court and the legislatures in *Charter* litigation has been described as a "dialogue." "[D]ialogue occurs where a judicial decision striking down a piece of legislation for inconsistency with a *Charter* right or freedom is followed by some action by the competent legislative body." See Peter W Hogg et al, "*Charter* Dialogue Revisited — Or 'Much Ado about Metaphors'" (2007) 45 Osgoode Hall LJ 1 at 45 and generally. While this discussion focuses on *Charter* cases, the logic applies equally to division of powers cases. In what is perhaps the clearest example, as a direct result of the opinion in *Reference Re Secession of Quebec*, [1998] 2 SCR 217, Parliament passed *An Act to Give Effect to the Requirement for Clarity as Set out in the Opinion of the Supreme Court of Canada in the Quebec Secession Reference*, SC 2000, c 26. This view is supported by McLachlin J (as she then was), in McLachlin, above note 13, where she discusses how the *Charter* was changing the Court's involvement in policy, especially in the context of judicial references.

15 See discussion in Radhakrishnan Persaud, "Resort to the Supreme Court through the Reference Procedure: Use of the Judicial Advisory Mechanism in Canadian Political Law" (2011) 5 J Par & Pol L 261.

who will be directly affected by the decision.[16] This allows the Court to address broader and perhaps more abstract questions, in order to resolve difficult intergovernmental issues, without being strictly constrained by a fact-specific evidentiary record.[17] At least theoretically, these decisions represent only non-binding, advisory opinions.[18] In practice, however, governments have relied on the Court's opinions to craft appropriate legislation, policy approaches, or responses. The process of referring a specific question or set of questions to a court for its opinion avoids the time, uncertainty, and financial costs of resolving constitutional issues through private litigation.[19] A constitutional Reference can relate to virtually any constitutional matter, including those which engage *Charter* principles and those which require analysis under the Constitution's division of powers. The approach taken by the Court in responding to the question (or questions) referred will be determined in large measure by the legal principles the questions engage. A Reference is often the first stage of an ongoing policy interaction. The decision of the Court either confirms or alters a policy direction; it can evoke a legislative response, prompt a change in policy, or serve as the starting point for consultation and negotiation between governments or affected interest groups.[20] Although directed to the "advisory opinion process" that exists in some American states, Jonathan Persky's words are equally applicable to the Canadian context:

---

16 Hogg, above note 11, ch 8 at 17.

17 Radhakrishnan Persaud, above note 15 at 269; Robin Elliot, "References, Structural Argumentation and the Organizing Principles of Canada's Constitution" (2001) 80 Can Bar Rev 67 at 139–40.

18 However, no government has acted contrary to the decision rendered in a reference. Hogg, above note 11, ch 8 at 18: "[T]here do not seem to be any recorded instances where a reference opinion was disregarded by the parties, or where it was not followed by a subsequent court on the ground of its advisory character." Similarly, courts have tended to treat reference opinions as if they were binding (see Carissima Mathen, "Mutability and Method in the Marriage Reference" (2005) 54 UNBLJ 43 at 57).

19 James L Huffman & MardiLyn Saathoff, "Advisory Opinions and Canadian Constitutional Development: The Supreme Court's Reference Jurisdiction" (1990) 74 Minn L Rev 1251 at 1278; Katherine Swinton, *The Supreme Court and Canadian Federalism* (Toronto: Carswell, 1990) at 67; Mathen, above note 18 at 58–59; Persaud, above note 15 at 274–75.

20 Persaud, above note 15 at 273–82; Patrick J Monahan, "The Public Policy Role of the Supreme Court of Canada in the Secession Reference" (1999) 11 NJCL 65 at 93–94; Swinton, above note 19 at 17–20.

In many respects, the advisory opinion process is an ongoing conversation between two branches of government: the requesting authority outlines the situation, explains the constitutional issue involved, and delineates the question; the justices respond by clarifying the question, establishing jurisdiction, and providing an answer. In many cases, however, the advisory opinion is merely an intermediate step in this larger conversation. Often, the dispute alluded to in the advisory opinion request is "effectively remand[ed] . . . back to the other branches" for further disposition. [21]

Like advisory opinions, References form an integral part of the policy dialogue between different levels of government and, therefore, of policy dialogue with the public.

C. The *Securities Reference*, 2011

The federal government referred the proposed *Canadian Securities Act* to the Supreme Court by a proceeding commenced on 26 May 2010.[22] Prior to this, however, the governments of Quebec and Alberta had already referred the question of a national securities regulator to their respective Courts.[23] In referring the proposed Act, the federal government sought to obtain legal certainty from the Court on the implementation of a policy priority:

"The Government strongly believes that Parliament has the constitutional authority to enact a comprehensive *Federal Securities Act* and is initiating preparatory steps in that direction," said Minister Nicholson. "In coming to this view, the Government is supported by many of Canada's foremost constitutional experts. However, for greater certainty, we will be asking the Supreme Court for its opinion, which is why we are proceeding with this reference."[24]

---

21 Jonathan Persky, "Ghosts That Slay: A Contemporary Look at State Advisory Opinions" (2005) 37 Conn L Rev 115. The US Supreme Court, however, is prohibited from hearing references under Article III, section 2, of the US Constitution, since the jurisdiction of the Court is limited to "cases and controversies." For discussion, see Mathen, above note 18 at 55–56.

22 Proposed *Canadian Securities Act*, as set out in Order in Council PC 2010-667 (26 May 2010).

23 *Reference Re Securities Act (Canada)*, 2011 ABCA 77; *Québec (Procureure générale) c Canada (Procureure générale)*, 2011 QCCA 591.

24 Department of Justice, News Release, "Government of Canada Intends to Seek Opinion of Supreme Court of Canada on Consti-

The Supreme Court was asked "whether the proposed *Securities Act . . .* falls within the legislative authority of the Parliament of Canada."[25] The Court limited itself to addressing the very specific question asked and the arguments advanced in support of the federal government's position, namely, that the proposed Act was valid under the general trade and commerce clause of section 91(2).[26] In answer to that specific question, a unanimous Court rendered a narrow but clear answer: the proposed *Securities Act* was not within the legislative authority of the Parliament of Canada to enact within the general branch of Parliament's power over trade and commerce under s. 91(2).

Again, for context, the *Securities Reference* was argued and decided under the division of powers, not the *Charter*. The Court was not asked whether it is constitutionally permissible to have a national securities regulator; nor was it asked whether such an initiative would make sound policy sense. Rather, the Court was limited to deciding issues of legislative competence:

> The courts do not have the power to declare legislation constitutional simply because they conclude that it may be the best option from the point of view of policy. The test is not which jurisdiction – federal or provincial – is thought to be best placed to legislate regarding the matter in question. The inquiry into constitutional powers under ss. 91 and 92 of the *Constitution Act, 1867* focuses on legislative competence, not policy.[27]

Notwithstanding the outcome, it is clear that the Court did not tell Canada that the policy aspirations reflected in the proposed Act could not be achieved legally. As well, in limiting itself to the specific arguments advanced, the Court did not address the question of whether the proposed Act was within Parliament's authority outside of its general trade and commerce power. It did not consider whether the proposal was within Parliament's authority to regulate interprovincial and international trade and commerce: "No doubt, much of Canada's capital market is inter-

---

tutionality of Proposed Canadian Securities Legislation" (16 October 2009) online: Canada News Centre news.gc.ca/web/article-eng. do?crtr.sj1D=&mthd=advSrch&crtr.mnthndVl=11&nid=490539&crtr. dpt1D=&crtr.tp1D=&crtr.lc1D=&crtr.yrStrtVl=2008&crtr.kw=&crtr. dyStrtVl=7&crtr.aud1D=&crtr.mnthStrtVl=11&crtr.yrndVl=2009&crtr. dyndVl=17.

25 *Securities Reference*, above note 2 at para 1.
26 *Ibid* at para 6.
27 *Ibid* at para 90.

provincial and indeed international. Trade in securities is not confined to 13 provincial and territorial enclaves."[28] Nor did it address any other basis that could possibly ground the initiative's constitutionality.[29] The decision is consistent with the conversation historically fostered by cases such as this one, and should be seen in the context of such conversation. It should not be seen as the end of the matter; rather, it may define the beginning of a policy conversation.

The decision and its implication are discussed in greater detail elsewhere in this volume, but it is worthwhile to highlight three points here. First, the Supreme Court explicitly found that, notwithstanding the historic view of securities regulation as being within provincial jurisdiction, the federal government has a constitutionally sound role to play in securities regulation.[30] Second, the Court said that at least some areas of securities regulation can be regulated only by the federal government, not by the provinces, whether acting alone or in concert.[31] Finally, the Court suggested an approach for comprehensive securities regulation that is consistent with the division of powers:

> It is open to the federal government and the provinces to exercise their respective powers over securities harmoniously, in the spirit of cooperative federalism. The experience of other federations in the field of securities regulation, while a function of their own constitutional requirements, suggests that a cooperative approach might usefully be explored, should our legislators so chose, to ensure that each level of government properly discharges its responsibility to the public in a coordinated fashion.[32]

---

28 *Ibid* at para 115.
29 *Ibid* at para 129.
30 *Ibid* at paras 114–121.
31 *Ibid* at para 121:

> The provinces, acting in concert, lack the constitutional capacity to sustain a viable national scheme aimed at genuine national goals such as management of systemic risk or Canada-wide data collection. This supports the view that a federal scheme aimed at such matters might well be qualitatively different from what the provinces, acting alone or in concert, could achieve.

32 *Ibid* at para 9.

It is arguable that these three points are at least as pertinent to the public policy conversation as the answer given to the very specific question before the Court.[33]

D. Conclusion

All the public policy reasons that existed for pursuing a national regulator before the Supreme Court's decision existed after it, neither strengthened nor weakened. As noted above, the Court, by its own statements, said nothing about the relative merits of having a national securities regulator:

> At this juncture, it is important to stress that this advisory opinion does not address the question of what constitutes the optimal model for regulating the securities market. While the parties presented evidence and arguments on the relative merits of federal and provincial regulation of securities, the policy question of whether a single national securities scheme is preferable to multiple provincial regimes is not one for the Courts to decide. Accordingly, our answer to the reference question is dictated solely by the text of the Constitution, fundamental constitutional principles and the relevant case law.[34]

The referral of the proposed *Securities Act* to the Supreme Court of Canada, and the Court's response, represent part of a dialogue: the federal government expressed its desired approach to pursuing a policy objective, and the Court expressed its opinion on the constitutionality of that intended approach, based on the arguments put to it. What remains to be seen is how the federal and the provincial governments react and respond to this decision. It is a matter of government policy. The ultimate impact of the

---

33 Recently retired Supreme Court Justice Ian Binnie, a member of the Court that authored the decision, has suggested that the decision's essence is greater than the result. When asked about the legal potential for a national securities regulator, he replied: "[M]y wish is that more commentators would actually read the decision instead of simply the outcome. They will find in that decision a large part of the answer to your question." Jacquie McNish, "The Supreme Court's Retired, But Hardly Retiring, Ian Binnie" *The Globe and Mail* (10 April 2012).

34 *Securities Reference*, above note 2 at para 10.

Securities Reference will be determined not by the decision itself but by how governments, both provincial and federal, respond.[35]

---

35 The federal government responded to the decision by announcing in the 2012 Budget: *Fostering Stable, Competitive, Fair and Efficient Capital Markets* that it was consulting with provinces and territories on the basis of the *Securities Reference* (Canada, House of Commons, Department of Finance, *Jobs Growth and Long-Term Prosperity: Economic Action Plan 2012* (29 March 2012), online: Government of Canada www.budget. gc.ca/2012/plan/pdf/Plan2012-eng.pdf).

The federal government subsequently expressed its intention to pursue a cooperative arrangement, of the sort contemplated by the SCC decision, with willing provinces. It extended the mandate of the Canadian Securities Transition Office, whose mandate is to "assist in the establishment of a Canadian securities regulation regime and a Canadian regulatory authority," for an additional year beyond its statutory July 2012 end date to assist in that effort (*Canadian Securities Regulation Regime Transition Office Act*, SC 2009, c 2, s 297). The Minister of Finance has stated publicly that a number of provinces have expressed interest in pursuing these discussions.

Theresa Tedesco, "Ottawa pushes for national securities regulator within year" *Financial Post* (27 April 2012), online: Financial Post business.financialpost.com/2012/04/27/ottawa-pushes-for-national-securities-regulator-within-year.

Contributors

ANITA ANAND is a professor at the Faculty of Law at Toronto and served as associate dean (JD program) at the faculty from 2007 to 2009. She is the academic director of the Faculty of Law's Centre for the Legal Profession. Professor Anand has conducted research for the Five Year Review Committee, the Wise Person's Committee, and the Task Force to Modernize Securities Legislation in Canada. She is the inaugural chair of the Ontario Securities Commission's Investor Advisory Panel. Her main research areas relate to the regulation of capital markets and include a focus on corporate and securities law, as well as prudential regulation.

CRISTIE FORD is assistant professor at the University of British Columbia Faculty of Law. She teaches and researches in the areas of securities regulation, administrative law, and regulation and governance theory. Professor Ford joined UBC in 2005 from Columbia Law School, where she pursued her graduate degrees and taught in a variety of capacities. She has practised securities, regulatory, and administrative law in Vancouver (with Guild Yule LLP) and in New York (with Davis Polk & Wardwell LLP). She is co-authoring the forthcoming fifth edition of *Canadian Securities Regulation* (Toronto: LexisNexis) with His Excellency David Johnston and Kathleen Rockwell, and is at work on a monograph on regulation and innovation for Cambridge University Press.

HARDEEP GILL completed his PhD in mathematics at the University of British Columbia in 2011, concentrating on probability theory. He has been the recipient of multiple awards over the course of his studies, including NSERC Canada Graduate Scholarships at both the master's and doctoral levels. He will be receiving his JD from UBC in 2014.

ANDREW GREEN is an associate professor at the University of Toronto Faculty of Law. His areas of interest focus on environmental law; administrative law (including the design of regulatory agencies); instrument choice in environmental law (including instruments for fostering renewable energy); the role of law in fostering individuals' environmental values; and international trade (including how international trade rules constrain countries' ability to implement climate change policies). He also analyzes judicial decision making and has undertaken empirical studies of the decisions of the Supreme Court of Canada and the Tax Court of Canada.

PETER W. HOGG, Q.C., is the scholar in residence of Blake, Cassels & Graydon LLP, where he provides counsel to the firm in his areas of expertise, including governmental liability and constitutional law. He is a professor emeritus of the Osgoode Hall Law School at York University, where he taught from 1970 to 2003, and served as dean from 1998 to 2003. He is the author of numerous articles and publications, notably *Constitutional Law of Canada* (Toronto: Carswell). He also appears as counsel in constitutional cases including counsel for the Government of Canada in the *Securities Reference*.

EDWARD M. IACOBUCCI is Professor, Associate Dean Research, and Osler Chair in Business Law at the Faculty of Law, University of Toronto. He was visiting professor at New York University Law School in 2007, visiting professor at University of Chicago Law School in 2003, and a John M. Olin visiting fellow at Columbia University Law School in 2002. He won a teaching prize at the Faculty of Law in 2000 and was a joint winner with his co-authors of the 2002–2003 Doug Purvis Prize in Canadian economics for *The Law and Economics of Canadian Competition Policy*. His areas of interest include corporate law, competition law, and law and economics more generally.

MAHMUD JAMAL is a litigation partner with Osler, Hoskin & Harcourt LLP. He represented the Canadian Bankers Association as an intervener supporting the federal position in the *Securities Reference* before the Quebec Court of Appeal, Alberta Court of Appeal, and Supreme Court of Canada.

IAN B. LEE is an associate professor at the Faculty of Law and is currently the associate dean of the JD program. He clerked with Justice Claire L'Heureux-Dubé of the Supreme Court of Canada and Justice Mark MacGuigan of the Federal Court of Appeal, and practised with Sullivan & Cromwell LLP in Paris, France, and New York, New York, before joining the Faculty of Law in 2003. His teaching and research interests are in the areas of constitutional law and corporate law.

JEFFREY G. MACINTOSH holds the Toronto Stock Exchange chair in capital markets law at the University of Toronto Faculty of Law and is a past associate director and director of the Capital Markets Institute at the University of Toronto. He was appointed a John M. Olin fellow at Yale Law School in 1988–1989. He also served as a member of the Ontario Securities Commission Task Force on Small Business Financing. Professor MacIntosh specializes in corporation law, corporate finance, securities regulation, venture capital, and small firm financing.

CHRISTOPHER C. NICHOLLS holds the Stephen Dattels chair in corporate finance law at Western University. He is the author of numerous articles in the business law field as well as five books: *Financial Institutions: The Regulatory Framework* (Toronto: LexisNexis, 2008); *Mergers, Acquisitions and Other Changes of Corporate Control* (2d ed.) (Toronto: Irwin, 2012); *Corporate Law* (Toronto: Emond Montgomery Publications, 2005); *Corporate Finance and Canadian Law* (Toronto: Carswell, 2000); and *Securities Law* (with Jeffrey G. MacIntosh; Toronto: Irwin Law, 2002). Professor Nicholls has been consulted by law firms and government departments and regulators, and has lectured to academic and professional audiences in Canada, the United States, the United Kingdom, and South America.

POONAM PURI is one of Canada's most respected scholars and commentators on issues of corporate governance, corporate law, and securities law. She is associate dean, research, graduate studies, and institutional relations and professor of law at Osgoode Hall Law School, York University. She is co-director of the Hennick Centre for Business and Law, a joint initiative of Osgoode Hall Law School and the Schulich School of Business at York University. She has also served as research director at the Capital Markets Institute at Rotman School of Business, University of Toronto. Professor Puri was the co-research director for the Task Force to Modernize Securities Legislation in Canada, as well as the expert panel on Securities Regulation, and she has conducted extensive research on issues relating to the Canadian capital markets.

LAWRENCE E. RITCHIE is the executive vice president and senior policy advisor to the Canadian Securities Transition Office, the federal statutory organization charged with leading the transition to a common securities regulator for Canada, and has held that role since the opening of that office in July 2009. Mr. Ritchie is on secondment from the Ontario Securities Commission (OSC), where, as vice-chair since 2007, he has served as a member of the Commission's Board of Directors, and the Executive Management and Adjudicative Committees, and has sat on and chaired adjudicative panels. Prior to his appointment to the OSC, Mr. Ritchie was a litigation partner with Osler Hoskin & Harcourt LLP, where his practice included a range of securities litigation.

STÉPHANE ROUSSEAU holds the chair in governance and business law and is full professor at the Faculty of Law of the Université de Montréal. He has been director of the Centre for the Law of Business and International Trade since 2008. He specializes in corporate law, corporate governance, securities law, and law and economics. He has given conferences in academic and professional settings in Canada as well as abroad in numerous countries (Argentina, Australia, Brazil, China, France, United States, and Tunisia).

JANIS SARRA is professor of Law at the University of British Columbia (UBC) Faculty of Law and director of the Peter Wall Institute for Advanced Studies at UBC. She was founding director of the National Centre for Business Law. She served as associate dean of the Faculty of Law from 2003 to 2007 and was senator of the university from 2003 to 2008. She researches and writes in the areas of corporate finance, securities law, corporate law, and commercial insolvency law.

DAVID SCHNEIDERMAN is professor of law and political science at the University of Toronto where he teaches Canadian and US constitutional law and international investment law. He has authored numerous articles and edited several books on Canadian federalism, the *Charter of Rights*, Canadian constitutional history, and constitutionalism and globalization. He has authored *Constitutionalizing Economic Globalization: Investment Rules and Democracy's Promise* (New York: Cambridge University Press, 2008) and co-authored *The Last Word: Media Coverage of the Supreme Court of Canada* (Vancouver: UBC Press, 2006).

LORNE SOSSIN is dean of Osgoode Hall Law School. Prior to this appointment, he was a professor with the Faculty of Law at the University of Toronto. His teaching interests span administrative and constitutional law; the regulation of professions; civil litigation; public policy; and the judicial process. Dean Sossin was a law clerk to former Chief Justice Antonio Lamer of the Supreme Court of Canada, a former associate in law at Columbia Law School, and a former litigation lawyer with the firm of Borden & Elliot (now Borden Ladner Gervais LLP).

MICHAEL J. TREBILCOCK holds the chair in law and economics at the University of Toronto Faculty of Law. He has written widely on issues in international trade law, internal barriers to trade, and economic and social regulation. He is a former president of the American Law and Economics Association and is the recipient of the premier's Discovery Award for the Social Sciences.

Index